M000022171

EARLY CHILDHOOD L
Sharon Ryan, Editor

ADVISORY BOARD: Celia Genishi, Doris Fromberg, Carrie Lobman, Rachel Theilheimer, Dominic Gullo, Amita Gupta, Beatrice Fennimore, Sue Grieshaber, Jackie Marsh, Mindy Blaise, Gail Yuen, Alice Honig, Betty Jones, Stephanie Feeney, Stacie Goffin, Beth Graue

(continued)

Understanding the Language Development and Early Education of Hispanic Children

Eugene E. García
&
Erminda H. García

Teachers College, Columbia University
New York and London

Published by Teachers College Press, 1234 Amsterdam Avenue, New York, NY 10027

Library of Congress Cataloging-in-Publication Data

García, Eugene E., 1946–
  Understanding the language development and early education of Hispanic children / Eugene E. Garcia, Erminda H. Garcia.
    p. cm. — (Early childhood education series)
  Includes index.
  ISBN 978-0-8077-5346-0 (pbk. : alk. paper)
    1. Hispanic American children—Education (Early childhood) 2. English language—Study and teaching (Early childhood)—Spanish speakers. 3. Language acquisition. I. Garcia, Erminda H. II. Title.
  LC2670.2.G37 2012
  371.829'68073—dc23   2012004052

ISBN 978-0-8077-5346-0 (paperback)

Printed on acid-free paper
Manufactured in the United States of America

19 18 17 16 15 14 13 12   8 7 6 5 4 3 2 1

Contents

Acknowledgments

A volume like this one would not exist without the opportunity that provided the authors to work with young Hispanic children and their families, teachers, and schools. To them we owe a great debt of gratitude. They have taught us more than any organized form of education about the education of Hispanic children in the United States. To our readers, we remind them that this contribution does not take the place of real experience, but our hope is that it helps to enhance that experience. We owe a great deal to other professionals whose work served as a basis for what is in this volume. To Mr. Scott Miller, for his incisive data generation and overall analyses as the director of the National Task Force on Early Childhood Education for Hispanics; Ms. Melissa Castillo, who continues to ask the hard question, "Why isn't good instruction occurring in all classrooms for all children?" and to the countless teachers, administrators, and research colleagues who assisted and supported our research and practice. Last but not least, to our daughters (Marisol and Ava) who wondered, after more than 40 years of marriage, why we would want to write a book together; and to our grandchildren, Joaquin, Vicente, and the twins, Jiana and Julian, who from the day they were born, have continued to learn what *familia* is and how it informs what they learn every day.

What's in a Name?
What's in a Culture?

Some decades ago, one of Eugene's elder sisters looked forward to her first day at school. Accompanied by her mother on her first day, her family reminded her of the importance of school. Her school was a small one-room schoolhouse, and although it was not red, it, like the teacher, was held in high esteem by the local community—a rural Colorado community of farm/ranch owners and farm/ranch laborers. While her siblings had picked up some English, her mother and the majority of the family spoke Spanish primarily. The European and indigenous ancestors, dating back before the arrival of the Pilgrims on Plymouth Rock, had decided to stay in the territory seceded to the United States by Mexico in the Treaty of Guadalupe Hidalgo in the mid-1800s.

Eugene's sister will never forget that first day of school. She was asked by the teacher, "What is your name, little girl?" She responded, "Ciprianita." The teacher tried to pronounce the name and then respectfully requested, "Can I call you Elsie?—it is my favorite name." In that one instant, her linguistic and cultural heritage was politely and unintentionally challenged, and in her mother's presence, her child's "raíces" were metaphorically severed. The teacher's intent was positive. She meant no harm. It did not seem like a significant incident since scenes like this were common then and are still common today.

Ciprianita has repeatedly told this story with tears in her eyes. Over time, this incident marked an important attribute of schooling for her and other Hispanic children like her who came to school not speaking the schooling language, English. In the most positive interpretation of such actions, changing a name when one enters school could signify the general educational philosophy that who you are—poor, rich, Anglo, Hispanic, and so forth—does not matter in school. Everyone is treated as equals and changing a name really is not that important. In other words, students, not names, are important. On the most negative side, a change in name may signal an unwillingness to respect a student's cultural and linguistic background, and set the stage for still other instructional and institutional practices that do the same. Last, it might also suggest to the student and the family that they may not belong in the school.

For Elsie and the García family and the students that we serve today, the interpretation of this one action on Ciprianita's first day of school was somewhere in between these positive-to-negative interpretations. It is so important to understand the cultural and linguistic roots of our students—a place to start is to ask them about the origins of their names, their parents' names, their grandparents' names, and to respect and honor the diversity of those origins. This can be done both informally by asking students (or asking their family members) or formally, looking for linguistic and cultural origins on websites. This never happened for Ciprianita—Elsie never did well in school nor did she graduate from high school. And her mother often refused to make school visitations with any of her sons or daughters. However, neither that same mother, or the García family, or Elsie lost the notion that education was important.

Can this happen to you? When Erminda went to school not so long ago, a very interesting name-change event also characterized her first intersection with the place called *school*. Erminda was not sure when she fully realized why her parents named her Marierminda. Her father's youngest sister had died as a young woman and he wanted her name to be carried on by his daughter. Marierminda realized she should feel special whenever she was identified as Marierminda. Her mother prepared her for school by teaching her how to form letters of her name and even suggested that she could use the name "Minda" as a short version of her full name. She had concluded that five letters would be easier than eleven letters for a 1st-grader.

During the first week of school, she was asked to write "Marie" on her work by her 1st-grade teacher. She indicated that "Marierminda" was too long to write on the work she finished. So she had made the decision to respectfully shorten the name by using the first five letters. This seemed okay at the time. Marierminda still remembers the afternoon she proudly shared the first set of papers that she had completed in school. Her mother asked, "Who is Marie?" Marierminda was surprised and shared that her teacher had asked her to shorten her name. Her mother then announced that she would be going to school with her the next day. Marierminda knew it was about how she had written her name on her school papers and that her mother was not happy. After hearing why the teacher had decided to shorten her name, Marierminda's mother stated, "My husband and I are the only ones who have the right to choose what name Marierminda will use in and out of school." Marierminda's teacher agreed and from then on she was "Minda."

Later in Minda's educational experience, all sophomores in her high school were required to fill out a personality survey so that they could be placed on the "correct" educational track. This type of placement had two types of outcomes. Those students who were placed on the "work after graduation, no college track" did not take college-bound English or math. She was placed on the track that was "college bound." Within a few months, college-bound peers begin to call Minda, "Mindy." As one of them stated, "'Mindy' sounds like someone that would be in college." When "Mindy" enrolled at the university close to home and stated that she wanted to be a teacher, the counselor shared with her that she would need to take a speech class. This requirement was necessary so that as a teacher one was able to pronounce and articulate English correctly. Her last name "Holguin," even when accompanied by the "Mindy," was an indicator that Hispanics like her required diction lesson to overcome Spanish accents—something "Mindy" did not have. She was a little surprised to be given the additional requirement, but she wanted sincerely to be a teacher, so she took the diction class. The instructor was quite young, from the East Coast, and struggled with all of the "strange names" that she would attempt to pronounce when calling roll. The instructor quickly began to use the name "Mindy" and Marierminda quickly began to resent the way she pronounced Hispanic student names. After enduring the ridiculous pronunciations, the entire class refused to acknowledge the names she called out. In fact, students used class time for "teaching" the instructor what they wanted to be called as well as how to pronounce the names. On that day "Mindy" asked that she be called "Erminda."

As we reflect on these experiences, we realize our name has always impacted our interactions with others. Whether shortening our names, changing our names, or pronouncing them incorrectly, they all affected us. We realized that people make assumptions about who you are and what you are capable of by utilizing your name. We have made it a mission to never change a student's name, to ask students and/or parents about names, and to practice the pronunciation of names throughout our 30-plus years of teaching. In our own experiences, "Ciprianita" could not be pronounced. "Minda" could not go to college, but "Mindy" could. A significant amount of research indicates that welcoming students and treating them in a respectful manner, enhances academic achievement, particularly for Hispanic children. (García, 2001a; García, 2005)

Our first effort to link research to practice, with some accommodation to our own experiences, allowed us to introduce a lesson framework associated with addressing the important issue of names and provide a way to be specifically responsive to the diverse names in a classroom. The framework we introduced here identifies the key content and language objectives along with the academic standards addressed—this we will repeat as we address instruction that has been shown to help Hispanic children master the academic language of U.S. schools. The lesson framework also identifies vocabulary terms that are to be addressed/ learned along with the sentence framework that will be the focus of the lesson. We believe these are key ingredients in addressing the success of instructing Hispanic children.

NAME LESSONS

Your name is your identity. It is how you are called and respond to the caller. It is how you engage with someone as well as label someone when talking to or about that person. Beginning always with understanding who the children are is the message we wish to reinforce. Learning their names are a critical part of this task. But that is not enough. In the search for educational equity and social justice, simple answers to complex questions are always prized. You are being asked by us to *complexify* this understanding. This is not to suggest that the search for simple and straightforward *explanations* is to be disregarded. Einstein is credited, rightly or wrongly, as saying, "We need to simplify explanations, but avoid making them too simple." We should not fear complexity. Rather, we should attempt to use it to better our own analytical processes. In complexifying the issue of Hispanic students in early learning circumstances, we can move away from superficial tip-of-the-iceberg analysis and more fully understand the course of events through more comprehensive articulations of these circumstances. In that way, the phenomenon can be treated more interactively and becomes more comprehensible. Once comprehensible, it becomes more possible to act in ways that affect undesired outcomes exposed in the analysis. Maybe it is more than just what is in a name.

THE EDUCATION OF HISPANICS IN EARLY CHILDHOOD

As a researcher working a research agenda predominantly with Hispanics, and as a teacher with some 30 years of early education experience similarly dominated in the service of Hispanics, we are often asked to address the links between research and practice in support of young Hispanic children and their families. In attempting to address that link, we have often found it useful to engage our professional experience and expertise (our "professional selves") with our cultural and linguistic experience (our "personal selves") to address national educational challenges and opportunities for Hispanic populations. The professional side of each of us has been nurtured at some of the best educational institutions in the United States—you can check out our biographies, while the non-professional side of us has been nurtured in the Mexican American family. Each of us was born in the United States, speaking Spanish as our first language, as our families have for generations in the southwestern United Sates. We are clearly Americans, but with a significantly different immigration history than most Americans—remember most Americans are of immigrant stock as are most Hispanics.

Bringing these personal and professional selves together is not always easy, but we have learned that the mixture has been quite helpful to the wide variety of people we interact with in our local, regional, and national roles as sometimes identified "experts." By bringing together these selves, we communicate with individuals in ways not possible had we spoken only with one voice or the other. This book presents our intersecting but distinct voices to help further the understanding of life in a diverse society— particularly for Hispanics growing up in the United States during their early childhood years. The historical pattern of the education of Hispanics in the United States is a continuous story of underachievement. It need not continue to be that way.

Our approach to the education of Hispanics in their early years recognizes the multiple selves that are a reality for all of us. It is useful to recognize that we walk in varied and diverse cultures. There is great diversity within each individual, just as there is diversity among individuals and the many cultures they belong to or represent. We all live with diversity, some of us more than others. No one escapes this challenge or its advantages and disadvantages. Hispanic children and families are no different in that they are in many ways similar and in many ways diverse. Our effort is not to stereotype this cultural group, but to understand the way in which similarities and differences are related to education so that we might build towards their advancement. At the heart of our approach is the belief that cultural and linguistical diversity, a characteristic of many Hispanics in the United States, is to be considered a resource not a problem (García & García, 2010). In so doing, successful education interventions for this population includes respecting the cultural and linguistic roots of this population, and sustaining and utilizing those roots in their education.

We also realize that our own analysis and assessment of the education of young Hispanics is not the only set of views held by others regarding Hispanics in the United States. Linda Chavez (1991)—adviser in the Reagan Administration, journalist, commentator, and author of *Out of the Barrio: Toward a New Politics of Hispanic Assimilation*—suggests that

> Every previous group—Germans, Irish, Italians, Greeks, Jews, Poles—struggled to be accepted fully into the social, political and economic mainstream, sometimes against the opposition of a hostile majority. They learned the lan-

guage, acquired education and skills, and adapted their own customs and traditions to fit an American context. (p. 2)

The key for Hispanic success in America, Chavez argues, is minimizing the public/governmental recognition of Hispanic roots and the individual and governmental promotion of assimilation. She chides the federal government, particularly federal bilingual education programs, and Hispanic leaders for promoting permanent victim-status and vying with Black Americans for the distinction of being the poorest, most segregated, and least educated minority, thereby entitling them to government handouts. These actions in turn, her conclusion advances, encourage Hispanics to maintain their language and culture and their specific identity in return for rewards handed out through affirmative action and federal, state, and local educational policies that thwart assimilation. This does not sound like my father's concern for the importance of roots or my mothers' emphasis on wings.

Yet another Hispanic author, Richard Rodriguez, is very eloquent in his description of his upbringing in a Mexican home and a Catholic school where the English-speaking nuns literally "beat" the Spanish language and the "Hispanic-ness" out of him. His book *Hunger of Memory* (1982) describes this forced assimilation, painful as it was, that propelled him to new heights of education achievement. Although he himself never articulates the conclusion, he leaves open the suggestion that such treatment of Hispanics is exactly what they need to get over their "problems." We reach a very different conclusion in this discussion. But you should know that the debate exists.

We turn now to a brief overview of important issues related to understanding the early education of Hispanics. Beginning in the middle 1980s, efforts to improve educational outcomes for Hispanics and other historically disadvantaged racial/ethnic groups in the United States, including African Americans and Native Americans, began to expand on a sustained basis. This expansion was stimulated in large measure by intensifying concerns about the long-term competitiveness of the nation's economy; greater awareness that these groups continued to do much less well educationally than Whites; and widespread recognition that their collective share of the population had already become quite large and was increasing rapidly, owing in large measure to growth among Hispanic populations.

Although much serious work to improve educational outcomes for Hispanics and other groups has been ongoing at all levels of the education system since that time, it has not made as much progress as many people had hoped would occur. For example, very limited progress has been made since the early 1990s in reducing gaps in standardized test scores on the elementary and secondary levels between Hispanics and Whites.

At this juncture, while much work continues from preschool through higher education, possibly the greatest emphasis is now being placed on the early childhood years, as evidenced by the movement to expand state-funded pre-Kindergarten. A major reason is the growing understanding that the foundations for educational outcomes are established when children are very young—particularly during the period from birth through age 8. In that regard, during their earliest years, many Hispanic children do not have the opportunity to acquire the knowledge and skills needed to get off to a good start academically when they enter Kindergarten. Subsequently, many develop low academic achievement patterns in the K–3 years, which continue for the rest of their formal schooling.

Adding to the tendency to give greater attention to the early childhood years, is growing evidence that high-quality pre-Kindergarten programs and well-conceived and executed school improvement efforts during the K–3 years can raise achievement. This is especially (but not exclusively) true for low-socio-economic status (SES) children—youngsters from families that have low parent educational attainment and low family income levels. The fact that it has proven to be very difficult to develop middle school and high school strategies that markedly raise achievement at those levels of the system for disadvantaged students has been an additional reason for educators and policymakers to focus on the early years.

In response to these circumstances, the National Task Force on Early Childhood Education for Hispanics (to be known as the Task Force throughout this book) was established in 2005 to determine how early childhood education could be expanded and strengthened in ways that would improve the school readiness and academic achievement of Hispanic children. It published its comprehensive report of its efforts in March 2007 (National Task Force on Early Childhood Education for Hispanics, 2007). We will rely heavily on the pioneering work of this Task Force in this volume. We will cite its efforts and its research often and have used it as a basis for this volume. In pursuing their work, the Task Force was very concerned with finding ways to improve outcomes for Hispanic children from low-SES immigrant families. The SES profiles of these children would place many of them at risk in schools in their parents' countries of origin. In the United States, most of these youngsters have the added challenge of becoming proficient in academic English (García, 2005; García & Frede, 2010).

In this volume, we, like the Task Force, have been mindful that the lower educational performance of Hispanics is not simply a matter of lower standardized test scores. Throughout the elementary and secondary school years, Hispanics are also less likely to take challenging college preparatory courses in high school and to perform well in those courses. Furthermore, the percentages of Hispanics graduating from high school and earning college degrees are much lower than the percentages of Whites and Asians that are doing so.

There are serious negative consequences attached to these educational patterns for Hispanics and for the nation. The many young Hispanic adults with very low levels of educational attainment and achievement have limited prospects in a labor market that increasingly rewards those with high levels of human capital and penalizes those with low levels. Furthermore, the low percentages of Hispanics with bachelor, graduate, and professional degrees make it exceedingly difficult for Hispanics to become well represented in professional and leadership positions that require advanced education.

Viewed from the perspective of the United States as a whole, if the relatively low education level of Hispanics persists over the long term, it does have the potential to reduce the nation's economic competitiveness. Possibly more important, it could be a significant source of social divisiveness, owing to limits it would place on Hispanics' capacities to participate fully in American society.

EDUCATIONAL ATTAINMENT AND ACADEMIC ACHIEVEMENT

The Task Force's findings fall into three categories particularly related to this volume: (1) those concerned with educational attainment and academic achievement patterns of Hispanics; (2) those related to the foundations for Hispanic school readiness and academic performance; and (3) those regarding the potential for infant/toddler programs, pre-Kindergarten, and K–3 education to improve Hispanic school readiness and academic achievement.

The Task Force's (2007) major findings concerning educational attainment and academic achievement outcomes for Hispanics are:

1. Hispanics have made substantial gains in educational attainment on an intergenerational basis over the past several decades. Nationally, both high school completion and college graduation rates are now much higher among native-born Hispanics than among Hispanic immigrants. California data show that these rates are higher among third-generation Mexican Americans than among first- and second-generation Mexican Americans.

2. Similarly, there is evidence of intergenerational progress in academic achievement. National data for Mexican Americans show that third-generation children have higher levels of school readiness and higher levels of reading and math achievement in the K–5 years than first- and second-generation children.

3. Nonetheless, even among native-born and third-generation Hispanics, substantial gaps with Whites persist in high school graduation and college graduation rates. The gap in college graduation rates is very large.

4. Overall, Hispanics lag well behind Whites on measures of school readiness and academic achievement on the elementary and secondary levels. Hispanics are not only severely overrepresented among low-achieving students, they also are heavily underrepresented among high achievers. Moreover, the achievement of Hispanic students is far below that of students from most other industrialized nations.

5. In addition to the overall achievement gap, Hispanic achievement in such key subjects as reading and math lags somewhat behind Whites in all social class segments at both the elementary and secondary levels. Consequently, the need to raise achievement among Hispanics cuts across social class lines.

6. Because Hispanic children are disproportionately from low-SES circumstances (from families in which the parents have little formal schooling and low incomes), the low levels of school readiness and elementary and secondary school achievement in this social class segment are extremely pressing problems.

7. The most urgent need is to improve school readiness and achievement among low-SES Hispanic children from immigrant families. Many of these children speak little or no English when they start Kindergarten and, subsequently, achieve, on average, at very low levels during the early years of schooling in both reading and math. Moreover, it is likely that there will be a great many such children for a long time to come, owing to the ongoing high level of Hispanic immigration.

8. Although large educational attainment and academic achievement differences persist between Hispanics and Whites, there is considerable diversity in attainment and achievement patterns among Hispanic national origin groups. Some Hispanic national origin groups, including South Americans and Cuban Americans, are close to White attainment and achievement norms. Other groups, including the largest, Mexican Americans, are far below White attainment and achievement levels.

These findings have several broad implications. One is that the size and complexity of the Hispanic school readiness and academic achievement challenges provide a very strong incentive for the nation to make maximum use of the best available strategies for addressing them at every level of the educational continuum. Fortunately, there are a number of promising effective strategies. Another implication is that responding effectively to these challenges will not be easy. That is because educators will be required to substantially expand the capacities and expertise of the existing educational system—such as providing much greater pre-K opportunities. Finally, although there is a compelling need to increase the rate of educational advancement of Hispanics, even under the best of circumstances it will almost certainly take a substantial period of time to engage those who serve Hispanics and assist them in implementing new repertoires of designing, organizing, and implementing effective learning environments for this population of children and families. Better strategies, widely implemented, should accelerate the educational advancement process for Hispanics substantially.

Indeed, it is precisely because the educational advancement challenges for Hispanics are complex that the nation should maximize its efforts to address them. This volume builds on the work of the Task Force and other research, and attempts to systematically engage topics related to the expansion and improvement of early childhood education for Hispanics. However, it does not address some societal conditions that, although they impact educational outcomes, are difficult to address primarily through educational strategies and institutions. For instance, we do not consider what might be done to reduce extreme family poverty, which can produce various kinds of family duress, family instability, and health problems that may often undermine the children's learning, even when they attend high-quality preschools and effective elementary schools.

We also attempt in this volume to describe a very complex situation in which there are many difficult educational challenges along with some substantive educational advances for Hispanics. From a demographic standpoint, Hispanics are very diverse in terms of national heritage, social class, geographic distribution within the United States, length of time that they or their families have been in the United States, and primary language. They also are diverse in their academic achievement patterns: Many segments have very low-achievement patterns, while some segments are generally doing well. There also are proven strategies for improving Hispanic children's school readiness and raising their school achievement, although, as previously noted, they have important limitations.

ORGANIZATION OF THIS BOOK

This Introduction has previewed the issues, perspectives, and challenges that this volume addresses. The following chapters begin the process of more intricately inspecting the early learning circumstances of Hispanics and highlighting research-based and promising instructional alternatives as well as policies that may be associated with them. It is our attempt to construct for the reader a road map that not only describes the topography of the terrain but how to navigate that terrain. In doing so, the volume illustrates the link among research, policy, and practice that we envision for young Hispanic students, their families, and the educators who serve them.

Chapter 1 examines the present educational circumstances of young Hispanics. Knowing the landscape and circumstances of their early education experiences will help provide the necessary background for the intervention that may be necessary to enhance that educational landscape.

Chapter 2 focuses on the concept of culture and how the set of beliefs, values, and behavior that encompass the Hispanic culture intersect with the culture of schooling, particularly in the early years. We all swim in our cultures and intersect with other cultural waters—that is the essence of our everyday living.

Chapter 3 specifically addresses issues related to the development of language and literacy. This area of early learning has been the primary focus for Hispanics since they are more likely to experience exposure and development of more than one language. In fact, some 80% of Hispanic children in the United States are exposed to both Spanish and English (García & Jensen, 2009).

Chapter 4 is a highly interventionist chapter. We have come to realize that rich language environments are critical for all children in acquiring the academic discourses of schools, and that early learning venues within such environments are most necessary for our youngest Hispanic students, many learning English as their second language.

Chapter 5 introduces the significance of organizing learning and schooling in systematic measures that are particularly responsive to the cultural and linguistic character of Hispanic children and families.

Chapter 6 embraces the notion that the individual instructor/teacher and her or his linguistic, cultural, and professional expertise are critical for the educational advancement of Hispanics in early learning settings. These architects and implementers of instruction are absolutely critical for all students, but particularly important for Hispanics.

Chapter 7 turns to an often unrealized partner in early learning for Hispanics: the family. The family is a critical positive ingredient in the development of all children, but it plays a key role in the overall cultural attribute of U.S. Hispanics. Making evident how the early childhood educators can bring that family to engage as a partner in the educational enterprise is the goal of this chapter.

Chapter 8 realizes that learning support systems in formal educational arenas are guided and defined by policies at various levels. We discuss the omnipresent policy issues related to Hispanics and their education, including federal, state, and local policy issues.

The last chapter, Chapter 9, makes the extreme effort to summarize the volume's themes in a manner that embraces the link among research, policy, and practice. We also put forward a set of recommendations for further consideration related to this topic. We are quite aware that we are unable to address some of the important ingredients of an enhanced educational experience for young Hispanics because we just do not have, yet, all the answers to this challenge.

Yet we remain optimistic that the volume can add to that advancement and invite you to join us in that partnership. We have so much to gain by doing so, not only for Hispanics in this country, but for all our children and families. In short, there is a great deal more to do but much on which to build.

CHAPTER 1

Demographics and Educational Circumstances of Hispanics in Early Childhood

Hispanics come from varied family backgrounds—there is no standard family structure or organization. But researchers who have studied this population in the United States and in Latin America seem to agree that the family as a unit is a critical defining construct for individuals in that immediate and extended family (Tienda, 2005). This has often been referred to as the phenomenon of "familism" (García & Cuellar, 2006). We recently discussed this issue very informally among a group of Hispanic colleagues at a recent early childhood education conference. We were all sharing stories of our parents—how they were aging and we felt responsibility in assisting them; our children—how they were growing up and we still felt responsibility for them; and, for some of us, our grandchildren and how we felt a responsibility for them. The general theme was that family is a critical aspect governing our daily existence. One colleague indicated that her son has just been accepted at an Ivy League college. We were impressed and congratulatory since few Hispanics, even today, find their way to the Ivy League. She reminded us, however, appropriately so, that although her son would have a very good college education, there were so many other Hispanics who would not have that opportunity or even the opportunity to go on to college because of their underachievement in U.S. schools. She also reminded us that if this growing population of Hispanic students continue to be educationally unsuccessful, the future of her Ivy League graduate would not be as positive either—society as a whole needs this growing population of children to be successful. A sobering thought for us about our families and their interconnectedness to other Hispanics.

A GROWING POPULATION

Between 1960 and 2000, the number of Hispanics in the United States grew fivefold—from 7 million to 35 million people (Bean & Tienda, 1987).

In the process, they tripled their share of the nation's population, growing from less than 4% to 12.5%. By mid-2001, Hispanics numbered 37 million and had become the country's largest minority group (U.S. Census Bureau, 2003). By mid-2005, they had reached nearly 43 million (14.4% of the population) and had accounted for half the nation's population growth in the previous year (U.S. Census Bureau, 2006.) This rapid expansion is expected to continue for decades to come. By 2050, Hispanics are projected to number about 100 million and constitute about one-quarter of the nation's population (Passel, 2003).

The rapid growth of the Hispanic population is a product of several factors, including a high, sustained level of immigration; a large number of young adults who are in their family formation years; and a relatively high total fertility rate among Hispanic women (mainly among those who are immigrants) (Hernandez, 2006). Consistent with these factors, the Hispanic share of the nation's youngest children is considerably larger than their share of the population as a whole. For example, an analysis commissioned by the National Task Force on Early Childhood Education for Hispanics (2007) of the demographics of children in the 0 to 8 age group in 2000 found that among the 33.4 million children in the United States in that age segment, 6.8 million were Hispanic—20% of the total. Moreover, the Hispanic share of this age group is projected to reach 26% as early as 2030. Consistent with that projection, 25% of the 4.4 million babies born in the United States in 2007 had Hispanic mothers, up from 21% in 2000.

A large majority of the Hispanic population is of Mexican heritage. Yet, Hispanics also are quite diverse in terms of national origin. Among the Hispanic children in the 0 to 8 age group in 2000, about 68% were Mexican American, 9% Puerto Rican, 7% Central American, 6% South American, 3% Cuban, and 3% Dominican. In recent years, Hispanic births in the United States have continued to be generally consistent with this pattern (National Task Force on Early Childhood Education for Hispanics, 2007).

Owing to the high level of Hispanic immigration over the past 40 years, a majority of Hispanic children are either immigrants or from families in which one or both parents are immigrants. The Task Force's study of the 0 to 8 population in 2000 found that 64% (4.4 million) of the Hispanics were either immigrants themselves (first-generation Americans) or the children of immigrants (second-generation Americans). Only 36% (2.4 million) were children with two U.S.-born parents (third-generation Americans). Nevertheless, this pattern varied considerably among Hispanic national origin groups. The split for Mexican Americans was 66% first or second generation and 34% third generation, while the split was 91% and 9% for South Americans (National Task Force on Early Childhood Education for Hispanics, 2007).

Although it might be assumed that the majority of children in immigrant families are themselves immigrants, this is not the case, especially for the youngest children. Currently, among all immigrant families, regardless of their race or ethnicity, about 9 in 10 young children were born in the United States (Hernandez, 2006). Hispanics follow this pattern closely. About 88% of the 4.4 million first- and second-generation Hispanic children in the 0 to 8 age group in 2000 were U.S.-born.

Historically, Hispanics have been concentrated in a few states, and that is still the case. But, Hispanics currently have a rapidly increasing presence across the country. In 2000, about four-fifths of young Hispanic children lived in just nine states—California, Texas, New York, Florida, Illinois, Arizona, New Jersey, Colorado, and New Mexico, with half living in just two states—California and Texas. Yet, in that year, at least one in eight of the children in the 0 to 8 age group in 24 states were Hispanic. In 2004, babies born to Hispanic mothers accounted for at least 10% of the births in 27 states and the District of Columbia (National Task Force on Early Education for Hispanics, 2007). Some of the most rapid growth is taking place in states in the South and Southeast. For example, in both Georgia and North Carolina, the share of the babies born to Hispanic mothers grew from 2% in 1990 to 14% in 2004. In Virginia, it grew from 3% to 11% and in Arkansas, it grew from 1% to 9%.

PARENT EDUCATION LEVELS

The National Task Force on Early Childhood Education for Hispanics (2007) presented important analyses of parental education levels. Relative to non-Hispanic Whites, young Hispanic children are much more likely to have parents who have not graduated from high school and much less likely to have parents who have a bachelor's degree or more. For example, in the 0 to 8 age group in 2000, almost 46% of the Hispanic children had mothers who had not graduated from high school, while this was the case for only 9% of the Whites. Twenty percent of Hispanic children had mothers who had not gone beyond the 8th grade compared to only 1% of the White children. At the same time, less than 10% of the Hispanic children had a mother with a bachelor's degree or more, while 30% of White children that had a mother who was a college graduate.

These differences were even larger for Hispanic youngsters in immigrant families. About 54% of these children had a mother who had not completed high school; 29% had a mother who had not gone beyond the 8th grade; and, 9% had a mother who had no more than a 4th-grade education. Regarding higher education, only 8% of Hispanic children in immigrant families had a mother with at least a bachelor's degree. Not all Hispanic national-origin segments had weak maternal educational attainment profiles. Among Cubans and South Americans, the children in both immigrant and non-immigrant families had parent education profiles that were generally similar to that of Whites. However, together, Cubans and South Americans constituted only about 8% of the 6.8 million Hispanics in the 0 to 8 age group in 2000.

In contrast, among young Mexican Americans, the parent education profile in immigrant families was much weaker than the profile for Hispanics as a whole. Only 4% of the Mexican American children in immigrant families had a mother with a bachelor's degree or more, while 64% had a mother who had not completed high school. In fact, 36% of these youngsters had a mother who had not gone beyond the 8th grade, and 11% had a mother who had not gone beyond the 4th grade.

These parent education patterns meant that Hispanics were a very large share of the nation's young children from families in which parents had little formal education. Among the 33.4 million children in the United States in the 0 to 8 age group in 2000, about 6.1 million (18%) had a mother who had not completed high school, and about 1.8 million (6%) had a mother who had not gone beyond the 8th grade. Hispanic youngsters accounted for 49% of those with a mother who had not completed high school and 74% of those with a mother who had not gone beyond the 8th grade. By themselves, Hispanic immigrants accounted for 39% of the children with mothers who had not completed high school and 69% of those with mothers with an 8th-grade education or less.

CHILD POVERTY

The National Task Force on Early Childhood Education for Hispanics (2007) also provided informative analyses of poverty circumstances for Hispanic families with young children. Consistent with the large differences in parent education, a much larger percentage of young Hispanic children live in families that have incomes that fall below the federal poverty line. Among children in the 0 to 8 age segment in 2000, about 26% of Hispanics were below the poverty line, compared to only 9% for Whites. The gaps also were very large for children in low-income families (with "low income" defined as below twice the official poverty line). About 58% of young Hispanic children were from low-income families, while this was the case for 27% of Whites. Poverty and low-income rates were significantly higher for young Hispanic children from immigrant families than for Hispanics with native-born parents—63% versus 48%. Among Hispanic national origin groups, young Mexican American children with immigrant parents had the highest percentage in low-income families at 69%.

These high-poverty and low-income rates are not primarily a function of high unemployment rates—about 93% of the young Hispanic children in 2000 had fathers who were employed full or part time. Rather, they are mainly due to low-wage rates and relatively high levels of part-time employment, which are consistent with lower than average job attainment levels of Hispanic fathers and mothers.

ENGLISH LANGUAGE LEARNERS

Because a large majority of young Hispanic children have immigrant parents, a majority of these youngsters also have home environments in which Spanish is the primary or exclusive language. The National Task Force on Early Childhood Education for Hispanics (2007) analysis of Early Childhood Longitudinal Study-Birth Cohort (ECLS-B) data found that 56% of the Hispanics infants had a mother who was born outside the United States. Consistent with this pattern, 19% of the Hispanic parents said that only Spanish was spoken in their homes, while 35% described the language environment of their home as being mainly Spanish with some English spoken. About 21% said that only English was spoken in their homes, and 22% reported that mainly English was spoken with some Spanish. The tendency for Spanish to be the exclusive or primary language of the home was even greater for Hispanic families in poverty. About 28% reported that only Spanish was spoken, while 15% said that only English was used. The dominance of Spanish in the home environments was reinforced by the childcare arrangements of the families. Among the families that used non-parental childcare on a regular basis, 60% said that English was not the primary language used in childcare.

Consistent with these circumstances, a companion federal study to the ECLS-B, the Early Childhood Longitudinal Study-Kindergarten Cohort (ECLS-K), found that about 30% of the Hispanics in the national sample did not have strong enough oral English skills when they started Kindergarten (in the fall of 1998) to be given the test designed to assess their English literacy skills at that point. Moreover, because a large number of Hispanic children in immigrant families have parents with little formal education, many of these youngsters' parents may have weak Spanish academic capabilities. Thus, a substantial percentage of Hispanic children may be starting Kindergarten without the English or Spanish literacy foundations needed to get off to a good start in school. (It will be recalled that about 54% of the young Hispanic children in immigrant families in

2000 had a mother who had not completed high school; and 29% had a mother who had not gone beyond the 8th grade).

HISPANIC EDUCATIONAL PERFORMANCE PATTERNS IN EARLY CHILDHOOD

Consistent with the parent education, family income, single-parent family, and home language patterns discussed in the previous section, Hispanic students have had much lower levels of academic achievement than non-Hispanic Whites (and Asian Americans), at least since national achievement data first became available by race/ethnicity in the mid-1960s. Importantly, there is extensive evidence that these differences in achievement, whether measured by standardized tests or school grades, have their foundations in the infant/toddler and preschooler period. On measures of reading readiness, math concepts, and general knowledge, Hispanic youngsters are already behind their White peers when they start Kindergarten. By the end of the primary grades, the achievement gaps are essentially fully formed, including in reading and mathematics, both of which are central to academic progress in most areas of the school curriculum in the late elementary grades and at the secondary level.

These differences in academic achievement are most pronounced at low- and high-achievement levels. As students move into the upper elementary school grades, Hispanics are heavily overrepresented among low-achieving students and markedly underrepresented among high achievers. Consequently, viewed from the perspective of educational futures, Hispanics are overrepresented among students with such low achievement that they are at-risk of eventually not graduating from high school; and, they also are underrepresented among those who are on course to emerge from high school academically well prepared to attend college—and are severely underrepresented among those on course to be very well prepared to attend highly selective institutions.

Owing to these overall patterns and to the diversity of the Hispanic population, the National Task Force on Early Childhood Education for Hispanics (2007) provided an analysis of K–5 reading and mathematics achievement, using data from the ECLS-K. Such an analysis provides a much more detailed picture than has been available to date of how Hispanic academic achievement compares to the achievement of non-Hispanic Whites in the early years of school. In making these comparisons, the study looked at the achievement patterns of Hispanics on an overall basis and for a number of subpopulations, including (1) several Hispanic national origin segments, such as Mexican Americans and Central Americans; (2) first-, second-, and third-generation Mexican Americans; and (3) low-, middle-, and high-SES Hispanics. The White students in the study were limited to those who were third-generation Americans because they represent the "baseline" group within the White population (National Task Force on Early Childhood Education for Hispanics, 2007).

Table 1.1 lists the nine reading proficiency levels that were used in the ECLS-K study during the K–5 years.

Table 1.2 presents data on students' reading skills at the start of Kindergarten. The Hispanic data do not include the 30% of Hispanic children in the ECLS-K sample who did not have oral English skills strong enough for them to take the English-language reading readiness assessment as they entered Kindergarten. (The reading skills of the non-English-speaking group of Hispanic youngsters are discussed later in this section.) Yet, even with 30%

Table 1.1. ECLS-K Reading Proficiency Levels

Level	Proficiency
1	Recognition of letters
2	Understanding beginning sounds of words
3	Understanding ending sounds of words
4	Sight recognition of words
5	Comprehension of words in context
6	Literal inference from words in text
7	Extrapolating from text to derive meaning
8	Evaluating and interpreting beyond text
9	Evaluating nonfiction

Source: Princiotta & Flanagan, 2006.

Table 1.2. Percentage of Students Scoring at Levels 1, 2, 3, and 4 in Reading at Start of Kindergarten

Group	Level 1	Level 2	Level 3	Level 4
Whites—3rd Generation	73	34	20	4
All Hispanic	54	20	10	2
Mexican	51	19	10	2
Cuban	67	25	12	2
Puerto Rican	62	26	14	2
Central American	52	18	11	1
South American	60	26	15	5

Source: Reardon & Galindo, 2006.

excluded, the data in Table 1.2 show that the remaining Hispanics lagged well behind third-generation Whites in letter recognition, understanding beginning sounds of words, and understanding ending sounds. They also lagged behind Whites in sight reading words, although few children from any group had that skill at the beginning of Kindergarten.

Among Hispanic national origin groups, Mexican Americans and Central Americans lagged behind Whites to about the same extent as Hispanics overall. The strongest performing Hispanics at the start of Kindergarten were children of South American origin, followed closely by Cuban and Puerto Rican youngsters. As will be recalled, South Americans and Cubans have parent education levels that are generally similar to those of Whites, while the other Hispanic groups have much lower parent education levels.

Table 1.3 presents reading skill data for the end of 5th grade that also excludes the 30% of Hispanics who began Kindergarten with little or no knowledge of English. At the end of 5th grade, Hispanics overall and Mexican Americans and Central Americans had considerably smaller percentages of students demonstrating mastery of the more advanced reading skills than third-generation White students. However, the reading skill patterns for South Americans were virtually identical to those of Whites. The skill patterns of Cubans and Puerto Ricans were close to the White pattern also.

Although the achievement gaps between Hispanics and Whites are heavily related to the much lower socioeconomic status (SES) circumstances of Hispanics relative to Whites, this is only part of the story. Extensive research going back to the late 1960s has found that Hispanics achieve at somewhat lower levels than Whites (and Asian Americans) in all or most social class segments across the K–12 years. Moreover, the within-class gaps have often been found to be larger at high-SES levels than at low SES levels. (African Americans also lag behind Whites and Asian Americans within most social class segments.)

Table 1.3. Percentage of Students Scoring at Levels 6, 7, 8, and 9 in Reading at End of 5th Grade

Group	Level 6	Level 7	Level 8	Level 9
Whites 3rd-Generation	91	79	52	10
All Hispanic	86	69	41	5
Mexican	86	67	40	5
Cuban	92	80	48	5
Puerto Rican	92	78	48	6
Central American	90	76	43	3
South American	91	79	51	11

Source: Reardon & Galindo, 2006.

The data in Table 1.4 show that within-class gaps existed between Hispanics and Whites in all five social class segments at the start of Kindergarten. Yet, the data in Table 1.5 show a mixed picture at the end of the 5th grade. Hispanics continued to lag behind Whites somewhat in the top three SES quintiles. However, the Whites and Hispanics in the first SES quintile looked very similar in their reading skill patterns at the end of the 5th grade, while in the second quintile Hispanics had a slight edge. That is to say, low-SES Hispanic children who started Kindergarten with reasonable oral skills in English ended the 5th grade with about the same English reading skill levels as their low-SES White counterparts, at least as measured by the instruments used in the ECLS-K.

The caveat is that 30% of the Hispanic students were excluded from the 5th grade data in this analysis, owing to their limited English skills at the start of Kindergarten. Had their 5th-grade scores been included, Hispanics would have undoubtedly lagged behind Whites considerably in the lowest two SES quintiles for two reasons. First, most of the 30% were Hispanic children from families in the lowest two SES quintiles. Second, the reading scores of the 30% were far below those of Whites at the end of the 5th grade—over a full standard deviation in statistical terms. The implications of this are that, for Hispanics as a whole, meaningful within-class gaps with Whites would be predicted at all SES levels when students reach the secondary level.

Data in Table 1.5 also show that 27% of the lowest quintile Hispanics were unable to reach Level 1 (simple reading comprehension) compared to 12% of the Whites. Thus, over a quarter of low-SES Hispanic

Table 1.4. Percentage of Students Scoring at Levels 1, 2, 3, and 4 in Reading at the Start of Kindergarten, by SES Quintile, for Hispanics and Whites

SES Quintile	Group	Level 1	Level 2	Level 3	Level 4
First (Low)	Hispanic	37	8	3	0
	White	48	13	5	0
Second	Hispanic	54	17	8	1
	White	60	20	10	1
Third	Hispanic	54	20	11	3
	White	69	29	16	3
Fourth	Hispanic	72	33	17	2
	White	80	38	21	3
Fifth (High)	Hispanic	73	41	25	5
	White	86	50	33	8

Source: Reardon & Galindo, 2006.

Table 1.5. Percentage of Students Scoring at Levels 6, 7, 8, and 9 in Reading at the End of 5th-Grade, by SES Quintile, for Hispanics and Whites

SES Quintile	Group	Level 6	Level 7	Level 8	Level 9
First (Low)	Hispanic	77	51	29	1
	White	73	51	30	3
Second	Hispanic	89	74	44	6
	White	86	68	40	4
Third	Hispanic	86	66	38	2
	White	91	77	48	7
Fourth	Hispanic	92	81	51	9
	White	94	86	55	9
Fifth (High)	Hispanic	95	87	59	13
	White	96	91	64	20

Source: Reardon & Galindo, 2006.

sophomores evidently were reading far below the level required to do high school academic work.

The data presented here make it clear that promoting greater educational progress for Hispanics will require improving the school readiness and early academic achievement of Hispanic children from all SES levels, not just those from low-SES circumstances. Because they represent about two-thirds of young Hispanics, it also is essential that significant improvements be made in the readiness and early achievement of Mexican Americans. Furthermore, since a large segment of Hispanic children from immigrant families are starting Kindergarten with little or no knowledge of English and, subsequently, are lagging far behind Whites in the early years of school, it is imperative that ways be found to meet their language development needs much more effectively.

These data also make it clear that the challenge is not simply one of markedly reducing the percentage of Hispanics who are low academic achievers from the time they start school. There is a pressing need as well to substantially increase the percentage of Hispanics who are high achievers. Full participation of Hispanics within all sectors and organizational levels of American society requires both. Both also are increasingly required to maintain the international competitiveness of the U.S. economy.

Finally, the need to improve outcomes for Hispanics is made more pressing by the continued relatively low academic achievement of African Americans. Although data for Blacks have not been presented here, their overall achievement patterns also are generally much lower than those of Whites, and they have substantial within-class gaps with Whites as well

(National Task Force on Early Childhood Education for Hispanics, 2007). Because together, Hispanics and African Americans now account for about two-fifths of the nation's births, the overall low-achievement patterns for these two groups make it increasingly important to accelerate the rate of intergenerational educational advancement of both of them.

Sources of School Readiness and Achievement Gaps

School readiness and school achievement patterns have their foundations in the period from birth to age 3, a time at which the home and family typically play the dominant role in the development of children. One of the most important ways in which the home environment differs for Hispanics and Whites is in literacy-related parenting practices. For example, there is evidence that, on average, Hispanic mothers talk less to their children than White mothers. They also read less to their infants and toddlers than White mothers; this is especially true for Hispanic mothers who do not speak English as their primary language in the home. In addition, there tend to be fewer literacy-related materials, such as children's books, available in Hispanic homes than in White homes (National Task Force on Early Childhood Education for Hispanics, 2007).

These differences in Hispanic/White parenting patterns are partly associated with social class differences, that is, Hispanic children are more likely than Whites to be from low-SES families as measured by parent education and family income levels. This is important, because research has documented large SES-related differences, not only in mothers' book reading to their children, but also in mother–child talking patterns. On average, low-SES mothers talk with their children much less than middle-class mothers talk to their youngsters, and even less than professional-class mothers talk to their youngsters. One influential study of low-, middle-, and high-SES (professional class) families with young children estimated that, by age 3, low-SES children have heard only one-third as many words spoken as children with professional-class parents.

That study also found large SES differences (in favor of the high-SES youngsters) in the number of different words that the children heard, in how words were used, in the length of sentences, and in the range of topics that were discussed. Parents' modeling of the use of language differed by SES in terms of such things as the kinds of questions that were asked and how things or events were described. The children were also exposed to different amounts of information on a wide range of topics. These differences also meant that there were large SES differences in the ways that the parents acted as teachers of their children. The mothers in the professional-class families were much more likely than those in the low-SES families to ask their child to elaborate on comments. They also were more likely to ask their children questions concerned with promoting thought and reflection and to elicit behaviors rather than directing the youngsters to do things. Furthermore, they were much more likely to make positive comments to their children and much less likely to make negative comments. These patterns did not stop when the children reached their third birthdays. They simply continued on, because they were fundamental characteristics of the families' lives.

That study, as well as others, has found that these substantial early differences in oral language experiences and vocabulary development are correlated with the large differences in oral vocabulary sizes between low- and high-SES children in the early elementary grades. High-SES children have much larger oral vocabularies than low-SES children in the early elementary grades, and an advantage in this area persists into the upper elementary grades and beyond. These vocabulary differences are important, because the vocabulary that children have, as they start 1st grade, is not only a predictor of their reading skills at the end of the 1st grade, but also of their reading comprehension skills through high school. Moreover, it is not just that high-SES children generally have larger vocabularies than low-SES youngsters on which to draw when they read a textbook in, say, the 4th grade; they also have larger stores of knowledge on many topics related to understanding their schoolwork that were partly acquired while acquiring the larger vocabularies.

The Task Force's study of data on the infants being tracked in the ECLS-B found that literacy-development-related parenting differences between Hispanics and Whites exist during the 1st year of children's lives. The initial assessment of the sample of children in the ECLS-B was undertaken when they were, on average, about 9 months old. At that point, the White mothers were more likely than the Hispanic mothers to tell their children stories, to sing to them, and to read to them. Moreover, these differences existed to some extent at all SES levels. Other research also has found that differences in the percentages of Hispanic and White mothers who read to their children exist at most SES levels. Research also indicates that these differences are particularly large between White mothers and Hispanic mothers who do not speak English as their primary language in the home. One study found that, among White mothers with less than a high school diploma, only 13% reported never reading to their children, while this was the case for 21% of the Hispanic mothers who spoke English at home, and for 48% of the Hispanic mothers who did not speak English. Similarly, among mothers with a bachelor's degree or more, 5% of the White mothers did not read to their children compared to 9% of the Hispanic mothers who spoke English at home and 30% of the Hispanic mothers who did not.

The importance of these differences in the language and cognitive development of infants and toddlers has recently been documented in a study of about 2,600 low-income mothers and their children who participated in a randomized trial of 17 Early Head Start programs across the United States. Frequent, regular reading of books to the children by their mothers from the time the children were 14 months old was correlated with their language and cognitive development at 36 months. This was true both for children with English-speaking and Spanish-speaking mothers. However, the Spanish-speaking mothers were much less likely to engage in frequent book reading to their children than the English-speaking mothers were.

Some researchers have estimated that these and related parenting differences account for between one-quarter and one-half of racial/ethnic readiness gaps at the start of kindergarten. Clearly, these are consequential differences for Hispanic children (García & Jensen, 2009).

Pre-Kindergarten Access Challenges for Hispanics

Apart from the need to improve the quality of pre-Kindergarten programs available to Hispanics, it also is essential to expand their access to pre-K. As Table 1.6 shows, while 59% of White and 66% of Black children ages 3 to 5 attended some form of center-based childcare or preschool program in 2005, only 43% of Hispanics did so. Moreover, the percentages for each group had changed very little over the previous 15 years. In 1991, they were, respectively, 39%, 54%, and 58%.

As Table 1.6 also shows, attendance by Hispanics lagged well behind that of Whites and African Americans among both poor and non-poor children. Thus, Hispanics' need for greater access to preschool reaches across social class lines. Although the reasons for the relatively low attendance of Hispanics have not been firmly established, several factors seem to be involved. One evidently is inadequate preschool capacity to meet demand in many Hispanic communities. For example, an analysis commissioned by

Table 1.6. Percentages of Children Ages 3 to 5 Who Attended Center-Based Early Childhood Care and Education Programs in 2005, by Race/Ethnicity and Economic Status

Group	Economic Status of Children		
	All	*Poor*	*Non-poor*
Hispanic	43	36	48
White	59	45	61
Black	66	65	68

Source: National Center for Education Statistics, 2007.

the Task Force of the preschool supply-demand situation for Hispanics in two large urban areas (Los Angeles and Chicago) found an overall shortage of center-based preschool seats in Hispanic neighborhoods.

A survey of Hispanic adults' views on pre-Kindergarten asked the respondents what they think accounts for the low enrollment rates of Hispanic children. The two most cited reasons were (1) Hispanic parents' lack of knowledge about program availability in their communities (one-third of the respondents held this view); and (2) the inability of Hispanic parents to afford to pay for preschool for their children (one-fifth gave this reason) (García & Gonzalez, 2006).

Because a large segment of Hispanic parents have limited knowledge of English, getting information about preschool programs would be expected to be difficult for many of them. Also, the cost of preschool is likely to be an obstacle for many middle-class and lower middle-class Hispanic families—just as it is for similar families from other groups. Such families have incomes that are too high to qualify for Head Start or other programs that target low-SES children but are too low for the families to have the discretionary income to pay for their children to attend a good pre-school program. These circumstances may help explain why a majority of the respondents to that survey said that government-funded preschool should be available to all children, not just youngsters from low-income families.

The survey also identified another obstacle of potential importance: About one-eighth of the respondents believed that many parents do not have the documents required to enroll their children in preschool. The extent to which this is a real obstacle in many cases is unclear. However, because many Hispanic parents and some of their children are undocumented, an appreciable number may be reluctant to enroll their children in pre-Kindergarten. Because there is not yet a full explanation for why Hispanics lag far behind African Americans and Whites in preschool attendance, much more research and analysis is required in this area. Nonetheless, policymakers almost certainly will need to address the supply and affordability issues described here. Providing much better information about available preschool opportunities to immigrant parents with limited English proficiency also will probably be necessary.

Early Childhood Education and Low-SES Hispanic English-Language Learners

As was noted earlier in this volume, across the industrialized world, children with parents who have relatively little formal education generally achieve at much lower levels in school than children who have parents with a great deal of education. Consequently, societies with large numbers of children from families in which the parents have low educational attainment levels have a very strong incentive to provide these youngsters with high quality early childhood education.

Certainly this incentive applies to the United States, especially with regard to improving educational outcomes for Hispanics. In 2000, about 46% of the nation's young Hispanics—nearly 3 million youngsters—had mothers who had not graduated from high school and more than one-third—about 2.4 million—were from immigrant families in which the mother had not completed high school. Moreover, Hispanic immigration is projected to continue at high levels and a high percentage of Hispanic births in the United States continue to be to women with relatively little formal schooling. This suggests that, for a long time to come, an enormous number of young Hispanic children will be from families in which there is relatively little human capital; and many of these youngsters will be from homes in which the primary language is Spanish.

Such circumstances would undoubtedly present complex educational challenges in most industrialized nations. Adding to the complexity here in the United States is the fact that Hispanics are heavily underrepresented among children who attend preschool. As Table 1.6 indicates, only 43% of all 3 to 5-year-old Hispanic children were attending center-based early childhood care and education programs in 2005; and only 36% of Hispanics from poor families were doing so. Furthermore, this situation has changed relatively little over the past decade. This means that essential developmental opportunities that can be provided by high (or even average) quality pre-Kindergarten are simply not available to many of the nation's children in most need of those opportunities.

Under these circumstances, it is almost inevitable that a substantial percentage of Hispanic children would enter Kindergarten each year with very weak English language skills along with school readiness gaps in other areas. Owing to the limited human capital possessed by a large percentage of the parents in immigrant Hispanic families, it also seems likely that many Hispanic children would enter Kindergarten with relatively weak Spanish skills. This combination would place many of these children at risk of low-level academic achievement throughout their elementary school years and beyond.

There are no national data on the Spanish proficiency levels of Hispanic children as they enter Kindergarten. However, the ECLS-K, which was discussed extensively earlier, provides data on the English proficiency of a national sample of children, including Hispanics, as they started Kindergarten in the fall of 1998. In addition, findings from the Task Force's analysis of ECLS-K data provide information on the math and English-reading achievement patterns of the children as they have moved through elementary school. The ECLS-K data are quite consistent with the circumstances described here. As noted earlier, about 30% of the Hispanic children in the ECLS-K did not speak English well enough to be assessed in it as they started kindergarten. Among the 30%, seven in ten of the children were from families in the bottom SES quintile and nearly nine in ten were from the bottom two SES quintiles. Also, a large majority were from homes in which Spanish was the only or primary language spoken.

CONCLUSION

Overall, given the circumstances described above, it would seem that the home-based human capital and home language patterns coupled with the immigrant attributes of Hispanics had much to do with how young Hispanics performed academically. As these children have moved through elementary school, their math and reading achievement levels have been very low. At the end of the 5th grade, the 30% of Hispanic children who had weak or essentially no English skills at the start of Kindergarten were, not only performing below White children's averages in reading and math, they also were well below the averages for the other 70% of Hispanic children.

A major theme in this volume is that time is one of the most important factors in developing early childhood education strategies that are more effective in promoting school readiness and school achievement for Hispanics. The case for full-day pre-Kindergarten for 3- and 4-year-olds also may be especially strong for Hispanic ELLs from immigrant families in which the mother has relatively little formal education. These youngsters seem to have language development needs in Spanish that are similar to the English development needs of low-SES children from English-speaking homes. In addition to the exposure to early learning opportunities, the quality of those opportunities seems to be significant. We will turn to those in the chapters that follow.

NOTE

The statistics presented in this chapter were derived from tabular databases overseen by L. Scott Miller as director of the National Task Force on Early Childhood Education for Hispanics.

CHAPTER 2

The Concept of Culture in the Classroom

When we speak of the "culture" to which an individual belongs, our reference is generally to the system of understandings (values, prescriptions, proscriptions, beliefs, and other constructs) that are characteristic of that individual's society, or some subgroups within the society—that is, ethnic minorities, social classes, countercultures, generations, genders, and occupational groups. This is the traditional notion of culture employed by functionalist anthropologists in their analyses of the behavioral patterns and normative customs of groups.

The culture concept, with its technical anthropological meaning, was first defined by Edward Taylor in 1871 as "that complex whole which includes knowledge, belief, art, law, morals, custom, and other capabilities and habits acquired by man as a member of society" (Kroeber and Kluckhohn, 1963, p. 81). Since Taylor's time a great variety of definitions of culture have been advanced by anthropologists. These definitions commonly attempt to encompass, as did Taylor's, the totality (or some subset of the totality) of humanity's achievements, dispositions, and capabilities. And virtually every anthropologist considers culture to be something that is learned, as it is transmitted from generation to generation.

Most definitions of culture include another social dimension, the notion that culture is something that members of a group share in common. A recently published anthropology textbook states, for example, that behaviors and ideas may be considered cultural only insofar as they are shared among members of a social group. This formulation is useful for anthropological comparisons between societies or subgroups within societies. Its basic assumption, however, is that of uniformity in the cultural equipment of individual members of societies and their sub-groupings. In this formulation, the ontological locus of culture is some kind of group.

At the same time, all anthropologists acknowledge that members of all sorts and sizes of societies display differences in their behaviors and ways of thinking and valuing. That is to say, societies are characterized to some extent by intra-cultural heterogeneity. But such discussions remain most often at the level of the group, as in statements about the "loose-ness" or "tightness" of societies' cultural systems. When these researchers proceed to write their ethnographies, they tend to ignore inter-individual variations as they abstract what they apparently consider to be "an es-sential homogeneity from the background noise of insignificant diversity" (Schwartz, 1978, p. 419).

CULTURAL PERCEPTIONS AND EXPECTATIONS

Anthropologist Ralph Linton defined culture as "the sum total of ideas, conditioned emotional responses and patterns of habitual behavior which the members of [a] society have acquired through instruction or imita-tion and which they share to a greater or less degree" (quoted in Kroeber and Kluckhohn, 1963, p. 82). Although acknowledging that cultural items (ideas or learned behavioral habits) need not be totally shared by everyone in a group, in this concept it is, nevertheless, the property of sharing that defines the domain of culture.

This emphasis on shared traits is relevant to any consideration re-garding a definition of culture. But such an emphasis on shared traits leaves little, if any, room for the conceptual recognition of each student's individuality within the framework of the culture concept. Individuality becomes the domain of psychology, relevant only to discussions of per-sonality, while the culture concept is reserved for behavioral and ide-ational features of the individual's group.

The relevance of this problem lies in the possible consequences of the group-oriented culture concept for the perceptions and expectations of teachers in their interactions with children of a different culture than their own. It is our contention that a group-oriented notion of culture may serve to detract the teacher's attention from the process. The connection between teacher–student interaction and the culture concept derives from the fact that assumptions about the student's culture—whether right or wrong—may serve to stereotype the student and thus preclude the flexible, realistic, and open-minded quality of teacher–student interaction needed for effective in-struction. This possibility becomes more apparent when one realizes that the educational process is fundamentally one of social interaction.

Picture, if you will, a situation where a teacher is perplexed by some action or response on the part of a student who "is not like him or her." If the teacher has studied some of the anthropological ethnographies of the student's ethnic culture he or she may leap to an interpretation of the student's behavior in terms of idealized or modal characteristics attrib-uted to that culture. To construe an individual's behavior solely on the basis of generalization about group traits is to stereotype the individual, no matter how valid the generalizations or how disinterested one may be. It would be better for the teacher to pursue the meaning of the student's behavior in the way ethnographers most often come to understand the people they study. Even though they write about cultures in collective terms, they come to know about them through observations of individuals. Of course, the teacher's efforts to understand the individual student could (and should) benefit from knowledge of cultural orientations that are widely, or typically, held in the student's ethnic community. But this fund of knowledge should be viewed only as background information. The question of its applicability to the particular student should be treated as inherently problematical. Many investigations of culture and schooling also caution educational personnel against hasty ethnographic/cultural generalizations on the grounds that all linguistic-cultural groups are continuously undergoing significant cultural changes.

Thomas Carter's early research (1968) along with Matuti-Bianchi and Ogbu's (1988) and Steele's (1994) research on expectations on student learning and classroom behavior—namely that Chicano students may sometimes actualize in their behavior the negative expectations held for them by educators—confirms the concerns expressed here.

The Individual-Oriented Culture Concept

Fortunately, anthropological theory contains a parallel individual-oriented conception of culture developed and used by a number of psychologically oriented anthropologists. An early expression of the individual-oriented concept of culture is seen in the work of a now-forgotten anthropologist, J. O. Dorsey. The individual-oriented approach to culture frequently describes a society's culture as a "pool" of constructs (rules, beliefs, values) by which the society's members conceptually order the objects and events of their lives. The individual's own portion of a society's culture is termed by Goodenough (1981) as a "propriocept," by Wallace (1970) as a "maze way," and by Schwartz (1978) as an "idioverse."

For purposes of understanding Hispanic culture it seems most appropriate to simultaneously recognize a Hispanic's ethnic culture (that is, what individuals share with their ethnic peers and not with out-group members) and those characteristics that define each person as a relatively unique individual (all individuals are in some ways different from their ethnic peers). It also permits recognition of traits shared with members of the larger culture, such as those acquired through acculturation.

Cultural integration is a crucial variable in the analysis of Hispanics, and its process contributes significantly to the existence of the heterogeneity of Hispanic cultures. Writing of Chicano culture, Garcia (2001a) notes, for example, that among Chicanos, many have ancestors who came to North America several centuries ago, but others are themselves recent immigrants. Hence, a simple cultural characterization of [this] ethnic group should be avoided. He also cautions against a simplistic view of the process of cultural integration, noting that integration may not be linear, in the sense that one simply loses certain Mexican attributes and replaces them with new attributes. The process may be characterized by more complex patterns of combination and by ongoing recombination than by simple substitution and, in addition to the fact of degrees of integration among individuals, would contribute to the cultural heterogeneity of the Chicano population, which is to say, the relative uniqueness of its members.

I might add, parenthetically, that some people are likely to respond to the individual-oriented conception of culture with the question, "What about customs?" Some Hispanics, for example, might point out that they recognize certain *costumbres*, or customs, that distinguish them as a group from the larger society. This indicates a realm of culture that is highly shared and more likely to belong to the public sphere rather than the individual's subjective orientation. Referring to the "layered" nature of culture, anthropologist Benjamin Paul has observed that

> What we call customs rest on top and are most apparent. Deepest and least apparent are the cultural values that give meaning and direction to life. Values influence people's perceptions of needs and their choice between perceived alternative courses of action. (1965, p. 200)

What we wish to emphasize here is the problematical nature of the variability and sharing of values and other constructs as internalized by individuals. The individual's participation in culture reflects his or her unique set of life experiences. This variable participation and the relative uniqueness of the individual that it engenders is important for education as are the generalized cultural differences between ethnic groups. Educators must deal with both. This is true for all students, but is particularly relevant for educators who serve learners who come from a culture(s)—learners who have internalized a different set of experiences—significantly different than their own culture(s).

Rogoff (2011), in her extensive research related to understanding culture and culture change in Guatemala, cautions educators in particular to stay away for the "Box Problem"—a tendency to put individuals from non-familiar cultural groups in distinct ethnic "boxes." In the United States, due to U.S. Census categories, these usually relate to ethnic groups such as Asian, Hispanic, Southeast Asian, and so forth. In the Hispanic "box," a wide variety of children and families could be included—some speaking Spanish, some bilingual in Spanish and English, some from Mexico or Cuba (some born in the United States, others born outside the United States), others from South America, and the list of diversity can go on and on. For this reason Rogoff (2011) recommends we focus on specific cultural practices of those who we normally put in the ethnic "boxes." This requires that we operate with an open mind to examine how people live rather than use predetermined labels to attempt to understand who they are. This will allow us to see cultural integration and cultural change at work. We need to remind ourselves that no culture is homogenous or static; changes occur across generations and within cultural contacts that shape individual's cultural integration right before our eyes. We also need to remind ourselves that those interactions that we shape as educators are critical in the overall cultural integration process and may have both immediate and long-term influences. Those can be positive and negative with regard to the individuals—something we often reflect on in our everyday teaching. Yet for all our children, and particularly Hispanics and others whom we might want to put into ethnic boxes, we are agents of cultural integration and change whether we realize it or not. It is best to understand your role as an educator in this process. Let us examine how you might do that.

Americanization

Historically, "Americanization" has been a prime institutional education objective for Hispanic children (Gonzalez, 1990; García, 2005). Schooling practices were adopted whenever the population of these students rose to significant numbers in a community. This adaptation established special programs, and was applied to both children and adults in urban and rural schools and communities. The desired effect of Americanizing students was to socialize and acculturate the diverse community. In essence, if schools could teach these students English and American values, then educational failure could be averted. Ironically, social economists have argued that this effort was coupled with systematic efforts to maintain disparate relations between Anglos and "minority" populations. Indeed, more than anything else, past attempts at addressing the "Black, Hispanic, Indian, Asian, and so forth, educational problem" have actually preserved the political and economic subordination of these community (Spencer, 1988). Coming from a sociological theory of assimilation, Americanization has traditionally been recognized as a solution to the problem of immigrants and ethnicity in the modern industrialized United States. Linda Chavez (1991, 1995) continues to champion this solution for Hispanics today.

Americanization was intended to merge small ethnic and linguistically diverse communities into a single dominant national institutional structure and culture. It can be argued that Americanization is still the goal of many programs aimed at culturally diverse students (Weis, 1988; Rodriguez, 1989; García, 1994). Americanization for these students unfortunately still means the elimination not only of linguistic and cultural differences but of an undesirable culture. Americanization programs seem to assume a single homogeneous ethnic culture in contact with a single homogeneous American culture, and the relationship between the two is not that of equals. The dominant community, enjoying greater wealth and privileges, claims its position by virtue of cultural superiority (Ogbu, 1987). In one way or another, nearly every culturally diverse child—Hispanic, Asian, African American, and even White, non-English-speaking immigrants—whether born in the United States or elsewhere, is likely to be treated as a foreigner, an alien, or an intruder. The Americanization solution has not worked. Moreover, it depends on the flawed notion of group culture. The Americanization solution presumes that culturally different children are as a group culturally flawed. To fix them individually, we must act on the individual as a member of a cultural group. In essence, the groups should "melt" into one large and more beneficial "American" culture. The previous discussion regarding group-versus-individual oriented concepts of culture suggests that our educational efforts have been responding quite ignorantly with regard to the processes in which individuals and groups come together to form culture, and how that understanding should inform educators. The challenge facing educators with regard to Hispanic students is not to Americanize them, but instead to understand them and to act responsively with respect to what they bring.

Given the previous understanding of culture and schooling conceptually for Hispanics, we must address the cultural diversity of these children and their families in order to properly assess and improve learning environments designed for this population (García, 2005; Fuller, 2007; Portes, 2007; García & Frede, 2010). This cultural significance position is supported by a rich contribution of research that suggests that the educational failure of "diverse" child populations is related to differences in practices between home, school, and other community services. In essence, researchers have suggested that without systematically attending to the distinctiveness of the child's culture, endeavors to assist and support the development and learning of Hispanic children are likely to fail. We steer away from the notion that understanding "general" principles of development alone can help us understand the diversity of children and families and respond to them in ways that are supportive of their own positive efforts to enhance development and learning.

The challenge is to identify critical differences between and within our Hispanic populations and individuals within those groups, and to incorporate this information into practice. In this manner, the individual and the cultural milieu in which that individual resides receives practical attention. Advances in research design (particularly in developmental science), analysis, and theory have produced principles concerning how children from diverse cultural histories develop in environments designed for care, teaching, and learning (Gardner, 2006; Gutierrez & Rogoff, 2003; García, 2005). Among this work, some consensus has emerged. For example, at the conclusion of their efforts to synthesize the scientific knowledge base of development, Bransford, Brown, and Cocking (2000) argued that scientific understanding of learning and development includes understanding about developmental processes, developmental environments, instruction, and sociocultural processes that contribute to gains in cognitive, social, and emotional functioning in early childhood.

Sociocultural Contexts of Learning

Building development and learning opportunities for Hispanic children and families requires a strong theoretical framework concerning the social and cultural context of learning (Nasir & Hand, 2006). We need a thorough and shared understanding of the cultural processes that shape learning inside the home and classroom—ways in which environments within and outside of school interact to shape children's engagement and learning (Gutierrez & Rogoff, 2003). And understanding, as noted above, necessitates a well-organized structure of knowledge.

To date a comprehensive, unitary model of sociocultural processes that shape student learning has not been put forward (Nasir & Hand, 2006). However, various models emphasize different elements of what could be a unifying model. For example, the work of Cole and Engeström (1993) emphasizes ways in which knowledge is historically accumulated and culturally organized. This is relevant to student development and learning because information shared outside of the home is filtered by children through their personal histories and family cultures. Another example can be found in the work of Barbara Rogoff (Rogoff, 2003; Rogoff, Mistry, Göncü, & Mosier, 1993), a psychologist interested in activity participation and the collaboration between children and adults across different cultures. Her work has introduced important concepts to psychology, including "guided participation" in cultural activity, by which adults with little formal schooling parent (and teach) their young children much differently than those with extensive schooling experience (Rogoff et al., 1993).

Additional pieces to an underlying model of sociocultural student learning have been put forward, including the notions of "situated cognition"

(Brown, Collins, & Duguid, 1989), "cognitive apprenticeship" (Brown & Campione, 1994), "intersubjectivity" (Vygotsky, 1978), "engagement" (Skinner, Pappas, & Davis, 2005), "learning as shifts in social relations" (Nasir & Hand, 2006), "power in social structure" (Freire, 1970; McDermott & Varenne, 1995), "meaning in cultural tools and artifacts" (Cole, 1996), and "responsive pedagogy" (García, 2005). Each of these pieces is important to the whole. We rely heavily in our approach on these conceptual and theoretical underpinnings, and place heavy emphasis on issues of language and culture and its antecedents as mediating variables.

As mentioned, conflict occurs when different cultural communities share time and space to engage in a shared activity (Rogoff, 2003). "Difference" does not equate to "deficient," though the two are often confused by persons projecting their own cultural values onto others. Typically, these persons are detached from the metacognitive exercise of "cultural understanding" (García, 2005). To avoid cultural differences in school, communities frequently segregate themselves by race, ethnicity, and/or socio-economic class (Boulton, 1995; Ellis, 1997).

As different communities share space and activity within schools, however, cultural practice evolves over time, whether the change is recognized or not (Valdés, 1996). While change in cultural practice attributable to conflict and differentiation is, and will continue to be, typical of the human experience, understanding, predicting, and even shaping that change within schools so as to build engaging learning environments is necessary—and must be deliberate—in order to provide equitable educational opportunities to all students (Lesgold, 2004).

In terms of developmental science, building cultural bridges is critical for early childhood educators and means connecting situated experience in early learning environments with students' prior knowledge (Bransford, Brown, & Cocking, 2000; Bransford, Derry, Berliner, Hammerness, & Beckett, 2005; Driscoll, 2000, pp. 218–255; Lesgold, 2004). An assessment of prior knowledge must consider their family histories (Cole & Engeström, 1993); and adapting to fit with family cultural practices necessitates an assessment of developmental history (Rogoff et al., 2003). Cultural fit, in order words, entails a three-prong effort: (1) an assessment of child/family history; (2) evaluating formal care and early schooling history; and (3) a negotiation of cultural practices. The third is perhaps the most challenging (Greenwood, Horton, & Utley, 2002; Guthrie, Rueda, Gambrell, & Morrison, 2008; Gutierrez & Rogoff, 2003).

This work and other studies of cultural practice in education (Gonzalez, Moll, & Amanti, 2005; Guthrie et al., 2008; Gutierrez & Rogoff, 2003; Well & Mejía Arauz, 2005) combine to clarify theoretical constructs related to learning and associated cultural practices in the home and formal "developmental/learning" environments. They demonstrate that development and learning must be understood in terms of institutional and family histories. We cannot ignore the role of families as they engage with the formal activities constructed by society for care and development of their children.

In order to improve early development and learning through responsive policies, programs, and practice there must be a merger of cultural and inferential research. In his book on culturally oriented and empirically supported solutions to the learning gap between at-risk children (particularly children of racial and ethnic minority backgrounds) and their peers, Portes (2005, p. 98) asserts that "the three most important predictors of school success remain parent involvement, adult-child ratios, and academic learning time." Referring to these predictors, he continues,

> These are no accident since they are quite interrelated. All three maximize learning activity related to what schools expect, teach, and value and are directly related to social class and tests. The adult present or level of assistance in the home and school available for tasks and experiences valued at school seems, in fact, to account for how parental involvement is defined. . . . What is needed then is a brainy, reliable way to ensure that combinations of factors are maximized and integrated in the lives of [students placed at risk] from underrepresented groups at multiple levels. We need to understand the reasons why some variables such as teaching characteristics (content and instructional expertise), leadership, collaboration, and similar school factors differ from others structured socially from a multifaceted view. It cannot be expected that interventions focusing on individual level factors such as self-esteem or character can close the gap any more than vouchers or high expectations at other levels. A comprehensive plan must direct strategies toward a common purpose and anticipate the social impact and costs of altering learning or economic outcomes. (pp. 98–99)

Imbedded in this is the understanding that language, culture, and their accompanying values are acquired in the home and community environment; that children come to early care and early learning environments with some knowledge about what language is—how it works and what it is used for; that children learn higher level cognitive and communicative skills as they engage in socially meaningful activities; and that children's development and learning is best understood as the interaction of linguistic, sociocultural, and cognitive knowledge and experiences in consistent and positive socio-emotional contexts. A more appropriate perspective of development and learning, then, is one that recognizes that development and learning is enhanced when it occurs in contexts that are both socioculturally and linguistically meaningful for the child and the family. García (2005) and Fuller (2007) further emphasize that children learn best, and parents and teachers feel most satisfied when they are encouraged to become allies in the care and learning process of children. Therefore, a more appropriate practice approach is one that recognizes that development and learning are enhanced when they occur in contexts that are emotionally, socioculturally, linguistically, and cognitively reflective of the child's and families' history/culture.

Such meaningful contexts have been notoriously inaccessible to linguistically and culturally diverse children, particularly young children exposed to two languages that we will refer to as dual language learners (DLLs). On the contrary, schooling practices and teachers who are the architects and engineers of instruction often contribute to educational vulnerability (Valenzuela, 1999). The monolithic culture transmitted by common forms of care, pedagogy, curricula, instruction, classroom configuration, and language dramatizes the lack of fit between the culturally diverse child and the experience of that child. The prevailing "culture" is reflected in such practices as:

- The systematic exclusion of the histories, languages, experiences, and values of these children.
- Segregation, which limits access to academic courses and which justifies learning environments that do not foster academic development and socialization or perception of self as a competent learner and language user.
- A lack of opportunities to engage in developmentally and culturally appropriate learning in ways other than by teacher-led instruction.

Constructing Responsive Communities of Practice

The implication of this rethinking has profound effects related to Hispanics (García, 2005). This new approach to developing responsive practices is one that redefines our efforts to better serve diverse children and families. It might be described by some as practices of empowerment, by others as cultural learning, and by others as a cultural view of providing developmental assistance/guidance. In any case, it argues for practices that respect and integrate students' values, beliefs, histories, and experiences and recognizes the active role that family and children must play in the processes of development and learning. It is therefore a *responsive community of practice*, one that encompasses practical, contextual, and empirical knowledge and a "world view" of learning and development that evolves through meaningful interactions among parents, family members, children, caregivers/teachers, and other community members. This responsive set of strategies expands children's knowledge and well-being beyond their own immediate experiences, while using those experiences as a sound foundation for appropriating well-being.

To further examine this challenge, Figure 2.1 summarizes the conceptual dimensions for high-performing responsive communities as formal interventions in early care and early learning circumstances.

Figure 2.1. Conceptual Dimensions of Addressing Cultural and Linguistic Diversity in Responsive Development and Learning Communities

Agency-Wide Practices

- A vision defined by the acceptance and valuing of diversity
- Treatment of classroom practitioners as professionals, colleagues in school development decisions
- Characterized by collaboration, flexibility, enhanced professional development
- Elimination (gradual or immediate) of policies that seek to categorize diverse children thereby rendering their experiences as inferior or limiting
- Reflection of and connection to surrounding community— particularly with the families of the children served

Caregiver/Teacher Practices

- Bilingual/bicultural skills and awareness
- High expectations of diverse children and families
- Treatment of diversity as an asset
- Ongoing professional development on issues of cultural and linguistic diversity and practices that are most effective
- Basic of services to address cultural and linguistic diversity:

1. Attention to and integration of home language cultural practices
2. Focus on maximizing children and family interactions across categories of language proficiency, academic performance, immigration status, etc.
3. Regular and consistent attempts to access and build on family/ community resources
4. Thematic approach to early learning activities—with the integration of various skills, events, learning opportunities
5. Focus on language development through meaningful interactions and communications combined with direct skill-building in content appropriate contexts

CONCLUSION

Constructing responsive communities of practice for Hispanics in early education recognizes that care and learning has its roots in processes in varied contexts and circumstances. Such a conceptual framework rejects the Americanization strategy, extends beyond the policy and practice frameworks of "equal opportunity," and concludes that a focus on broader issues of culture is useful but not enough. Instead, a focus on responsive engagement with communities, families, and children encourages the positive construction and reconstruction of meaning and allows reinterpretations and augmentations to past knowledge within compatible and nurturing contexts. Diversity is perceived and acted on as a resource for enhancing development and learning instead of a problem. A focus on what children and families bring generates a more asset/resource-oriented approach versus a deficit/needs approach.

This mission requires an understanding of how individuals with diverse sets of experiences, packaged individually into cultures, "make meaning," communicate that meaning and extend that meaning, particularly in social contexts designed for early learning. Such a mission requires in-depth treatment of the processes associated with producing diversity and issues of socialization in and out of formal early learning experiences, coupled with a clear examination of how such understanding is actually transformed into care, pedagogy, and curriculum that results in enhanced social, emotional, cognitive, and linguistic development for Hispanic children. We now ask you to join us as we move further into specific instructional activities cognizant of Hispanic cultural and linguistic diversity.

CHAPTER 3

Language Development and Early Education of Young Hispanic Children

Young Hispanic children come from diverse racial, linguistic, and cultural backgrounds. However, current estimates suggest 60% of young Hispanic children are raised in home environments in which variable amounts of Spanish and English are spoken. Considering the burgeoning size of the young Hispanic child population, and the large number of them being raised in multilingual environments, it is critical that researchers, policy-makers, and practitioners address basic questions related to language, culture, cognition, and educational opportunity for this population. This chapter provides a synthesis of empirical work that spans several decades and conceptual frameworks associated with the linguistic development and the early education of young Hispanic children in the United States. Linguistic, psycholinguistic, anthropological, psychological, sociological, and educational contributions that underscore research and practice are reviewed.

Because language is a central feature to the cognitive development and early learning of young Hispanics (García, Jensen, & Cuellar, 2006), topics explored in this chapter are linked to questions of language use and practice. Bilingualism, second language learning, and related issues, therefore, appear and reappear throughout this synthesis. We recognize that not all Hispanic children are English language learners (ELLs). Many are raised in English-only homes. Moreover, Hispanic children represent various racial groups, national origins, social classes, geographical locations, and immigrant generations. While we are aware of the incredible diversity found within this group, there are general trends, patterns, and themes significant to young Hispanics as a whole. Such are important to understand as efforts are made to improve educational opportunities for young Hispanics. To avoid gross generalizations, we discuss key characteristics of Hispanic children in terms of proportional representation, and provide, where possible, descriptions of Hispanic samples of children in the studies reviewed. As in most reviews, the evidence must be weighed, critiqued, and understood in its proper context where applications are made to individuals or small groups.

This chapter reviews a diverse set of issues associated with the language development and early education of young Hispanic children in the United States, ages 0 to 8. Theory and qualitative and quantitative research incorporating multiple academic disciplines—linguistics, education, anthropology, psychology, and sociology—underscore historic and concurrent work reviewed in this paper. This review is organized thematically, and responds to the following questions:

- What is the range of linguistic proficiency of young Hispanic children in the United States?
- How do the linguistic properties of Spanish and English relate and develop for young Hispanic children?
- What relationship does social context have with the language and literacy development of young Hispanic children in the United States?
- What instructional options are available to young Hispanic children learning English, and what does the evidence show in terms of programmatic features that promote literacy, academic achievement, and "academic" English proficiency?

VARIATIONS IN LANGUAGE ENVIRONMENTS

Due to this variety in immigrant national origin and related social factors, language development and language use vary. Some young Hispanics, for example, acquire English as their first language and maintain monolingual proficiency throughout their lives. These children are more likely to have native (U.S.-born) parents. Others speak Spanish as their first language and learn English as they enter public schooling—often referred to as "sequential bilinguals." The proportional size of this subpopulation has been growing rapidly over the past few decades. In a recent report, the Grantmakers for Education (Grantmakers for Education, 2010) indicate that one in ten pre-K–12 students in the United States are "officially" categorized as English language learners (ELLs), a total of 5.3 million students, and that a sizable achievement gap exists between these students and their English-proficient peers. According to the 2009 National Assessment of Education Progress (NAEP), only 6% of 4th-grade ELL students scored at or above proficiency in reading in English, compared to 34% of non-ELL 4th-graders. It is important to note that some 2 to 3 million children, ages

0 to 8 in the United States are learning English as a second language, and some 25% of the U.S. birth cohort in 2007 was born to mothers who did not speak English as a primary language, mostly to parents of Hispanic origin (National Task Force on Early Childhood Education for Hispanics, 2007; García & Jensen, 2009). Figure 3.1 summarizes the student language population in the United States—Hispanics make up over 70% of that population.

Moreover, the increasing presence of native Spanish-speaking children in U.S. schools is a function of high immigration and birth rates among the Hispanic population (García, Jensen, Miller, & Huerta, 2005). A final (and smaller) subset of Hispanic children develops English and Spanish fluency simultaneously and at comparable levels in the home and in school. Differences in language development are most commonly attributable to differing linguistic practices in the home.

In an analysis of data from the Early Childhood Longitudinal Study-Birth Cohort (ECLS-B), López, Barrueco, and Miles (2006) describe the home language environments of Hispanic 9-month-olds in the country. Representing a national sample of children born between December

Figure 3.1. U.S. English Language Learners

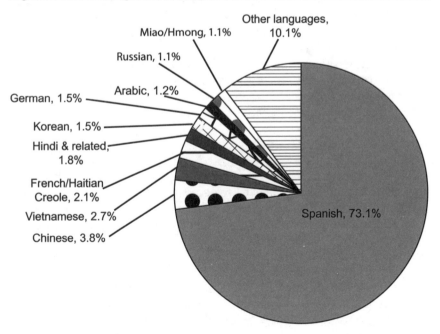

2001 and January 2002, López et al. found that Hispanic infants (constituting 26% of the total infant population) resided in various sorts of home language environments. The largest group (34%) of Hispanic infants lived in a home in which Spanish was the primary language, with some English. Twenty-two percent lived in a home in which English was primarily spoken, with some Spanish; 21% in English-only homes; and 19% in Spanish-only homes. The "other" category (4%) includes homes in which languages other than Spanish and English (e.g., indigenous Central American languages) are used. In other words, approximately 75% of all homes of Hispanic children 9 months of age spoke at least some Spanish. It should be no surprise, therefore, that the United States is the fifth largest Spanish-speaking country in the world (González, 2005).

In another study, data from the U.S. Census reveal that many parents of young Hispanic children have limited English proficiency (Hernandez, 2006). For example, three-fourths of young Hispanic children in immigrant families (71%) live with at least one parent who is limited English proficient (LEP), not speaking English exclusively or very well, and one-half (49%) live with two such parents (Hernandez, 2006). Young children in immigrant families from Mexico (78%), the Dominican Republic (73%), and Central America (70%) are the most likely to live with a parent whose English is limited. On the other hand, only 3% of young Hispanic children in U.S.-born families live with two parents who are limited English proficient (LEP), and 11% live with at least one such parent. Hispanic children raised by monolingual, English-speaking parents are often exposed to Spanish-language environments through grandparents, other relatives, and/or neighbors involved in the child's care and upbringing (Zentella, 2005).

Intergenerational Trends

It is not surprising that Hispanic children from native families (3rd-generation or more) are more likely to demonstrate English proficiency than children of immigrant families (children who have at least one foreign-born parent). On the other hand, Hispanic children born to immigrant families (first- or second-generation) are more likely to show bilingual proficiency between 5 and 8 years old, compared to children in native-born families. Indeed, 40% of Hispanic children from immigrant families are proficient in English and Spanish, compared to 18% of children from native families—a trend present in every country-of-origin subgroup.

This general decrease in bilingual proficiency of Hispanic children from immigrant to native families exemplifies a phenomenon linguists and bilingual researchers call "language shift." It also typifies Lambert's (1974) notion of "subtractive bilingualism." With empirical evidence as early as the mid 1970s (Lieberson, Dalto, & Johnston, 1975), the language shift occurs when a language minority group gradually changes its language use and preference from the minority language to the locally dominant language. In the context of this paper, Census data indicate that Hispanic children of U.S.-born parents are more likely to be monolingual English speakers, and that children of immigrants (first- and second-generation) are more likely to maintain bilingual proficiency (Hernandez, 2006), even when they demonstrate a preference for English in school settings (Oller & Eilers, 2002). Thus, the language shift—from Spanish to English in this case—as Veltman (1983) suggested, tends to occur by the third generation after a family migrates from one country to another with a different majority language. In addition, some research suggests that a preference for English occurs in immigrant children attending U.S. schools within the first generation, by grade 3.

Bilingualism, therefore, for many Hispanic children in the United States tends to be of the subtractive sort. Lambert (1974) was the first to differentiate between subtractive and additive bilingualism. The basic distinction between the two depends on whether second language proficiency *replaces* native language proficiency (i.e., subtractive bilingualism) or *adds* to it (i.e., additive bilingualism). Data suggest that the linguistic development of many Hispanic children exemplifies the latter type. In other words, competence in English has tended to come at the expense of Spanish proficiency (the heritage language) both for individuals and across generations.

In a mixed-method design study evaluating home practices that influence dual-language proficiency, López (2005) highlighted the roles of immigration status, parent education, and motivation on the language development of young Hispanic children. Analogous to findings by Hammer, Miccio, and Wagstaff (2003) regarding the role of immigrant history on language development, López concluded that parents who have been in the United States the longest are the most likely to use English and see this language as an important consideration to schooling success. On the other hand, Hispanic families who have been in the United States less time had a better grasp on Spanish, and felt generally that their children would benefit more from learning Spanish skills rather than from the parents trying to teach a language they were not familiar with themselves. Parents with more formal education were also more likely to value the child's bilingual development and to motivate their children to maintain their native language while pushing English development as well.

Summary of Findings

The following points capture the essence of the intersection among demographics, contextual factors, and linguistic proficiency of young Hispanic children in the United States.

- The proportion of English language learners (ELL) in U.S. schools continues to grow. From the 1993–1994 to the 2003–2004 school year, K–12 enrollment of ELL grew more than 65% while the total K–12 population grew less than 7%. A majority of this growth is attributable to immigration and the rise of the Hispanic population.
- Young Hispanics are raised in linguistically diverse home environments. More than half are raised in mostly Spanish environments, and two in five in mostly English environments. Approximately three in four are influenced by Spanish in the home; and three in four are exposed to English in the home.
- Linguistic proficiency (in English, Spanish, or both) among young Hispanic children in the United States is variable and strongly predicted by language use and practices outside of school and in the home.
- Young Hispanic children of Dominican, Central American, or Mexican heritage are more likely than those of other national origins to live with a parent whose English proficiency is limited.
- Language proficiency of young Hispanic children differs between geographical regions and states. In 2000, the highest relative proportion of bilingual Hispanic children was found in Florida and New Jersey; and the lowest relative proportion was found in Colorado, Arizona, California, and Illinois; Texas had the highest relative proportions of young Hispanic children who were limited in English proficiency.
- Differences in language proficiency of Hispanic children by generational status suggest an inter-generational shift toward monolingual English proficiency.
- Spanish maintenance within and between generations of Hispanic families is influenced by a combination of personal, familial, educational, and societal factors. Parent educational attainment is associated with the quality of non-English native language proficiency where more formal education is associated with language maintenance and stronger bilingual proficiency.

BILINGUAL LANGUAGE DEVELOPMENT

The intersection of Spanish and English language development is a critical feature for many young Hispanics. Our understanding of bilingual development and the specific development of English as a second language for Hispanics continues to expand. The accumulating body of evidence indicates that young children can attain proficiency in more than one language at early ages (Baker, 2000; Genesee, Lindholm-Leary, Saunders, & Christian, 2005). The process by which this occurs is quite complex, and linguistic properties between languages intersect in intricate ways.

As documented earlier, a clear majority of young Hispanics live in homes in which Spanish is spoken in the home, with fluctuating amounts of English. It is therefore important to note that most young Hispanics are influenced by both Spanish and English, and a growing number of them are positioned to be bilingual. In this section we draw from research that spans the past 3 decades to assess the development and interchange of linguistic properties between languages (i.e., English and Spanish). Focusing mostly on native Spanish-speaking children who learn English as a second language, these studies evaluate the developmental structure (phonology, morphology, and syntax) of language, showing that bilingual development is complex and varies between children as a function of their environment. Moreover, linguistic properties between language systems influence one another, suggesting that bilingualism cannot be viewed simply as "the arithmetic sum of two languages" (García, 2005, pp. 21–38).

Transferring Linguistic Skills

The studies reviewed below support the notion that, for young Hispanic children learning two languages, linguistic skills tend to transfer. Indeed, current research and scholarly discussions of first- and second-language relationships emphasize transfer theory, which tend to be "the most powerful and most frequently cited frameworks" (Genesee, Lindholm-Leary, Saunders, & Christian, 2006). However, transfer theory does not account for all associations among linguistic attributes for young Hispanics. That is, common underlying abilities, typological differences between languages, unique features of the target language, and well developed oral and literacy skills in the first language all contribute to second language learning to some extent (Genesee et al., 2006). Moreover, with regards to children ages 3 and 4 years, there is little large sample research available to suggest that the process of cross-linguistic transfer functions in the same way as for older children.

In an early analysis of bilingual development in young children, Padilla and Liebman (1975) reported a longitudinal linguistic analysis of Spanish-English acquisition in two 3-year-old children. By conducting an analysis of several dependent linguistic variables (phonological, morphological, and syntactic characteristics) over time, the authors observed gains in both languages, although several English forms were evident while similar Spanish forms were not. They also report the differentiation of linguistic systems at phonological, lexical, and syntactic levels. They concluded:

> The appropriate use of both languages in mixed utterances was evident; that is, correct word order was preserved. For example, there were no occurrences of "raining esta" or "a es baby," note there was evidence for such utterances as "esta raining" and "es a baby." There was also an absence of the redundancy of unnecessary words, which might tend to confuse meaning. (Padilla & Liebman, 1975, p. 51)

García (1983) also reported developmental data related to the acquisition of Spanish and English for Chicano preschoolers (3 and 4 years old) and the acquisition of English for a group of matched English-only speakers. The results of this study can be summarized as follows: (1) acquisition of both Spanish and English was evident at complex morphological levels for Spanish/English 4-year-old children; (2) for the bilingual children studied, English was more advanced based on the quantity and quality of obtained morphological instances of language productions; and (3) there was no quantitative or qualitative difference between Spanish/English bilingual children and matched English-only controls on English language morphological productions (García, 1983; García, 2005).

Code-Switching

Code-switching (CS) is a common phenomenon observed in bilingual populations of young Hispanic children. It is a term used in linguistics to refer to the alteration between two (or more) language registers in a single conversation or utterance. In an early study of this phenomenon, Fantini (1985) noticed that his son Mario was able to switch easily between two languages according to characteristics of the addressee. If Mario knew that the person was a Spanish-dominant speaker he spoke Spanish, and he would speak English to an English-dominant speaker. An exception that Fantini noticed was when both his children became close and felt comfortable with an English-speaking person: They had an inclination to switch to Spanish, which was the language they related to intimately and comfortably with loved ones. It has also been found that young bilinguals have a tendency to switch languages when talking about a specific topic (Zentella, 1997). They tend to switch to the more comfortable language. For some this might be their first language, but this is not necessarily for everyone since some bilinguals become dominant in their second language.

The evidence to date concerning the development of CS behavior in young bilingual children consistently shows that both knowledge of the grammatical capabilities and sensitivity to the norms of code choice upheld by their flexible use of grammar are major factors determining language choice. Grosjean (1982), Fantini (1985), and McClure (1981) stress the importance of the child's social role. If a child is taking care of younger siblings, she will tend to switch to the language with which the youngest child feels most comfortable. In addition, older children tend to use CS as a clarification device when other children do not seem to understand. Similarly, García (1983) observed that mothers used mixed utterances in Spanish and English when speaking to their young children "as a teaching aide" to clarify from one language to the other.

The fact that children use two languages seems to make them more aware of the available possibilities for multiple language use with community members who speak their two languages than with those who do not. This awareness to understand and use two languages is referred to as the child's "meta-linguistic" awareness (Bialystok, 2001; Jensen, 2008b). With time children achieve and maintain a level of fluency in each language skill that in general reflects the need for that skill in a particular language (Grosjean, 1982).

The above linguistic findings can be summarized as follows:

- Children can competently acquire two or more languages.
- The acquisition of two languages can be parallel but need not be. That is, the qualitative character of one language may lag behind, surge ahead, or develop equally with the other language. The relationship of linguistic properties between languages is complex.
- Transfer theory is the most widely accepted theory used to explain the linguistic and literacy development of young bilingual Hispanic children in the United States.
- A broad range of variables moderate cross-linguistic processes. These include individual factors, such as personality, as well as contextual factors, such as language practices in the home and instructional practices in the school.
- Code-switching is a common occurrence among bilingual children. Children acquiring two languages are likely to mix those languages in regular, systematic ways that assist in the enhancement of meaning. Language choice of bilingual Hispanic

children depends on characteristics of and the particular relationship with the addressee(s) as well as attitudinal features of the child.

- The quality of literacy skill development in the second language is associated with the developmental quality of parallel skills in the native language. Oral skills (i.e., the integration of vocabulary, grammar, and semantics driven by contextual circumstances [Saunders & O'Brien, 2006]) in the second language do not appear to transfer in the same way, but are greatly influenced by second language exposure and language use in the home.

THE EFFECTS OF POLICIES AND PRACTICES ON ACADEMIC ACHIEVEMENT

The knowledge-base reviewed in previous sections is directly related to understanding instructional programs and teaching strategies that seek to provide optimal literacy and academic outcomes for young Hispanic children. The demographic data, for example, demonstrate that most young Hispanic children in the United States are exposed, at some level, to Spanish in the home—approximately three in four (López, Barrueco, & Miles, 2006), and that the home environment is likely to be characterized by aspects of the immigrant experience. This set of circumstances is very important given that home language practices—different from "language use"—are highly relevant to early literacy outcomes (Goldenberg, Rueda, & August, 2006; Nord, Lennon, Liu, & Chandler, 1999; Tabors, 1997; Tabors & Snow, 2002). Moreover, given that higher order cognitive and literacy skills tend to transfer from native to the second language (August, Calderón, & Carlo, 2002; Genesee, 2003; Genesee et al., 2006; Goldenberg, Rezaei, & Fletcher, 2005), it is critical that educators adequately assess, develop, and leverage the child's non-English native language skills. This means tailoring instruction, curricular content, and schooling practices in general to meet the child's particular language development circumstances—based on individual, school, and family factors—as well as the social and cultural contexts to take full advantage of the child's home resources and parental support (Shannon, 1995; Reese, Garnier, Gallimore, & Goldenberg, 2000; Goldenberg, Gallimore, Reese, & Garnier, 2001; Scheffner Hammer & Miccio, 2004; Goldenberg, Rueda, & August, 2006).

In this section we discuss the present status of young Hispanics' academic achievement levels—including early literacy skills—and discuss how policies and practices play a part in these outcomes. We comb the literature and our own experience to highlight the programs and, more specifically, the features and strategies of the most effective programs used to leverage young Hispanic children's strengths to produce the most favorable outcomes, with a particular exploration of preschool participation.

Because socio-demographic conditions differ—and local and state policies demand assorted objectives from their schools and teachers—no single program works best in every situation. When selecting a program, one of the most fundamental decisions should be whether bilingual proficiency is an objective. Clearly, given the cognitive and economic advantages of bilingual proficiency in a world that is becoming increasingly globalized, promoting bilingualism is an intuitive ambition (García & Jensen, 2006). However, the development of balanced bilingualism depends on state and local policies as well as the availability of teachers and course curriculum to meet the need. Indeed, the feasibility of bilingual promotion varies among schools.

A second feature that should be considered when selecting a program designed for bilingual Hispanic children is optimizing individual achievement and literacy development. Academic performance continues to be the driving force behind educational policy reform and practice in the United States, and programs developed for young Hispanics should strive to reduce achievement gaps. It is also important, however, that programs support the development of the whole child, simultaneously sustaining the cognitive, social, emotional, and psychological development of children—a holistic approach is especially important during the early years (i.e., pre-K–3) of schooling (Zigler, Gilliam, & Jones, 2006).

"Teaching" Language

Children acquire language by engaging in meaningful conversations as they communicate with adults or other children. There is cultural, social, and individual variation in the nature and quality of the communication that they take part in when it comes to adults. Considering the effects on children's acquisition of language and verbal literacy, the quality of the communication between teachers and children in preschool and primary grades has a decisive impact on language development.

This broad recommendation regarding instruction of bilingual Hispanic children resonates very well with the ten cornerstones articulated by the World-Class Instructional Design Consortium (WIDA) related to language development and the national CORE Standards, a set of academic standards now adopted by more than 40 states (WIDA, 2011). These cornerstones recognize that every child is learning a language or languages, but that for many children, the access to academic language—that language created for and utilized in U.S. schools, mostly in English—is differentially available to children outside the schooling environment. As the previous discussion in Chapter 1 has described, young Hispanics, through no fault of their own, are likely to be characterized by more limited access to the academic aspects of language development, particularly in English. This is at the center of the WIDA cornerstones:

1. Students learn language and culture through meaningful use and interaction.
2. Students use language in functional and communicative ways that vary according to context.
3. Students develop language proficiency in listening, speaking, reading, and writing interdependently, but at different rates and in different ways.
4. Students' development of social, instructional, and academic language is a complex and long-term process and is the foundation for their success in school.
5. Students' development of academic language and academic content knowledge are interrelated processes.
6. Students' academic language development in their native language facilitates their academic development in English and vice versa.
7. Students' access to instructional tasks requiring complex thinking is enhanced when linguistic complexity and instructional support match levels of language proficiency.
8. Students draw on their metacognitive, metalinguistic, and metacultural awareness to develop proficiency in multiple languages.
9. Student's home, school, and community experiences influence their language development.
10. Students' languages and cultures are valuable resources to be tapped and incorporated into schooling. (WIDA, 2011; www. wida.us)

These cornerstones are serving for WIDA, as they should serve for all educators of Hispanic children. They provide a critical foundation upon which to generate specific academic language, literacy, and content standards that are then associated with student instructional opportunities and the assessments generated that measure student progress against those standards.

In short, we wish to emphasize that instruction must consider teaching practices that facilitate both primary- and second-language learning including the following:

- Language interactions that respond to the child's lead;
- Expand and extend their response to questions in complete sentence;
- Create pairing where a child is with other child who speaks that child's language;
- Introduce vocabulary words in contexts of their experiences using complete sentences;
- Establish consistent routines labeling them orally as they begin and end;
- Use pictures or regalia to explain activities;
- Sing familiar songs daily and add new materials gradually; and, teach new vocabulary while singing them in a familiar tune.

We cannot emphasize enough how important it is for the designers and implementers of instruction to plan rich communication experiences. Successful development of language and literacy includes a learning environment that reflects an optimal response to their educational needs and signs of communication as they develop their language. Teachers need to responsively plan quality instructions that can occur in this type of environment. Their enthusiasm about a topic that is being studied helps convey the meaning of the subject and support their students' learning. Teachers also need to extract meaning from what they are learning and relate it to their other experiences in the past, present, and future.

Teachers must have an understanding of the stages of language development, in all aspects of teaching and learning at all times, and this knowledge should help to form the basis for all activities that teachers plan. Therefore, we are including a modified chart outlining language-development stages that has helped teachers in selecting teaching opportunities they might create for their students. Note that the chart begins with what students are orally doing, then listing the stage of language and what verbal literacy they are engaged in. More important, the chart includes a short list of what teachers should be able to do with the information they have acquired about their students. An initial chart was shared at different professional activities led Markos (2006).

Teachers must also express an enthusiasm for what their students are communicating. Children continually share experiences, family happenings (a new baby), favorite books or topic ("Teacher, can we learn about sharks?") or connections that they are making to their recent learning. When these are voiced by their students it is crucial that teachers take note. Often this type of communication occurs while they are in large groups or in center work with their peers. Knowing that these are important and motivating for students, a teacher should plan a Conversation Table as part of their center time. Figure 3.2 provides a set of considerations for this type of table.

During the week, teachers invite children to an "appointment" at the Conversation Table where individually they can talk with their teacher. Students look forward to being able to sit next to their teacher around a small table and share what happened at home or outside, what book they really like and would like to hear again, who recently visited at home, and so forth. This 5-minute opportunity needs to be taught early in the year so that students will understand the importance of remaining in their centers, allowing their teacher and peers to engage in a meaningful conversation. Teachers should help them realize that sometime during that week they will participate in the center and "talk" with their teacher. Later in the year, students often remind others during other learning contexts that they can share their comments with their teacher at the Conversation Table. Teachers soon understand that this 5-minute or so opportunity becomes a critical source of information when planning lessons, choosing books or vocabulary words, selecting students to respond to different levels of questions, and so forth. Teachers should create a notebook and date the individual conversations that they have with their students. These entries become developmental histories of language and learning for each student.

Language Development Activities

In addition to the organization to enhance language development, we ask teachers to consider some often utilized activities that follow.

Sharing from Home. This is a show-and-tell language activity that supports development of oral language with the oral language assets at home as a base. Recall that children advance language by following a protocol to gain practice as they orally present in front of their peers, using an established sentence frame. The sentence frame scaffolds children's understanding of who, what, where, how, and why and supports them as they practice at home prior to presenting in the classroom. These homework language frames are sent home prior to sharing and practiced with their family. Figure 3.3 is an example a homework language frame that was sent home to parents.

The homework language frame sheet can then be included in a class book alongside a picture of the child and a drawing of what was shared at school. Throughout the year, the "Sharing from our Homes Book" is read by the children.

Vocabulary Work in Language. In classrooms where students are being academically challenged as well as being successful, two types of vocabulary learning occur. Students incorporate new words from centers and small-group work on the Internet into their oral and written communications. The second type of learning is planned, occurring daily at the same time. An example of how you might teach three to five words weekly in a teaching routine organized over 5 days is briefly described in Table 3.1 (See Chapter 6 for a more extensive description of this vocabulary development routine). The vocabulary words may come from any of the content areas, selected by the teacher, and the work is done in a 5-by-8-inch booklet stapled together by the teacher. These booklets often go home, to be shared with families, and returned to the classroom.

Figure 3.2. Conversational Considerations

Instructors need to consider the following:

What I know:

- Listening is important and is optimized when it is one to one.
- Relationships are strengthened when experiences are shared.
- Shared content informs instruction and lessons.

What I can do:

- Engage in dialogue that allows me to extend and expand language.
- Document the language growth of individual children over time.
- Create a list of interests and experiences for individual children.
- Listen and list/note new learning that children experience.

Figure 3.3. Example of a Homework Language Frame Sheet

Sharing From Our Homes: A Show-and-Tell Activity   **Date** _____

My object is from my home. It is a _____ .

It is/has _____ . (describe by color, shape, size)

I/We use it to _____ . (make a special food, to remember when . . .)

It helps me remember _____ . (when, who, where, why)

These booklets are used by the teachers introducing target words in different content areas. They have more than one booklet. A teacher may use a learning-math-vocabulary booklet during math time, introducing math words and following the 5-day routine. During the structured routine, students are able to work in whole groups or pairs, at centers, and by themselves. The key here is that vocabulary instruction requires planning, consistency, and time.

Promoting Transfer

Early childhood educators are seeking guidance in how both to respect the child's language and culture and to introduce academic English. When a child's home language has the same writing conventions as English, the child will most likely apply these principles to reading and writing in the second language. Young Hispanic children who see, hear, and perhaps speak Spanish are able to transfer many language skills. The stronger the language and literacy skills in the home language, the more likely the child will transfer these skills successfully to his or her second language.

For children in preschools, Kindergarten, and the early grades, several basic cognition abilities have been found to transfer across languages and facilitate the process of second language literacy development. These skills/abilities include:

- Using information that is being discussed in the new language and connecting it with information they already know in order to make sense of new concepts.
- Accessing words and their meanings from memory including cognates that also support decoding print.
- Using reading/print skills that might include reading from left to right and top to bottom. (Pictures often show the meaning of the words; punctuation marks support literacy in the same way.)
- Asking questions of self and others when they do not understand the story or text that is being read.
- Putting thoughts in writing, including generating texts in various genres of writing.

Children can transfer all of the above skills to their understanding of decoding and strategies for determining when they are reading text in English. In regards to phonic skills, some of the basic decoding processes that transfer include letter recognition, phonological awareness, phonics, as well as blending sounds into words.

Table 3.1. A 5-Day Vocabulary Plan

Day 1	Teacher introduces words pictorially, sounding them out, and states the meaning. Then uses the word in a complete sentence that embraces the individual backgrounds and experiences of the students.
Day 2	Students draw or glue in small pictures representing the meaning of the word. Then they write their own complete sentence or fill in a writing frame about each word.
Day 3	Students read their sentences with each other. Their structured conversations are focused on listening and describing what they hear from each other.
Day 4	Student identifies the target words by circling them in a text that is selected from reading material or created by the teacher.
Day 5	Teacher introduces a word strategy that focuses on previous word work. An example of this strategy might have students categorizing the target words as verbs or nouns.

Teachers also need to find materials that make connections with the child's first language. For example, some books use both languages in the text, allowing the teacher to make those connections explicit in lessons. Some texts label specific objects in two languages within the text, while others may have different characters "speak"a different language. All of these forms of texts are now available and should be utilized to maximize transfer as well as a student's "meta" understanding of the relationship between his/her own language and English. Many Hispanic students will recognize environmental print in Spanish and English from signs, logos, labels, and television. (The Logo's lesson described in Chapter 5 can also address the issue of transfer.) We also recommend that you visit the following websites that we have found to be very useful in addressing early childhood instruction materials relevant to the issues we have discussed. These websites are http://colorincolorado.org and http://edition.tefl.net.

From the general recommendations to the specifics of instruction identified in the above discussion with regard to issues of language development, we come to better understand the complexities of language development and "teaching." We turn now to program-level understandings that can positively promote the language and academic outcomes of Hispanic children acquiring the demanding academic English in the classroom.

Dual Language Programs

Dual language (DL) programs—also known as two-way immersion (TWI)—are relatively new in the United States. Unique among program alternatives, the goals of DL programs are to provide high-quality instruction for students who come to school speaking primarily a language other than English, and simultaneously to provide instruction in a second language for English-speaking students. Schools offering DL programs thus teach children language through content, with teachers adapting their instruction to ensure children's comprehension and using content lessons to convey vocabulary and language structure. Striving for half language minority students and half native English-speaking students in each classroom, DL programs also aim to teach cross-cultural awareness. Programs vary in terms of the amount of time they devote to each language, which grade levels they serve, how much structure they impose for the division of language and curriculum, and what populations they serve. The Center for Applied Linguistics (CAL, 2005) has compiled research-based strategies and practices associated with DL program development and implementation. Entitled *Guiding Principles for Dual-Language Education,* seven dimensions to help with planning and ongoing implementation of DL programs are discussed: (1) assessment and accountability, (2) curriculum, (3) instruction, (4) staff quality and professional development, (5) program structure, (6) family and community, and (7) support and resources.

There are two widely adopted models of language division in DL programs: the 50-50 and the 90-10 models. In the 50-50 model, instruction is given half the day in English and half the day in the child's non-English native language (i.e., target language) throughout the grades. In the 90-10 models, children spend 90% of their Kindergarten school days in the non-English minority language, and this percentage gradually decreases to 50% by 4th or 5th grade.

The installation of DL programs is based on a strong theoretical rationale and supported by empirical research findings concerning both first- and second-language acquisition (Genesee, 1999). This rationale grows out of sociocultural theory, which maintains that learning occurs through naturalistic social interaction (Vygotsky, 1978). That is, the integration of native English speakers and speakers of other languages facilitates second-language acquisition because it promotes natural, substantive interaction among speakers of different languages.

Currently in the United States, there are over 400 DL programs, and the number is growing rapidly (García & Frede, 2010). While the vast majority offers instruction in Spanish and English, there are also DL programs that target Korean, Cantonese, Arabic, French, Japanese, Navajo, Portuguese, and Russian (Howard, Sugarman, & Christian, 2003; García, 2005).

Typically, there are three major goals for students in these programs:

1. To help children to learn English and find success in U.S. schools;
2. To help these children become competent in their own language without sacrificing their own success in school; and,
3. To promote linguistic and ethnic equity among the children, encouraging children to bridge the gaps between cultures and languages.

These goals are naturally interdependent, and relate to the individual student at differing levels, depending on his or her particular socio-linguistic and cultural background. For example, a native English-speaking child benefits by coming to understand that another language and culture hold equal importance to his or her own. A Spanish-speaking Hispanic child who is enrolled in a DL program is given equal school status due to his or her knowledge of the home language, rather than being penalized and segregated because of it.

Research evidence suggests that DL programs can be an excellent model for academic achievement for both language-minority and majority children. Studies have shown DL programs to promote English-language learning as well or better than other special programs designed for language minority children. For example, 100% of Spanish-dominant children in the Key School, a 50-50 DL school in Arlington County, Virginia, demonstrated oral English fluency by 3rd grade, as shown by the LAS-O Oral English Proficiency measure and classroom observations (Christian, 1997). English writing samples collected from native Spanish speakers in 5th and 6th grades were indistinguishable from those of native English speakers, and all were of high quality (Christian, 1997). In a separate study of four DL schools following the 90-10 program model in California, it was found that by 5th grade most students were clearly fluent in English and made gains in English reading at most school sites (although they did not attain grade level performance in reading) (Lindholm, 1999).

Comprehensive longitudinal data for DL students showed that both native English speakers and native Spanish speakers in the study showed progress in their language and literacy skills from the beginning of 3rd grade through the end of 5th grade. In addition, native Spanish speakers demonstrated more balanced language and literacy skills in the two languages, while native English speakers demonstrated clear dominance in English; yet, the DL program produced academic functioning for both groups of students over the period studied.

Positive effects of DL programs have also been found for Hispanics during the earliest years of schooling. Figueroa (2005) conducted a study with 24 Spanish-speaking Kindergartners (10 girls, 14 boys) in a

DL program looking at associations between the development of pre-reading knowledge in the child's native language and the development of the English skills. The researcher examined means and standard deviations from tests of phonological reasoning and oral fluency during the fall, winter, and spring of Kindergarten. She found that participants made significant gains in Spanish and English for every subtest of phonological awareness, in both languages, and at each of the three waves of data collection. Moreover, all participants were meeting or exceeding district requirements. Though the sampling methods in this study don't allow for robust generalizations to the larger population of young Hispanic ELLs, the results support what we know regarding the relationships between first- and second-language acquisition: Meaningful use and development of the primary language in the early years facilitates pre-reading skills in a second language. This is because higher-order cognitive skills tend to transfer between language and, during the early years, an acquisition of fundamental language and cognitive skills is very important (Genesee et al., 2005).

In an experimental study Barnett, Yarosz, Thomas, and Blanco (2006) compared the effects of a DL and a monolingual English immersion (EI) preschool program on children's learning. Children in the study (n = 150) were from both English and Spanish home language backgrounds. Eighty-five were randomly assigned to the DL program and 65 were randomly assigned to the EI program in the same school district. The two programs were compared on measures of children's growth in language, emergent literacy, and mathematics. Compared to those in the EI group, children in the DL program produced large and significant gains in Spanish vocabulary. In addition, all children (including native Spanish and native English speakers) in the DL program made greater phonological awareness gains in English, yet no group differences were found on measures of English language and literacy development. This study, therefore, suggests that early DL programs can provide support for native language development without sacrificing gains in English language development. Moreover, native English-speaking children in the DL program also made gains in Spanish language and literacy without hindering native language development. Additional analyses would be needed to determine the longitudinal impact of preschool DL programs on literacy development and academic outcomes throughout the elementary years.

Thus, the present knowledge base demonstrates that DL programs bear positive achievement outcomes for both language minority and language majority students, especially for young children developing fundamental language and literacy skills. Research supports the notion that higher-order cognitive and literacy skills transfer between languages, that developing native language skills can improve second-language skills, and that the DL program model corresponds well with these findings. Yet, the question remains: What specific programmatic features predict variation in quality among sites offering DL programs? To answer this question, Christian, Genesee, Lindholm-Leary, and Howard (2004) offered an in-depth examination of DL programs. Specifically, they evaluated the variation in educational attainment among school sites, the characteristics of effective classroom instruction, and the skills and knowledge required of professionals to work in DL programs. To get at these issues, researchers followed 484 students in 11 DL programs across the United States for 3 years, from 3rd through 5th grade—this is the same sample mentioned above. In this study authors looked specifically at features and practices of the DL programs that contributed to levels of English language proficiency for Spanish-speaking ELLs. Specifically, this study considered student outcome differences across DL program types (i.e., 90-10 versus 50-50), relative performance of at-risk students in three schools, and teacher characteristics and strategies deemed critical to effective program implementation.

Christian et al. (2004) analyzed particular teacher characteristics and strategies deemed important to effective implementation of DL programs. More specifically, they conducted classroom observations and focus groups with veteran teachers to investigate school- and classroom-level practices found to support language and literacy development in DL programs. Analyses of their data provided a list of key teaching strategies and teacher characteristics. They found that successful teachers "prioritize balanced literacy, cooperative and student-centered learning; focus on strategies that can be used across the content areas and language, thematic units, integrating language and content," and use "sheltered instruction strategies" (Christian et al., 2004, p. 6). Moreover, successful teachers prioritize the development of thinking, reading, and writing skills, emphasizing that these skills are not language specific, per se. The authors continue,

> Thematic instruction reinforces concepts in multiple contexts. Lessons are not repeated in both program languages, but the same language and literacy skills can be reinforced through the various activities that are done in different content areas. This type of teaching requires a great deal of coordination and joint planning time for the teachers involved. Teachers plan lessons with language and content in goals in mind and reinforce reading and writing skills taught during language arts by applying them to content areas. (p. 7)

Teachers able to implement these successful strategies, in general, shared the following characteristics: (1) fluency in both languages of instruction in order to model high language performance; (2) awareness of second-language acquisition patterns allowing the teacher to identify students' needs and tailor lessons to meet those needs; (3) a mastery of instructional strategies (i.e., cooperative learning, sheltered instruction, differentiated instruction, and strategic teaching); and (4) strong organizational and communication skills.

Critical to the success of pre-Kindergarten programs for Hispanic children—three of four of whom are exposed to Spanish in the home—are ways in which language and culture are integrated. More specifically, a trademark of high-quality pre-Kindergarten programs for young Hispanic children is the provision of dual-language (English and Spanish) content and instruction by school staff who are bilingual and culturally competent (Barnett et al., 2006; Borman, Hewes, Reilly, & Alvarado, 2006). This approach validates the child's cognitive and linguistic abilities while bridging home-school cultural differences—establishing an environment in which parents feel comfortable and are able to communicate with teachers.

CONCLUSION

Issues covered in this chapter about the intersection of early schooling, learning, and development of bilingual Hispanic children indicate that demographic circumstances of bilinguals in the United States should serve as an impetus to develop and support schooling programs and practices that recognize the conditions and strengths of these children and families. In terms of academic achievement, bilinguals lag behind their monolingual peers at the beginning of Kindergarten, and the gap closes very little thereafter. Socio-economic status, low parent education, limited English proficiency of parents, and other home circumstances, bear strongly on student performance. Home language practices strongly influence early student achievement. Also, in order to accurately determine language and cognitive competency of young Latino students (as well as other culturally and linguistically diverse student populations), appropriate tests and testing procedures are necessary. Assessment tools and procedures should systematically link learning outcomes with various contextual features, and should be used primarily to improve learning outcomes and service provision for these children. Studies in literacy development demonstrate that word- and text-level skills cross-transfer between languages. Letter learning, phonemic awareness, word reading, and passage comprehension in Spanish are strongly correlated with parallel skills in English. Moreover, the integration of the students' heritage language in the classroom has been shown to strengthen transfer. As the process of transfer takes time, literacy for emergent bilingual students, on average, takes longer than for native English speakers. Also, schooling program options for bilinguals differ in terms of their goals (e.g., whether bilingual proficiency is an aim), requirements for staff competency, and the student populations they are meant to serve. The effectiveness of a given program depends on local conditions, choices, and leveraging the cognitive benefits of bilingualism. In terms of student academic achievement, meta-analyses and best evidence syntheses suggest that programs supporting bilingual approaches to curriculum and instruction are favorable to English-only or English-immersion programs. These programs provide sound instruction in both the heritage language and English, and demonstrate, on average, academic benefits of 0.2 to 0.3 standard deviations over and above English-only programs.

Driven by sociocultural notions of language and learning, dual-language (DL) programs integrate native Spanish speaking students with native English speakers in the same classroom. Educators in DL programs use English-plus-Spanish (EPS) approaches to teach both languages through course content. Studies suggest that language minority and language majority students in DL programs perform academically at equal levels to their peers and, in many cases, outperform those in other programs. Finally, preliminary evidence suggests that high-quality pre-Kindergarten programs can improve school readiness for young bilingual children and decrease achievement differences between racial/ethnic groups at Kindergarten entry.

CHAPTER 4

Rich Language Environments

Because young Hispanics are highly likely to be raised in homes with limited educational capital (parents and relatives with limited schooling success), ways in which language is used at home and in preschool and early elementary settings will continue to be important. Moreover, the compatibility or cultural congruence of language environments between home and school is relevant. Empirical research reveals associations among literacy outcomes for bilingual Hispanic children and the extent to which teachers' discourse and interaction patterns resemble those found in the home (García, 2005; Goldenberg, Rueda, & August, 2006). The ongoing attention to rich language environments, therefore, will need to attend to both frequency and quality of language use (in Spanish, English, or both languages).

In terms of frequency, research on cognitive development, language, and early experiences shows that the amount of talk and conversational exchanges between adults and young children are strongly associated with school readiness and academic success in formal schooling (National Task Force on Early Childhood Education for Hispanics, 2007). However, there is limited empirical information on the vocabularies and the number of opportunities for linguistic exchanges within home and school environments of young Hispanics across levels of SES (including parent education) and immigration status.

During the last decade or so, many educational theorists have become interested in the social contexts of children as a critical variable related to overall learning and development (Nasir & Hand, 2006; Rogoff, 2003). This empirical interest is tied conceptually to sociocultural theory, an international intellectual movement that brings together the disciplines of psychology, semiotics, education, sociology, and anthropology. This conceptualization draws on work done earlier in the 20th century by the Russian theorists L. S. Vygotsky and Mikhail Bakhtin (Cole & Cole, 2001), and relates it to the thought of such theoreticians and philosophers of education as William James, John Dewey, C. S. Pierce, and Jean Piaget (García, 2002). The aim of this theoretical perspective is to find a unified way of understanding issues of language, cognition, culture, human development, and teaching and learning.

Sociocultural theorists posit that the psychology of the individual learner is deeply shaped by social interaction—in essence, that both children and those with whom they interact are engaged in the process of constructing knowledge primarily through social activity. Therefore, knowledge is created among individuals primarily through social interaction. Higher-order mental processes, the tendency to look at things in certain ways, and values themselves are produced by shared activity and dialogue (Rogoff, 1990). In a broader sense, these social interactions are highly determined by culture and directly affect language, cognitive, and social development as well as the acquisition of any new knowledge and behavior—that phenomenon we call "learning."

The focus of sociocultural theory holds particular import for understanding development and early education, partly because this population brings to the formal schooling process a language and culture with distinct social contexts that deviate in many cases from the norm in the United States. Educators of culturally diverse students—including young Hispanic children learning English as a second language—often find this theoretical framework helpful because it conceives of learning as an interaction between individual learners and an embedding context. That embedding context may be as immediate as the social environment of the classroom or as indirect as the traditions and institutions that constitute the history of education. Both contexts and many other factors come into play whenever teachers and students interact. Important contexts for teaching and learning range from (1) close detailed instruction of individual learners to (2) concern for the social organization of classrooms to (3) a consideration of the cultural and linguistic attributes of teachers, students, and peers. These contexts interweave, and we can follow their strands to gain a new understanding of the relationship between language, culture, and cognition.

It is useful, therefore, to consider co-occurring linguistic, cognitive, and social character of a child's development as inherently interrelated (Hart & Risley, 1995, 1999; García, 2005). As children develop their ability to use language, they absorb more and more understanding of social situations and improve their thinking skills. This in turn allows them to learn how to control their own actions and thoughts. It is through a culturally bound and socially mediated process of language development that children construct mental frameworks (or schema) for perceiving the world around them. If language is a tool of thought, it follows that as children develop more complex thinking skills, the mental representations through which language and culture embody the child's world play a significant role. This perspective is especially important for young children negotiating two or more languages (Scheffner Hammer, Miccio, & Rodriguez, 2004).

Empirical analyses indicate that young Hispanic bilingual children in the United States use cognitive and linguistic strategies to negotiate complex elements of social environments. Language use and social interactive strategies employed by children in such studies have been found to vary by the linguistic ability of the addressee(s) (García & Carrasco, 1981; Poplack, 1981; García, 1983; Fantini, 1985; Reyes, 1998), topic of discussion (Heath, 1983, 1986; Zentella, 1997), level of familiarity with addressee(s) (García & Carrasco, 1981; García, 1983; Dolson, 1984), the child's shared history with the addressee(s) (Genishi, 1981; Zentella, 1997), and attitudinal features of the child (Ramirez, 1985). This research evidence supports the notion that language use and preference of a young bilingual child cannot be conceived solely in linguistic or cognitive terms—it is contextually dependent and predicated on attributes of cultural relevance.

HOME AND CLASSROOM CULTURES

If what Vygotsky proposed (Cole & Cole, 2001) and a child's cognitive schema for operating in the world is culturally bound, what are the effects of trying to learn in an environment where the culture of the classroom differs from the culture of the home? Do young Hispanic children exposed to Spanish and English in the home face the challenge of accommodating their existing schema or constructing new schema once they enter formal schooling? Indeed, when the educational focus is on transitioning culturally and linguistically diverse students to a mainstream culture rather than building on what they already know, students may be forced to change in order to meet the needs of the classroom. Georges Duquette (1991) concludes: "Children need to be understood and to express themselves (in the same positive light experienced by other children) in their own first language, home context, and culture. Their minority background brings out the limitations not of the children but of the professionals who are asked to respond to those needs" (p. 91).

Unfortunately, educational policy and practice discussions regarding the education of Hispanic students are often overly simplistic and focus only on the language difference of this population (Tharp & Gallimore, 1989; García, 2005; Rolstad, Mahoney, & Glass, 2005; Jensen, 2008a). They tend to neglect the complex interweaving of students' cultural, linguistic, and cognitive development. In their study of the possible effects of language on cognitive development, Hakuta, Ferdman, and Diaz (1987) recognize the importance of acknowledging these three important strands in children's development and addressing them in schools. They concluded that most of the variance in cognitive growth directly relates to the way in which society affects and manipulates cognitive capacities. Therefore, cultural and contextual sensitivity theories that examine the social and cultural aspects of cognitive development will best serve diverse students.

Research on Sociocultural Context and Literacy

Language and cognitive development are critical to the maturity of literacy skills. While there is agreement among scholars and researchers that social and cultural features also play important roles in the literacy development of young children, paradigms and methodologies used to investigate the role of sociocultural contexts on literacy development and attainment vary. Some studies employ qualitative and ethnographic methods while others restrict themselves to quantitative and purely deductive models. Because sociocultural constructs (e.g., discourse patterns, attitudinal features, routines, etc.) are complex—interacting with cognitive and linguistic properties in subtle yet meaningful ways—research necessitates dynamic designs and multiple methods to account for ways in which contextual factors influence literacy learning (Ercikan & Roth, 2006; Smith, 2006). To date, this type of research is limited—most research has followed either quantitative, a priori models or has used only qualitative designs.

In a recent synthesis of empirical studies, commissioned by the National Literacy Panel on Language-Minority Children and Youth, Goldenberg, Rueda, and August (2006) present a research synthesis on the influences of social and cultural contexts on literacy development and attainment of language minority children and youth. They defined social and cultural influences broadly, as factors that contribute to the context in which children and youth go to school and live—including beliefs, attitudes, behaviors, routine practices, social and political relations, and physical resources connected with groups of people who share some characteristic (e.g., SES, educational status, race/ethnicity, national origin, linguistic group). Moreover, they evaluated studies using six operational definitions and domains of social and cultural contexts: immigration, home/school discourse differences, characteristics of students and teachers, the influence of parents and families, educational policy, and language status or prestige. Studies they reviewed reported data on (1) factors in one or more sociocultural domains and (2) student outcomes—including cognitive, affective, and/or behavioral—presumably impacted by one or more of these factors. Outcomes could be gauged in the child's first language, second language, or both. We focus our attentions specifically on studies that evaluated young Hispanics.

Only a few research studies have assessed the influence of immigration circumstances on literacy outcomes. These did not provide convincing evidence to suggest that Hispanic immigration, on its own, influences literacy achievement (Goldenberg, 1987; Monzó & Rueda, 2001; Rueda, MacGillivray, Monzó, & Arzubiaga, 2001; Arzubiaga, Rueda, & Monzó, 2002). Although there is clear evidence that immigration as a variable is associated with Mexican-origin students' academic achievement in the early grades (Reardon & Galindo, 2006), the "effects" of immigration (via generation status and circumstances associated with immigration) on literacy achievement appears to be mediated by various out-of-school processes. Moreover, "literacy outcomes are more likely to relate to home (and school) language and literacy learning opportunities, irrespective of immigration status" (Goldenberg, Rueda, & August, 2006, p. 255).

Differences in home/school discourse and interaction patterns were found between some language minority groups (Au & Mason, 1981; Rueda, August, & Goldenberg, 2006), but "the consequences of these differences for students' literacy attainment and the effects of attempts to address or accommodate these differences in the classroom are not clear" (Goldenberg, Rueda, & August, 2006, pp. 255–256). The few studies that claimed an association between literacy-related student outcomes and different discourse and interaction patterns between home and school for Hispanic youngsters (Huerta-Macías & Quintero, 1992; Kucer & Silva, 1999; Wilkinson, Milosky, & Genishi, 1986) bore certain methodological flaws. Problems in design, data collection, and analysis prevented clear interpretations. Goldenberg, Rueda, and August (2006), therefore, conclude,

> The most we can say given the available research is that bridging home-school difference in interaction can enhance students' engagement and level of participation in classroom instruction. This outcome is certainly not trivial, but it is not the same as enhancing student achievement or other types of learning outcomes—effects the existing data cannot confirm. (p. 256)

Related research on social and cultural characteristics of Hispanic students and their teachers, however, do lend some support to the notion that the cultural relevance of materials and testing procedures play a role in literacy outcomes (Jiménez, 1997; García, 1991; Reyes, 2001). García (1991), for example, offers compelling evidence that the lack of relevant background knowledge impeded Hispanic bilingual students on reading comprehension tests. In this study, qualitative and quantitative methodologies were employed to identify sociocultural factors that influenced the English reading test performance of 104 5th- and 6th-grade students from two elementary schools of similar socio-economic status (low to low-middle) in the same school district. Fifty-one of the children were identified as bilingual (Spanish-English) Hispanics, and 53 were identified as monolingual

(English-speaking) White children. Hispanic student reading test scores in this study were found to underestimate their reading potential. García (1991) concluded that test performance was affected by limited prior knowledge of certain test topics, unfamiliarity with vocabulary terms in test questions and answer choices, and their tendency to interpret the test literally when determining answers. Indeed, post hoc interviews revealed that Hispanic students tended to be more literal in their reading and did not use vocabulary they had to draw correct inferences. Furthermore, for the topic on which the Hispanic students had greater background knowledge (the word *piñata*), scores between bilingual Hispanics and Whites was equivalent. Though these data on comprehension outcomes, and the general notion that teacher and student characteristics influence literacy development, are compelling, further research is needed, particularly for younger children.

The body of research on the influence of parents and families on literacy outcomes is stronger—that is, more research has been conducted and written on this issue—and suggests three major findings. First, parents of language-minority students, in general, value literacy development for their children yet, for various reasons, school personnel underestimate and do not take full advantage of home resources and parents' interest, motivation, and involvement (Brooker, 2002; Goldenberg, 1987; Goldenberg & Gallimore, 1991; Goldenberg, Rueda, & August, 2006; Harry & Klingner, 2006; Shannon, 1995; Scheffner Hammer & Miccio, 2004; Scheffner Hammer, Miccio, & Wagstaff, 2003). Second, measures of parent and family literacy practices often predict literacy attainment of their children, but findings in this regard are not consistent across the board (Durán & Weffer, 1992; Goldenberg, Reese, & Gallimore, 1992; Pucci & Ulanoff, 1998; Reese, Garnier, Gallimore, & Goldenberg, 2000; Goldenberg Gallimore, Reese, & Garnier, 2001; Arzubiaga et al, 2002). Third, sociocultural studies suggest that the relationship between language use in the home and literacy outcomes of language minority students (in the school) is not clear (Dolson, 1985; Buriel & Cardoza, 1988; Hansen, 1989; Monzó & Rueda, 2001; Hancock, 2002). That is, it is unclear whether Spanish- or English-use in the home is preferable in terms of optimizing Hispanic students' literacy development. Again, this result appears to be associated with methodological problems and inconsistencies across studies. Most of the studies control for obvious confounds, such as parent education, but fail to do so for other critical factors, such as quality of instruction in school, parents' Spanish and English abilities, quality and quantity of language in the home, and parent attitudes regarding home language practices. As discussed later, studies in linguistics have considered in greater detail literacy and language development for Hispanic bilingual and emerging bilingual students. In general, these demonstrate that word- and text-level skills cross-transfer between languages. Moreover, the language system used in the home is not as important as the quantity of language used in the home and the quality of linguistic interactions. And literacy development appears to be associated with home literacy practices and parent educational attainment, where parents with less formal education, on average, read less to and engage their children less frequently in conversation (López, Barrueco, & Miles, 2006; Risley & Hart, 2006).

Rich Discourse Processes

With respect to overall instruction, the National Task Force on the Early Education for Hispanics (2007) concluded that an emphasis on content in our educational system has resulted in turning Hispanic students into "walking factual data bases" rather than "proficient problem solvers." This emphasis on content is perpetuated due to the extraordinary importance of achievement tests in the educational system. These tests measure content: "There is little incentive to emphasize process in the classroom given that the only meaningful measure used in evaluating a teacher's performance is how well their students perform in content based achievement tests" (National Task Force on the Early Education for Hispanics, 2007, p. 27). However, we see, in spite of this impediment, a positive trend in educational reform today that favors process along with content. In other words, we are seeing more thinking and problem solving within literacy, mathematics, and science (García & Frede, 2010).

Espinosa (2010) suggests that the interrelationship between language and performance on cognitive tasks could be particularly significant to the growing number of minority students populating our public schools. These children come to the schooling process with significant linguistic and problem solving experiences in a language other than the language utilized in schools. In school they meet for the first time academic-related language tasks in literacy, mathematics, and other content areas that may or may not be process oriented or in the student's home-based language(s). For all students, but specifically for Hispanic students, content must be taught, but the emphasis on process should be increased. To understand a process and be able to articulate it is to expand one's linguistic abilities. A product question ("What is this?") designed to measure content may be answered using "restricted code" whereas it is impossible to answer a process question without using an "elaborated code" ("Why did you pick the orange one?").

According to many researchers (see Chapter 4), the elaborated code of families with education experience runs more to subordination and modification than to a restricted code of the individuals with limited educational backgrounds. Elaborate codes include higher levels of vocabulary, more adjectives, adverbs, prepositions, and complex verbs as well as referents to the world of metaphors and analogies. It facilitates distinctions of all sorts, in particular logical ones. Elaborated code users distance themselves more from the immediate situation and from the content of their talk, through abstraction, through passives, through expressions of probability, through suppositions ("I think"), through questions and refusals to commit themselves quickly to definite interpretations of ambiguous experience. The elaborated code allows or encourages more individualization of a response and is less bound to the local, concrete situation. Restricted code meaning is implicit and dependent on prior understandings of the context . . . communal rather than individual, the concrete rather than the abstract, substance rather than the elaboration of processes, the here and now rather than exploration of motives and intentions (García, 2005).

However, to be clear, we all vary our speech (code) from situation to situation, but to be "at home" on every occasion, one would have to have a command of both the restricted and elaborated codes. Generalizing, we understand that formal schooling is not only based on elaborated codes and too often expect students to be versed in this code. We have argued that all students would benefit from more process oriented instruction, to include elaborated codes so as to aid academic language to natural language transitions and vice versa.

García and Barry (1990) report data from Hispanic, Spanish/English bilingual classrooms, which suggests that higher order teacher initiations and replies (process-related requests that emphasize "why," "how," etc.) lead to occurrences of complex language functions. This result is particularly important in language-minority classrooms in which one of the major curricular objectives is higher order, academic-related language acquisition. A greater emphasis on process-oriented instruction should turn students into "proficient problem solvers" and "enhance linguistic abilities." However, it is important to note that a study of literacy instruction in language-minority students (García, 2005) reported that higher-order cognitive and linguistic interaction was primarily found in student–student exchanges as opposed to teacher–student exchanges. It seemed that students were much more likely to engage in complex oral discourse and writing when teachers engaged Hispanic students in ways that were required answers to complex questioning—not the "what," but the "how" and "why" in teacher questioning.

CONCLUSION

We felt it important to devote an extended amount of space in this volume to address the significance of rich language environments for young Hispanics who participate in early learning environments. Our experience and our research, as well as robust theories of language, culture, development, and learning support the overall contention that complex modes of communication begin at home and are utilized in learning in school. For many Hispanic children, through no fault of their own, the only access to rich language experiences is within educational venues. They are likely to be absent in either Spanish or English in other non-educational venues of their experience. Therefore, it becomes incumbent on educators serving these children to enhance access to these process-related communication skills that we now realize are so important in attaining academic access as the content of schooling is delivered (Espinosa, 2010; García & Frede, 2010). Allow us also to remind readers of Head Start's efforts to address the complexity of education of our nation's youngest, and its specific attention to dual language learners. We refer you to Head Start's Revised Child Outcomes Framework available at http://eclkc.ohs.acf.hhs.gov/hslc.

The next chapters attempt to bring this understanding to the teaching process (Chapter 5) and to aspects of the educator who constructs and implements these learning opportunities (Chapter 6). For Hispanic children, constructing these rich language environments that connect academic discourses with academic content must be omnipresent in all occasions of schooling.

CHAPTER 5

Teaching and Learning for Hispanics in Early Childhood

Over the past 2 decades, there has been growing evidence from a few well-designed and rigorously evaluated model early childhood programs that high-quality preschool can make meaningful improvements in the school readiness of low-SES children and help them have better long-term educational outcomes in school. The two most influential model programs are the Carolina Abecedarian Project and the High/Scope Perry Preschool Program. Both have been tested using randomized trials; and both have followed the children in their studies into adulthood. An operating program, the Chicago Child-Parent Center (CPC) Program, also has been influential because it has conducted a longitudinal evaluation that has followed a large group of children into adulthood as well (Reynolds, Temple, Robertson, & Mann, 2001). Abecedarian provided a full-day, year-around, center-based program for 5 years, from early infancy to the start of Kindergarten, with some children getting additional support in the primary grades. Both the Perry Preschool and CPC provided a half-day program for 3- and 4-year-olds during the school year. CPC also provided support for some students during the primary grades.

Among the documented educational benefits of these three programs are higher academic achievement in school, less retention in grade, lower special education–referral rates, higher rates of high school graduation, and higher rates of college attendance (Barnett, 2006). Of the three, Abecedarian has shown the greatest capacity to raise participants' academic achievement, as measured by standardized tests, on a long-term basis. However, even Abecedarian was unable to help the participating low-SES children move on to educational trajectories in schools typical of middle-class children, much less than those of high-SES youngsters.

In addition to the empirical evidence of long-term positive outcomes, cost-benefit analyses of these programs have been generally very positive (Barnett, 2006). As a result, the economic case for preschool has been, and continues to be, a major reason for supporting its expansion in policymaking and advocacy circles. Yet, even as efforts to expand early childhood education for 3- and 4-year-olds have intensified over the past decade, there also has been growing recognition that it is very difficult to mount large-scale government-funded pre-Kindergarten programs that match the quality of the best model programs. This is in no small measure due to the fact that government per capita investment in large operational preschool programs has been much lower than the amount spent per child in the high-quality model programs. The largest government-funded preschool program, Head Start, is probably the most visible case in point. Its investment per child has always been much lower than the best model programs. However, Head Start also makes the case for most state-funded pre-Kindergarten programs (National Institute for Early Childhood Education Research, 2010). Without sufficient per capita investment, it is difficult to mount large-scale government programs that have high-quality features similar to the best model programs. Among these are well-educated teachers, favorable teacher-child ratios, relatively small class sizes, good ongoing professional development, and well-resourced classrooms (e.g., a large number of children's books).

EVALUATIONS OF HEAD START AND STATE PRE-K PROGRAMS

Most of these uncertainties are likely to persist to some degree for many years to come. However, over the past few years, much more research-based information has become available in many of these areas. Even more should become available in the years ahead. Much of this growing body of evidence is being generated by evaluations of a number of state pre-Kindergarten programs that have been recently established or expanded. Other information has been coming from the federal level, including results from a major evaluation of Head Start that is employing a randomized trial (National Task Force on the Early Education for Hispanics, 2007).

Because there is a great deal of variation among state programs, many opportunities have emerged to compare benefits of different amounts of preschool. For example, comparative evaluations have recently been undertaken of full- and half-day programs and 1- and 2-year programs. Many of these evaluations have included substantial numbers of Hispanic children. Thus, there now is much more information about "what works" for Hispanics (and what "what works" means in the way of developmental benefits) in the preschool years. For example, the initial results from the current Head Start randomized trial have produced evidence that Head Start programs overall do contribute to improvements in the school readiness of low-SES children, including Hispanic youngsters. However, the cognitive gains documented to date are generally moderate in size and concentrated in the verbal area. This is true for Hispanics as well, for example, 3-year-old Hispanics gained in letter recognition and vocabulary. Benefits for Hispanic 4-year-olds were very limited. While beneficial, the participating children in this evaluation were still well below national school-readiness norms (National Task Force on Early Childhood Education for Hispanics, 2007).

However, a rigorous evaluation of the public school component of Oklahoma's state pre-Kindergarten program (which serves 4-year-olds) has documented substantial school readiness benefits for children (Gormley, Gayer, Phillips, and Dawson, 2005). The findings from this evaluation, which looked at children in pre-Kindergarten programs in the Tulsa public schools, are important for several reasons. First, Oklahoma is one of the few states with a universal pre-K program; and, a larger share of 4-year-olds attend either a state- or federally funded preschool in Oklahoma than in any other state. Second, the evaluation has documented benefits for children from all racial/ethnic groups, including Hispanics. Third, the evaluation has found that both poor and non-poor children benefit from participating in the program. Fourth, substantial cognitive gains were documented on assessments of pre-reading, pre-writing, and math reasoning skills. In "age-equivalent" terms, the participants had scores equal to those usually registered by children 4- to 8-months older, depending on the skill area. Overall, the gains were not quite as large as the best model programs (Abecedarian and the Perry Preschool), but they were larger than the average gains documented in evaluations of other state programs. The authors of the evaluation of Oklahoma's universal pre-Kindergarten program have conjectured on why the readiness benefits of its program seem to be above average among state pre-K programs. One possible reason is that Oklahoma is providing a higher quality program in several important respects. For example, the state has required that teachers in public pre-Kindergarten programs have a bachelor's degree and be certified in early childhood education. Also, Oklahoma is paying public pre-K teachers' salaries that are the same as public school teachers in general. The authors also suggest that another reason may be that (based on their informal classroom observations) teachers in public school pre-K programs seem to be stressing academics. This suggestion is consistent with the fact that some of the largest gains were in such directly teachable pre-reading skills as letter-word recognition and spelling. Of course, that also raises the possibility that some of the gains may represent moderate acceleration of the acquisition of basic skills that would have been acquired anyway in Kindergarten. At this point, the investment that Oklahoma is making in universal pre-K looks very promising, especially for Hispanics.

As previously noted, a major unanswered question is whether it is beneficial to attend 2 years of pre-Kindergarten rather than 1 year. Recently, some findings have become available on this question from a test in New Jersey of the relative school readiness benefits for low-SES children, including low-SES Hispanics, of attending a full-day pre-Kindergarten program for either 1 year or 2 years. An analysis of the vocabulary, print awareness, and math skills of entering Kindergartners who had attended 1 year of pre-K and those who had attended 2 years of pre-K found that only in the area of vocabulary did 2 years of preschool produce greater benefits than one year (Barnett and Lamy, 2005). In a related vein, a recent analysis of ECLS-K data that included Hispanic children in California found that children who start attending a center-based program by age 3 (but after age 2) gain larger reading and math readiness benefits than do children who start at age 4 (Loeb, Bridges, Bassok, Fuller, & Rumberger, 2005).

Benefits of Preschool/Pre-Kindergarten

Six conclusions stand out from this brief review of research findings on school readiness and academic achievement benefits of preschool for young Hispanics:

1. The weight of the rapidly growing body of evaluation evidence indicates that high-quality, large-scale pre-K programs are producing meaningful benefits for low-, middle-, and high-SES children, including Hispanics.
2. The fact that benefits seem to accrue to middle- and high-SES children as well as to low-SES youngsters is potentially very important for Hispanics, because they are lagging behind Whites in readiness and school achievement at all social class levels.
3. Available evidence is beginning to support the conclusion that low-SES children benefit more from attending full-day pre-K programs than half-day ones and from attending 2-year rather than 1-year programs.
4. The actual extent of the long-term benefits of pre-Kindergarten is promising but still unclear, because the evaluations of the growing number of state pre-Kindergarten programs have not yet produced long-term information. It will be several years before there is extensive evaluation evidence through the end of elementary school and into high school.
5. Even the most promising pre-Kindergarten programs only partially close the differences in readiness and achievement

between Hispanic low-SES and middle-class children (and between Hispanic middle class and high-SES youngsters).

6. The best documented achievement benefits of pre-Kindergarten concern reducing negative outcomes, e.g., reducing the percentage of children who achieve at very low levels, reducing the percentage that are retained in grade, reducing the percentage that are assigned to special education, and so forth.

We wish to conclude, that for Hispanics, early educational experiences of the kind provided in Head Start and state-supported preschools produce important educationally related, positive outcomes. We turn now to specific instructional practices and program attributes that addressed the issue of quality and effective instruction that can lead to positive outcomes in preschool and early childhood education venues. This is the best example of research meeting practice.

READING WITH YOUNG HISPANIC CHILDREN

For Hispanic children's education success in U.S. schools, we believe that sophisticated academic English is the key to success. We discussed this in some detail in the preceding chapter. It is an equity issue for us. These students need a conscientious explicit focus on their language development in academic content domains of English. Many teachers focus on the content that they need to teach without realizing that each content area is contextualized by the language of that content. For example, social studies will utilize, almost consistently, the grammar of past tense; science will utilize, almost consistently, the grammar of passive voice; and language arts almost always deals in the present tense. If children cannot operate on language using these understandings, the content will not be successfully appropriated. Complex standards and related curriculum even at the earliest grades require students to identify, describe, differentiate, draw conclusions, and analyze. Any plan for student learning must take into account this set of complex requirements. As Chapter 1 so clearly emphasized, it is at these "complexity" levels that Hispanic children demonstrate achievement gaps. This is to say that present schooling and instruction are assisting Hispanic children at the "basic" levels, but they are failing at the more complex levels of instruction and learning. As previously noted in Chapter 3, robust levels of academic-related vocabulary and other aspect of academic English are critical. Let us draw on our experiences and related instructional practices that have worked to address these issues.

Phonological Awareness

Phonological awareness is the ability to detect and manipulate the sounds in words independent of word meaning. It improves school readiness skills and must be taught before children learn to read. Thus, children must be able to manipulate sounds as well as understand what is being read to them. What teachers should know is that phonological awareness teaches sound manipulation and text engagement storytelling teaches comprehension.

Phonological awareness proceeds sequentially along a continuum of skills beginning with sentence and syllable blending and segmenting, and proceeds to blending and segmenting individual phonemes in words. Teachers need guidance about how to organize and sequence phonological-awareness instruction so that children will develop more advanced phonological skills (e.g., those that involve deletion and substitution of sounds and linking of sounds and letters). Phonological awareness must be taught systematically, sequentially, and explicitly, and focus on identifying, detecting, deleting, segmenting, and blending segments of spoken words. Children must be able to blend and segment sounds before they can learn the relationship between sounds and letters in print. We must continue to create opportunities for children to explore spoken language through manipulations that are found in rhymes and songs. These will help build both the language and literacy skills that Hispanic learners need to be successful in our classrooms. Research continues to show that introducing the skills of phonological awareness, print awareness, and alphabet knowledge in brief, interactive, and multisensory activities are best done during the beginning years of school.

Teachers begin school with many chants, poems, or songs that may or may not be familiar: a good morning song to begin the school day and perhaps a good-bye song to end the day. Some of the poems are carefully chosen to introduce activities that ask children to state their name, favorite color, and so forth; and others are read together from a large chart that has the words written in large letters.

Table 5.1 provides teachers with a continuum of phonological skills that needs to be considered when they are planning their daily lessons.

Name Bingo

Teachers who share how they begin the school year always include name activities as their first way of establishing relationships and a sense of safety and belonging with their students. Young children often come home after one week of school and announce which friend did not share,

Table 5.1. Continuum of Phonological Skills

Activity	Teacher	Student
Sound Matching	Gives sound to child	Matches a word or generates a word beginning with that sound
Sound Isolation	Gives a word	Isolates a part of it: beginning/ middle/end
Sound Blending	Gives series of segmented sounds that form a word	Blends them together to produce the word
Sound Addition or Substitution	Gives a word with a new sound	Substitutes new sounds and produces a new word
Word Segmentation	Gives a word	Segments the word phoneme by phoneme

Adapted from P. Espinosa, 1996.

"Jiana would not let me use the red crayon," or that their best friend, Julian, "has a lunch box just like mine and he is my best friend." They realize the power of names and how important they are as soon as they begin to communicate what is happening in school. Names allow teachers to orally assign responsibility of actions to specific students and, more importantly, invite them to join you in learning. See Table 5.2 for an example lesson plan on names.

If a teacher *knows* the power of a name, what should she *be able to do* to ensure that names are being practiced? Name Bingo ensures this. Name Bingo can be implemented within the first month of school. This game begins with pictures of friends on a card, a teacher calling out names, and students covering up faces. Later the students call out names of students and students cover the beginning letter on a letter bingo card.

Friend Bingo

For this game/lesson, create bingo cards with a photo of each student. Glue photos in each square (nine squares per card). Each student should have one card and a few buttons to cover the pictures. The teacher calls out names, and students cover their friends' faces on the squares with their buttons. Once they cover all the squares they call out "friend bingo" and say their friends' names on their card. They use the language frame "The friend on my bingo card is _____, _____, _____, [etc]."

In this lesson, the power of hearing your name spoken by the teacher and friend strengthens the learning relationships they are forming each

Table 5.2. Name Lesson Plan

Week Date: _____   **Day:** M T W Th F

Content Area: Reading Writing Math Social Studies Science

Content Objective	Vocabulary
I can identify the name of my friend by using letters and their sounds in a "Peek-a-Boo" watercoloring activity.	*letter, sound, watercolor, appear, hidden*
Language Objective	**Sentence Frames**
I can name and sound out the letters of the alphabet.	Teacher or student: *"What letter is appearing?"* Students: *"I can see the letter ____ and it says _____."* *"My/The name is _____!"*
Standard	**Materials**
Identify one's name and associated letters and sounds	*chart paper, white crayon, watercolors, and brush*

MY TURN

Begin the lesson by having each child state their names using the sentence frame, "My name is _____." Introduce the notion of "Peek-a-Boo" and how they will do the same when they brush over the hidden letters. As they appear they will state the name and say the sound of the letter that appears.

OUR TURN

One student is chosen to color and is asked to state the name and sound of the letters first. Then the rest of the group can repeat and begin to put sounds together to figure out whose name is appearing on the chart paper. Remember the child watercoloring should be allowed to name and sound out the letters first as well as state the name of the child who was written in the white crayon. Use the sentence frame, "The name is _____."

YOUR TURN

Students identify name of peer in the "Peek-a-Boo" activity by sharing with a peer the sentence frame. Then they return to tables, copy the name, and draw their peer. The drawings will be collected and placed into a class book that will remain on the shelf to be read.

Total Response	Structure	Assessment
All students use sentence frame to name student (complete sentence) *All students complete page for book*	*Routine: once a week* *Whole Group* *Pairs* *Sentence frames for complete sentences*	*Teacher asks "Who agrees that the letter____ makes _____ (sound)?"* *The writing can also be included as a developmental history during the year.*

day at school. Friend Bingo can continue to be used during the beginning part of the year. As soon as students can read the names on the name cards the teacher no longer has to. The games can be used in centers. The key is that the language frame is more complex. Once a student calls "bingo," he or she uses the language frame "one friend on my bingo card is _____ and he/she like to _____."

Later, the bingo cards change, with just beginning letters of student's names. And pictures are used to call out names. The game can be done independently in a small group or in centers. It is important that children are asked to use the language frames when they call out "bingo." Consider the possibilities of what other pictures might be placed on teacher-crested bingo cards. They might be the vocabulary they are learning in a math unit, or just holiday pictures or maybe the planets of the solar system. It is important that the words are chosen carefully and practiced with purpose in mind. Will the students use these words as they "read" a book, as they describe their new understanding in their learning logs? Remember this strategy can become a context where vocabulary enhances, all beginning with the names.

Sound Word Wall

A phonological awareness activity that begins with students is a large wall space that is outlined with squares. In fact, many teachers create the wall with 26 spaces (one for each of the letters of the English alphabet) outlined on a large piece of bulletin board paper. The teacher then places pictures of each of the students, including his or herself and any other adults who might work in the classroom on the spaces. The teacher organizes the pictures by the initial sound in their names. It is important that no letter form is written in the outlined spaces. An example might be in a classroom where there are three students whose names begin with the sound /m/—Marissa, Marisol, and Myrtle, the teacher would place all three pictures in the same space. In fact, if the teacher assistant's name is Mike, then his picture would also be placed in the same space. The letter *M* would be the 13th letter, therefore these pictures would be placed on the 13th space. Remember, during sound wall there are no letters placed in the spaces. The sound wall becomes the ABC Word Wall when letters are placed in each of the 26 spaces.

During the next few days, other pictures are placed on the wall, and students join the teacher in sounding out the names of the pictures and listening for the beginning sound as well as identifying what other pictures might have the same sound. Pictures may come from home or a Sound Center. In the Sound Center students identify and cut pictures from magazines or newspapers. The teacher might ask a child to find a picture of his or her favorite food, animal, or perhaps a picture that begins with "your sound," the initial sound of his or her name. The class then follows the same routine of stating the word or label of the picture, saying the initial sound, and then identifying what space the picture should be placed on. Often, they will find pictures that begin with the friend's name because they like the picture (a soccer ball or movie character). The teacher should then ask the student to name the object in the picture and to state the friends' name and beginning sound. These are then placed by the group in the square with the pictures that begin with the same sound.

In the following months teachers will use the Sound Word Wall to teach the phonological awareness skills. The teachers begin by engaging children in sounding out their peers' names by rhyming the words they are working with, or counting the number of syllables in the name of a picture. Later, segment the names of the pictures and begin manipulating the beginning sound of some names. A phonological lesson script follows:

> "If I say Joaquin and take away or not say his first sound /j/ and use Veronica's sound the /v/ what word do I make?" The students yell out, "From Joaquin you get violin." The teacher responds with, "Yes, violin. And is that an object we know?"

It is always important to help children make connections with words that they might create and develop an understanding of what the new word might be. Manipulating sounds in words creates opportunities for teachers to introduce new vocabulary. Again, the Sound Word Wall is used for all of the phonological skills that students must learn, as well as vocabulary.

ABC Picture Word Wall

Finally, the Sound Word Wall is transformed into an ABC Picture Word Wall. The teacher begins the lesson by reviewing the purpose of the Sound Word Wall and practicing some of the skills students have learned. The teacher then asks if there might be a possibility of using the letters of the alphabet to show the sound of the pictures in the squares. Using the letter form, the teacher asks if there is a sound for the letter, X, shows a large uppercase letter *M* and the lowercase *m*. The students look up at the Sound Word Wall and call out the names of the objects and peers or teachers that are inside of a particular square. The teacher places the cutout letters and moves on to a new letter form. She continues in this same manner during the next few days. The Sound Word Wall now becomes an ABC Picture

Word Wall. (Remember some of the students' name might not begin with the sound in the English alphabet, and thus the teacher must make connections to the Spanish alphabet and what the letter might be for that sound (e.g., parents say *Jonathan* with the beginning sound /Y/ and the teacher should let the child and family know that his picture will be placed in the *J* letter square. Or it may be as simple as Joaquin's name being placed on the *J* because it is the sound that the Spanish letter represents.) This ABC Picture Word Wall becomes the first steps toward building sound symbol relationships and the students' initial introduction to phonics.

Logos

Logos of popular products and businesses in a literacy context can be used to develop skills between reading letters and sounds and reading text. This context should be implemented during the first week of school. Many connections are made with the students regarding how reading always has meaning. This activity quickly becomes a phonics activity where students use a picture logo or type of print text logo to represent what the object is. Students soon realize that they might be able to know what the name of the object is by what is around the letters. As they sound out the names of the objects they begin to connect the sound to the letter. Teachers need to understand that when students read logos they are reading with meaning and begin to understand the function of letters. When students share logos that they've created, other students then understand what their peer is reading. Below is a lesson using logos:

> Begin by bringing logos that you have chosen in a paper bag and take out one logo and state, "Yesterday I ate at _____. I can read _____." (Use a logo of an eating establishment that students will recognize.) Students will quickly join you in reading the logo. Then you might put out another logo and say, "This morning I brushed my teeth with _____ (toothpaste logo) and at lunch I am going to drink _____" (2% milk carton logo).

Teachers are continually surprised that the students will recognize what each logo represents. In fact many students will point to the first letters of the logo when asked what the logo is and others will point to the picture and think that the logo is the word. You can continue to do this but the purpose is to introduce logos. Students will then be instructed to identify logos at home that evening and bring them in to share them with the class the following day during morning circle. Figure 5.1 provides an example. It is important that you send home a letter informing parents

Figure 5.1. An Example of a Note for Parents

From the Desk of Erminda García

Dear Parent(s),

Today we spoke about logos, and the students were surprised that they could already read. Please help your child find a logo that they are able to read (examples: Crest toothpaste, 7-UP soda, Cheerios, potato chips, Scrub Net, Doritos, KMart, etc). Please help them cut out or remove the logo they can read. You can also use magazines. Please send only the logo, not the item with the logo on it. We will be using these logos to read and will make books to categorize them.

Thank you,
Sra. García

---

why their children will be bringing in logos the next morning and why it is important that they support their child's efforts.

When the students arrive the next morning with their logos, have large grocery bags ready for students to place them in. You'll be using these logos for the next few months. During the week that the logos arrive from home it is important that students "read' their logos using the sentence frame, "I can read _____(logo). Can you?" Students then join the "reader" and read the logo. You should also plan to stop once or twice during this beginning activity and ask students to talk about the logo and the letters they are reading.

After you have collected lots of logos, create a chart with large circles. Students will begin to classify the logos in groups. This classifying activity is much more then "thinking" about how you might form a group, it is also an opportunity for students to practice using language to describe their groups.

It is important to allow them to choose what group they are forming and to share how that group is formed. Students formed logo groups such as logos of toys and non-toys; logos for babies, for girls, for boys, and for partners playing together; and logos that begin with the letters of students' names. Categorizing logos can be done in a large group, in small groups, and in centers. Later in the year, students might place one near each letter and put them in alphabetical order.

Logos can also become part of a class book that is created during the first 2 weeks of school. It can be read by students all year long. Some will read it by using only the logo; others will point out letters they recognize. Each student is asked to select his or her favorite logo, and then read it to the class using the sentence frame "I can read _____ (logo). Can you?" They then glue it on a blank page that has the same written text pattern as the oral language frame that they used initially. Logos create a context where beginning readers understand that print has meaning and can quickly "read" logos throughout their homes.

These types of phonological awareness activities and phonics instruction will ensure that children can access print and build connections between letter sounds and symbols. Students very quickly begin to read and write from these experiences. Simultaneously, books and different text types need to be read and shared with students so that book talk is heard and vocabulary is learned.

All children need to be read to. When a young child hears the spoken word as it is used to label a picture or an object, language development occurs. When she/he hears a poem or song and sees the pictures of the words from the song, words and rhythm of the language begin to develop. Children begin to see visual cues in pictures around the print they understand, like logo reading. When they see the pictures in a book and follow the words that are being read, their literacy language is being developed. They begin to connect letters and sounds and form words they can read and write. Reading aloud to children using dialogic strategies and wordless books, are strategies that scaffold the skills that students need.

Dialogic Reading and Traditional Read Alouds

If you walk into any preschool you will see teachers reading a book to their students. In some classrooms teachers will read one or two pages and then ask questions (the traditional way). Often at the end of the story they will ask students, "What was the story about?" Often the same students answer the teacher's question using one- or two-word responses. In fact, the same types of questions are usually asked by the teacher. "Who was in the story? When and where did it happen? What was the story about?" You can quickly observe that the same students respond using the same short answers.

In classrooms where teachers are reading in a dialogic way, teachers will ask a question every two pages or so, evaluate the responses, and then extend the language through descriptive complete sentences and ask students to repeat what they have said. Again these teachers have purposefully planned what type of questions they will ask, always looking for the higher order questions that usually being with "why." They purposefully select who will be asked to use new vocabulary in oral sentence frames that they have created to expand the students' language use. All of the planned instruction is noted by Post-its, described below.

In the first classroom example, in a traditional read aloud, the teacher focused on the narrative/text and expected students to listen and respond to a common set of comprehension questions. Often the teachers will remember who answered and might make a written note of it. The comprehension questions are usually the same for narrative text, and a different set is used for nonfiction text. In the other classroom example, the teacher used interactive strategies to engage all the students in a conversation about what they were seeing and hearing, specifically, targeting their questions to students based on interest or literacy need. The information that teachers use to choose the questions might be gained from interactive journals, the conversation table, and the parent journals, and by observing and recording during centers.

Dialogic reading to children differs from a teacher reading a book to the class in a traditional way. It is a planned conversation where the teacher has thoughtfully considered the strengths and needs of her students. The book will have some sort of Post-it to remind her of a question or a vocabulary word. Of course she has read the book once or twice before beginning. Some of her questions might be asked to an identified set of kids because they have shared an interest in the topic of the book or need to respond to the types of questions she might ask. The teacher will read the book at least three times to ensure that all her students are engaged in the dialogue of the book.

During a dialogic reading of a book the reader will ask children to point to and/or label pictures, make predictions based on the storyline, other books, pictures, and past experiences. In dialogic reading, the focus is to have the students become the storytellers. The teachers' role is to be an active listener and questioner. Oral language is being developed as the teacher models vocabulary use and language frames that allow the students to practice the language that they are hearing. Recall that there is a critical connection between the oral language skills of preschoolers and how soon they acquire reading and writing. These types of conversations scaffold and support students who may bring a limited academic vocabulary and discourse to the teaching/learning enterprise. This type of interaction supports students who may not be read to as often as others and specifically have not been engaged in discussions or dialogues as stories are being read to them. For more information on Dialogic Reading, visit www.ed.gov. (See Appendix A and Appendix B for our recommended list of culturally relevant books and wordless books for the classroom.)

WRITING WITH YOUNG HISPANIC CHILDREN

In our own research and experience with young Hispanic children, we have concluded that "interactive journaling" is the most meaningful writing context for children. Whether it includes writing symbols, letters, or drawing pictures, the opportunity for students to talk about their experiences or certain topics opens windows for teachers. Those windows provide a view into their students' home life, family members, and cultural experiences. Often these experiences are not shared by the teachers, included in the books they read daily, nor are they a part of the learning contexts they create for their students. Moreover, interactive journaling ensures a context in which a teacher responds to the student in writing to what students have written. With emergent writers, the verbal conversations associated with the journal entry critically help inform the teacher about how they should respond. It is a win-win situation for all involved.

Keep in mind that a journal entry is the artifact of a student's life, and, with a response, it becomes an artifact of a teacher/student interaction. It includes experiences through pictures and writing. The journal might include scribbles, beginning letters of initial sounds that they are learning, and might have complex sentences. The teacher's response provides both a relationship-building opportunity and an opportunity to model formal written communication. The developmental history that is created by the students as they write throughout the year becomes an instructional scaffold for the teacher.

Interactive Journaling

We have included examples of interactive journal entries that we often share with teachers. These few artifacts demonstrate why this learning context is so powerful. Interactive journaling allows early writers to demonstrate their developing literacy behaviors.

These two journal entries reflect the level of development that students demonstrated throughout the year. In the first entry (Figure 5.2), the student clearly used scribbles to show writing. As he shared his entry he pointed to the picture and said in Spanish, "We have chicks at our home." When Erminda asked him where the word *pollito* ("chick" in Spanish) is on the page, he answered by pointing to scribbles at the end of his entry. Clearly he understood writing has meaning.

In the second entry (Figure 5.3), this 1st-grader was able to demonstrate her knowledge of "hopop" meaning "hope," and when asked where "hope" was written on the page, she answered by pointing to "hopop" and

Figure 5.2. Journal Entry of Beginning Writer

saying, "I know h-o-p say hop and that hope has more letters!" The knowledge of the word was clearly understood by this student. In this entry she
also used "feorart," and she sounded out the word "heart." After asking the
child where the first letter for heart was on the page, she pointed to the "f."
The teacher made a note of her /f/ sound for "heart" and wondered if she
still needed support in the sound-letter connection for "H."

Students begin to respond to journal entries when provided with a
question by the teacher. In Figure 5.4, a student describes what he sees
in his journal entry. After the teacher responds on the page in a "talking
bubble" with a question, he answers the question: "He's looking at the
heart." When teachers ask questions, children respond with more text.
When teachers respond with a statement as opposed to a question, the
written conversation ends.

Students use their first-language knowledge in creating journal response. Figure 5.5 shows a journal entry written by a 1st-grader that is
a wonderful example of language transfer. The student uses "da" for the
word "the." She is utilizing the Spanish sound-letter connections that
she "heard" in English. She did the same for the word "cheese." When we
look at the entry "lacx." It reminds us why "like" is taught as a sight word.

Figure 5.3. Journal Entry Demonstrating Knowledge of Words

Figure 5.4. Journal Entry Response from Student

Figure 5.5. Journal Entry Demonstrating Language Transfer

See Table 5.3 for an example lesson plan of how to respond to students' journal entries.

Developmental Door

Preschool teachers, in particular, need to establish a context or learning center where students can experiment with the tools of writing. A center area that has a table covered with layers of paper (resembling tables in a restaurant) should be established during the 1st month of the school year. On the table are crayons, all different kinds of pens and pencils, letter cards, and, later in the year, vocabulary word cards. Scribbles, strings of letters, and student names soon appear on the top layer of paper as students spend time "writing" on the table.

Teachers should observe and make note of who is writing and what they have written on the table. This is done by choosing one or two students' writing and labeling the section with the child's name and the month. This section is then ripped off and the top layer of paper is removed. This section then is taped on a door in the classroom with the label, "Becoming Writers." Each month, students' writing is labeled, torn off the paper on table, and added to the other writing pieces on the door. Soon

Table 5.3. Responding to a Journal Entry

Content Objective:	**Teacher vocabulary/sentence frame:**
Students will share with their teacher the written message that accompanies the drawing on their daily journal page. **Language Objective:** I can tell my teacher what my pictures are about by using the letter strings / sentence that I have written.	Read to me the sentence you wrote under your picture . . . . What letters did you use for the sounds/ words . . . _____ **Sentence frame for student:** My drawing is about . . . . The letter is/This is the word _____ and I know because it begins with a _____.
Beginning of the learning context: Ask children to share what they did yesterday/over the weekend with a partner. Let them know that you would like to hear all their stories and that as they draw and write you will circulate to a table and ask students to share their entries.	Writing journals are provided for each child. Half of the page is blank and the other half has writing lines. **Child's name on journal.** Dates can be stamped or written by teacher or students (this is important to establish development). Children draw their entries and are encouraged to voice their message including sounding out letters as they write their message.
Middle of the lesson: Teacher circulates throughout the class, selecting two or more students to share their journal entry, using the established frames . . . "My drawing is about_____." "The letter is a . . ."	Teacher moves to a table, asks one child to share with her/him what he/she has written. Child shares entry by placing his/her finger under the letters/words he/she is reading. Teacher then extends the sharing with questions that focus on the content and then asks one or two questions regarding letter/ sound from the written message.
End of the lesson: Teacher then stops at each table selecting one child to share his/her journal entry. While the child is sharing, the teacher asks questions and invites the children to join the interaction with their own questions. They often support the child who is sharing with sounds or letters he/she might use in his/her writing.	Students sitting at the table with the students who are sharing then join in the interaction with questions that require more talk by the writer. Students might go back and "edit" their thoughts by adding to their pictures or their letter strings.

a developmental door of the students' efforts in writing is compiled and becomes part of the classroom. Erminda has done these doors throughout her teaching career and has always used them as student progress informers. When parents or fellow teachers understand the purpose of celebrating students' writing development through this type of writing context they comment positively, and often teachers create their own developmental doors in their classrooms.

As discussed previously, writing should be planned in different contexts for different purposes throughout the day. A common group activity is the writing of an experience chart. Initially, the teacher is the writer as students share their thoughts about what they have been learning and creating in centers or about a common experience they have just had. Later, students become the writers once they understand that there are many writing conventions (spelling, punctuation, verb tenses, etc.) that still need to learned and that the teacher will act as a scaffold for them in their writing attempts.

An important practice that we have observed at the end of every month, requires children using experience charts to help create a representation of what they have learned that month. They include the calendar, pictures of events that occurred that month, and then an experience chart using words that describe their newly acquired knowledge. Initially, the teacher is the writer but soon children become the writers of the experience charts. These representations are placed across a wall in the classroom, providing the students with an example of how memories can be captured throughout the school year. This is yet another purpose for writing.

Writers Workshop

The previous contexts focus on how students share their personal experiences through writing. They are very meaningful to the students but often short on content. The writing workshop approach allows children blocks of time to write, focusing not on a finished product (a journal entry, a chart) but on the act of writing itself. They are not asked or required to finish a completed piece every day. They are encouraged to continue on a piece they are writing the next day and when they do finish a piece, to begin the writing process again.

This instruction endeavor requires teachers to teach and model the writing process: prewriting, writing, revising, editing, and then publishing. Teachers must model each of these steps. The teacher models the making of a "book" with a large version of what students will be using to write their story on. We recommend introducing the writing process steps with a large chart that is labeled with the writing process steps and placing the chart on the wall in a central place in the classroom. A writing folder is created for each student—a place to keep their writing products—with a small copy of the classroom chart in each folder. Every time students open their writing folders they are reminded where they are in the writing process. Our experience with Hispanic students is that this process, as well as the chart, is particularly useful in creating an understanding of the academic vocabulary that is necessary for these children to become accomplished grade-level writers. Figure 5.6 shows a sample writing strip for a folder.

This particular workshop approach to writing is different from other writing context because the child chooses the topic, decides what pictures will go on what page and what words he or she will need to write. The professional groups National Association for the Education of Young Children (NAEYC) and the International Reading Association (IRA) recommend that beginning writers have daily opportunities and teacher support to write many kinds of texts for different purposes. Writers Workshop is one of contexts that asks students to become authors using specific experiences that may be unique to them. Moreover, this type of writing activity allows children the opportunity to author narrative stories. For beginning writers, this genre requires an initial understanding of beginning, middle, and end.

In their homes and from their families, Hispanic children, like most children, hear a variety of stories—it is part of the cultural transmission process. This process builds on that set of cultural experiences. From the first day of the school year, teachers also have been reading quality children's literature with "stories" to their students and engaging them in a dialogue that helps build the understanding of "story features." The questions and discussions that follow picture book read alouds regarding the

Figure 5.6. Folder Strip Sequencing the Writing Process

character, the setting, the plot, and, the sequence of events happen as soon as a narrative story is read to students. This type of discussion supports how students will begin their transition from hearing a story at home and "understanding" a story in an academic sense, using academic vocabulary. The writing workshop extends this academic experience to academic authorship of stories as soon as students begin the writing process.

A step that we did not include in the writing process strip, but that should happen once or twice after students have finished a book and are ready to publish, is called the "Author's Chair." The author sits in a designated area, sharing the "first draft," and students ask questions about the emerging story. The teacher takes notes and later shares them with the author. The student might elect to change or add to the story or not. If the student decides to publish the story, the teachers will conference with the author, focusing on the editing process (sight-word spelling, some punctuation, sentence construction, etc.) Once the editing is done and the story is published, the second time the author takes "Author's Chair," it is to read the published book to the class. Eagerly, teacher and classmates listen to the author and wait for the clapping that follows the reading. This is clearly another win-win instructional opportunity, especially for young Hispanic students.

In our experience, we continue to be surprised by how easily all the children participate in the Writers Workshop. When students are sitting at their table, with their folders open and actively writing their stories, we see children who see themselves as writers, no matter what their developmental level of literacy is.

THE ASSESSMENT PROCESS

Classroom assessments may range from formative to summative, but they should all inform instruction. Evaluation of student academic growth through these assessments must be an ongoing and planned process. Recall that in our classrooms both academic language and content learning are the focus. The content objective and language objective that are written for each lesson are what needs to be assessed. Teachers can assess whether students can draw or write about the content or how many words they read on a sight-word list. The critical ingredient in this sharing is the complexity of the language and how it is shared. Teachers who know about language are better prepared to use these types of assessments to gather instructional information and create opportunities for complex language development.

It is important that we understand that language is what informs the instructor about what students have learned. They will use the language domains of speaking, reading, writing, and of course listening for what information you are asking for. On the other hand, through language acquisition, children build skills and content understandings about language and are able to share them through the language.

Rather than relying on a single test, teachers need to encourage the gathering of many sources of information in order to assess students' progress—what many have called "portfolio assessment." They need to gather these sources in a portfolio folder in a systematic way across the school year. The portfolio for each student always includes the first-day snapshot of their writing, a drawing of themselves, some picture and writing about a math concept and a self survey of likes and dislikes about school.

Continual systematic collections of information about students' learning must be included in the overall instructional activity. This means that every day and in each lesson, assessment must be planned as part of the instruction. The interpretation of these collections identifies areas that need instructional support and guides how instruction needs to be differentiated and adapted to individual students. It is a road map for instruction, individualized for each student. The assessment graphic organizer in Figure 5.7 depicts how this process must happen if it is to serve as such a guide. This process must always inform the teacher so that the next lesson meets the specific instructional needs of all students.

We have only touched lightly on assessment, but we consider it an important aspect of instruction. García (2005) is a good resource for the full discussion of the assessment process and how it can be utilized to enhance academic achievement in young Hispanics. Although we are not fans of accountability assessments, particularly for Hispanics, because of the intersections of language and content in those assessments, we realize that they are a reality. However, we are convinced that the use of ongoing assessments in reading, writing, and the content areas will bolster academic performance as measured by standardized tests, particularly for Hispanics. Our work and that of others confirms this conclusion (García, 2005; Freeman, 2009).

COOPERATIVE STRUCTURES

Kagan and Kagan (2007) reminds us that the use of cooperative structures can support academic language development as well as overall academic achievement, while building on the natural tendency for

Figure 5.7. Assessment Cycle

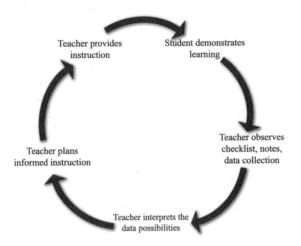

collaboration inherent in Hispanic cultural groups (García, 2001a) and on opportunities to create rich language environments. We have witnessed the significance cooperative-learning structures have and their relevance to the organization of classrooms, particularly for Hispanic children. The following structures are utilized by teachers to ensure that students are using listening, speaking, reading, and writing skills in collaborative and complex ways. For example, when sentence frames are included in the structures, teachers notice that the use of vocabulary and complete sentences are practiced more often. We recommend them to you and suggest you access the complete arsenal of cooperative-learning strategies at www.kaganonline.com.

> *Heads Together/Numbered Heads Together:* Students work together to ensure all members have the opportunity to share and understand what is being taught; it supports thinking and mastery.
>
> *Inside-Outside Circle:* In concentric circles, students rotate to face new partners and answer questions; it supports mastery, thinking, and information sharing, and provides opportunities to practice with peers a number of times using sentence frames.
>
> *Think, Pair, Share:* Students think to themselves on a topic or question provided by the teacher, and after a designated time, students turn to a partner and share their responses. This supports generating and revising answers by individuals and gives students an opportunity to learn by reflection and verbalization.

Corners: Students move to different corners depending on their expressed preference for a teacher-selected topic or answer to a question. (Some examples of questions might be related a favorite activity during free time or a favorite book.) Then students are given a short amount of time to think and then share their reason for their choice and any other information requested by the teacher. This supports thinking/reflection, expression of a point of view and oral defense of that point of view.

Jigsaw: Each student on the designated team of no more than four students becomes an "expert" on one area of a topic assigned by the teacher by working and sharing with each member of the team. This supports acquisition and presentation of new material in a group context.

Line-Ups: Students line up according to a value or unique position they are asked to take. (For example, a lineup could be by birth month.) The line is then split so as to pair up students, and the teacher asks these pairs to address a specific topic in the lesson and report out. The line can then be split in different ways to create new pairs and different topics can be discussed. This supports access to paired-level discussion regarding the lesson material and varied views on that material.

BEST PRACTICES THAT FACILITATE
LITERACY DEVELOPMENT

Allow us to conclude this overview regarding teaching and learning by identifying key ingredients that can meet the specific literacy deployment circumstance of young Hispanic children. In the examples provided in this chapter we have provided some specifics that can make a difference to Hispanic young children in acquiring academic literacy profiles. These, we admit, are examples. We realize it is difficult to provide a comprehensive set of instructional guidelines, however, based on our own experience and the best analysis of the empirical availability of learning opportunities, any classroom that implements the following key instructional ingredients will positively influence the academic outcomes of Hispanic students:

- Provide books in different genres with view of the world through different windows.
- Read books to and with children at least twice a day.
- Provide books that can be heard as well as read.
- Include singing and playing songs along with text charts.

- Provide activities daily that help recognition of letters, sounds, vocabulary, and sentences.
- Always provide paper and pencils in learning centers and promote writing at all centers.
- Ensure children create their own stories in books and allow them to share it.
- Provide activities daily that allow children to utilize those literacy constructs in meaningful ways.
- Utilize assessment to inform instruction.

PROMISING PROGRAM PRACTICES

Similar to the pre-K expansion movement, elementary school reform efforts over the past 20 years have been heavily concerned with improving outcomes for low-SES children, including low-SES Hispanics. These efforts have given high priority to improving K–3 outcomes, owing to the evidence that achievement patterns for most students are established in the early school years (Perie, Grigg, & Donahue, 2005; Reardon & Galindo, 2006). Because many factors contribute to learning outcomes, elementary school reformers have necessarily worked in many areas. Raising academic standards, developing better curricula and instructional strategies in several subjects, strengthening teacher-education programs, lowering teacher-pupil ratios, and providing more decision-making authority at the school level are but a few examples. Attention has been given to these and other factors on an individual basis and in combination. They also have been pursued at many levels, including by the federal government, state governments, school districts, and individual schools.

The "whole school reform," or "comprehensive school reform" (CSR), movement is one of the more influential, empirically oriented ways in which several factors are being addressed in combination at the school and district levels to raise achievement. Although CSR approaches vary, a core idea of CSR is that many aspects of individual schools have to change in a systematic, integrated fashion if children—especially low-SES youngsters—are to perform academically at markedly higher levels on a sustained basis. Consequently, many CSR initiatives work simultaneously to change curriculum and instruction in key subjects, such as reading and math; to strengthen school leadership and management; to improve student assessment; to strengthen staff development; and to expand parental involvement.

CSR has much in common with the model preschool program design, testing, and evaluation work exemplified by Abecedarian and the Perry

Preschool. Not only has CSR been concerned with empirically testing model programs designed to address a number of factors that influence achievement, the most effective CSR strategies provide benchmarks for elementary education reform similar to those that the best model preschool programs provide for the pre-K expansion movement. Two distinctive aspects of the CSR movement are that many CSR models have been tested in a large number of schools and many have also sought to improve their practices on an ongoing basis over a long period of time (Borman, Hewes, Overman, & Brown, 2003). Several CSR initiatives also have been conceived, not only as ventures to develop more effective strategies for raising achievement, but also as mechanisms for helping many schools and school districts learn to use the strategies and to implement them as designed over time. The very heavy emphasis that some CSR programs give to technical assistance and support among participating schools is a distinctive contribution in this period of school reform.

Over the past decade, many CSR strategies have been evaluated, in some cases numerous times. Although the quality of the evaluations has been uneven, the sheer number of them has made it possible in recent years to begin to gauge the overall impact of CSR strategies and to identify the ones that seem to be producing the largest achievement gains. Probably the most extensive and sophisticated effort to date to assess CSR programs examined 213 evaluations of 29 CSR approaches (Borman et al., 2003). That analysis found that, collectively, CSR strategies produce achievement gains, but they are, on average, small. Essentially, the average student in CSR schools was found to achieve at a higher level than 55% of the comparable students in the non-CSR schools in the comparison group. The analysis also found that only three CSR strategies have been able to demonstrate, via several rigorous evaluations, a capacity to produce considerably higher levels of achievement than the average for CSR strategies as a whole.

Because no major studies of CSR strategies have assessed their value specifically for Hispanics, the National Task Force on Early Childhood Education for Hispanics (2007) commissioned the authors of the study of 29 CSR models to conduct such an analysis. They found 12 CSR strategies with evaluations that allowed Hispanic outcomes to be assessed separately. The results for the 12 showed that, collectively, they produce small achievement gains for Hispanics—about the same size as the gains documented in the earlier study for all students. Only two programs, each of which uses a very well-known CSR strategy, had strong evaluation evidence regarding their impact on Hispanic achievement. In both cases, the achievement gains were moderate in size, but larger than the average gains for the 12 CSR programs as a group. In addition to better outcomes, these two programs, Core Knowledge and Success for All, are distinguished by a strong literacy development focus that can be tailored in ways that are culturally and linguistically responsive to Hispanics. In the case of Core Knowledge, teachers in participating schools have materials designed to support instruction responsive to cultural and linguistic diversity—incorporating culturally relevant literature, images, and language. Success for All has a full Spanish bilingual/bicultural version of its program. Thus, there are reading materials designed for Spanish and English instruction from pre-Kindergarten through 6th grade.

The above discussion has focused on work in the place called school. However, since the late 1970s, research has established that much of the growth in achievement gaps in the K–3 period between low-SES children and their middle class and high-SES counterparts takes place when school is not in session. Low-SES children experience "summer learning loss" in both reading and mathematics. In contrast, middle class and high-SES children tend to make gains over the summer in reading, while their learning losses in math are smaller than those experienced by low-SES youngsters. These patterns seem to be related to differences in family resources that tend to produce school readiness gaps in the first place. Over the years, many after-school and summer programs have been launched for the purpose of raising achievement of disadvantaged children, including many who have been having academic difficulty. Probably the most visible current use of summer programs in large urban school districts is to help reduce the number of children who do not pass tests required for promotion to the next grade.

The weight of the evaluation evidence is that summer programs in particular can raise achievement somewhat for both low-SES and middle class students. However, relatively few strategies have been evaluated rigorously, which means that there are uncertainties about the extent of their benefits (Borman, Hewes, Overman, & Brown, 2003). This is true for the student population as a whole, including Hispanics. In addition, many summer programs for low-SES students are remedial, reflecting the previously noted desire to reduce the number of students who are retained in grade. Although some of these programs seem to be helping a number of students move on to the next grade, little is known about whether and how non-remedial summer programs in the K–3 years might provide academic benefits to low-SES students who are average or above average achievers in school.

Recently, a major test was undertaken of a strategy for providing access to non-remedial summer programs over 3 successive years to low-SES children in the K–3 period. The test took place in Baltimore at the Teach Baltimore Summer Academy, which provides a 7-week, full-day, academically-oriented summer program for low-SES children in that city. It provides very extensive reading and writing instruction as well as hands-on math and science projects (along with substantial recreational activities) to participating students. The test involved a randomized trial in which several hundred children from ten high-poverty schools were assigned either to the participant group or to the control group. Although the program was voluntary, two-thirds of the participating children attended the program for at least 2 summers and one-third attended for all 3 summers. To date, the reported results from the evaluation have focused on reading. As prior research would predict, the control group experienced reading loses during the summer. However, participants who attended the program regularly for at least 2 summers had substantial reading gains. In the fall of the third year, the latter children had gains relative to the control group equal to three-quarters of a grade level in vocabulary, four-fifths of a grade level in comprehension, and seven-tenths of a grade level in overall reading skills. The vocabulary and reading comprehension outcomes are potentially quite valuable, owing to their importance for learning in the 4th grade and thereafter. The caveat to these results is that only about half of the participating children attended the summer program regularly enough over 2 years to experience meaningful benefits. Moreover, because the sample of students in this study was heavily African American, it needs to be replicated with low-SES Hispanic children, including ELLs from immigrant families (National Task Force on Early Childhood Education for Hispanics, 2007). Yet, efforts to expand opportunity to learn for Hispanics in their early schooling seem a viable intervention worth pursuing.

CONCLUSION

Early learning environments that consider the child's culture and language circumstances can serve Hispanic students well. In particular, early education efforts can maximize Hispanic children's access to academic vocabulary and discourse, particularly at the more complex levels. Educators can utilize both an understanding and the specific construction of learning opportunities that lead to enhanced academic learning that builds on the foundations Hispanic children bring from their non-schooling environments. This chapter has emphasized the research, best practices and programs that can lead to that enhancement. Recent research efforts have demonstrated clearly that practices and programs that address the linguistic and cultural resources Hispanics bring to the learning enterprise is important. Moreover, it seems clear that the early childhood programing for these students is critical in addressing achievement gaps that may exist at the beginning of school.

We have also addressed very specific best practices that relate to reading, writing, and overall language development, creating rich language environments in early learning settings. We have also provided descriptions of specific lessons and specific instructional strategies that well serve the learning activities for Hispanic children. This chapter is essentially the core transmission of our practice expertise in an effort to assist classroom personnel in their efforts to enhance the academic performance of young Hispanic students.

CHAPTER 6

Responsive Teaching for Hispanic Children

The education of Hispanics and other minorities has attracted national attention primarily with the Supreme Court rulings of *Brown v. Board of Education* and *Lau v. Nichols*. These cases indicate that adequate resources, particularly a qualified teacher workforce, be identified as key for effective program implementation (Gándara, Rumberger, Maxwell-Jolly, & Callahan, 2003; Reeves, 2004). And we, like others, would contend that the focal resource for young Hispanics is the teacher (Darling-Hammond, 2006; Faltis & Coulter, 2007; García & García, 2009). However, we have realized that there is a critical shortage of teachers prepared to respond to the needs of these students (Wong-Fillmore & Snow, 2002). In this chapter, we reflect on "effective" teachers for Hispanics, and articulate the importance of enhancing teacher knowledge through contact and collaboration with diverse ethnolinguistic communities. We build on recent research on the preparation of teachers for cultural responsiveness and linguistic diversity, and recommend a situated preparation that fosters the development of teacher knowledge of the dynamics of culture and language in children's lives and communities. We summarize the most recent research on culturally and linguistically responsive teacher preparation and focus on a framework, which includes developing teacher knowledge through contact, collaboration, and community, particularly for young Hispanic children.

DEVELOPING TEACHERS

There is a critical need for enhanced teacher development based on the demographic imperative (see Chapter 2). This need has been documented for close to 20 years. García (1990) reviewed and discussed the research pertaining to educating teachers for language minority students. That work noted the growing presence of students with Spanish language backgrounds and the critical need to prepare teachers for students' diverse educational experiences. He emphasized that language minority students can be taught in schools through effective teaching practices characterized by culturally appropriate interactions and instructions. This concern for effectively preparing teachers for language minority learners continues today (Márquez-López, 2005). Nevertheless, teachers who are ready to handle this demographic reality are no longer a luxury but a necessity (Menken & Antunez, 2001). The reality of teacher demographics is that teachers are very different from the students they serve.

As noted earlier, the demographic imperative is reflected not only in the growth and dispersal of Hispanics across the nation, but also by the fact that the teacher corps lacks diversity. According to data gathered by the U.S. Department of Education National Center for Education Statistics (2007) on the Schools and Staffing survey, the public teaching workforce is predominately female (75%) and of non-Hispanic White background (83%), and is expected to remain so. Teachers of racial and ethnic minorities rose from 13% in 1993–1994 to only 17% in 2003–2004. While the number of ethnic minority students grew by over 30%.

Overall, the demography of the U.S. teaching workforce is rather homogenous, while students attending schools are growing in their diversity, culturally, racially, and linguistically (Capps, Fix, Murray, Ost, Passel, & Herwantoro-Hernandez, 2005; Zumwalt & Craig, 2005; NCES, 2007). Current teachers and prospective teachers tend to teach children who are culturally and linguistically much like themselves and, as a result, growing linguistic and cultural differences between teachers and students continues, and diversity is viewed as an obstacle to overcome (Ladson-Billings, 1995). Rather than teaching students in the way they were prepared, these teachers often revert to the same traditional ways they were taught as students.

Teacher Preparation

Effective teachers are the key to meeting the needs of the diverse learners and critical in preparing these learners for the 21st century. Teacher-preparation programs can help prepare prospective teachers to teach these learners successfully. Darling-Hammond (2006) describes seven highly successful teacher-education programs that have prepared teachers to teach diverse learners to achieve high levels of performance. These colleges and universities include Alverno College; Bank Street College; Trinity University; University of California, Berkeley; University of Southern Maine; University of Virginia; and Wheelock College. Through her research and analysis of these programs, Darling-Hammond (2006) summarized common features of exemplary teacher-education programs.

Four of the seven common features connect specifically to the preparation of teachers working with linguistically and culturally diverse students:

- A common, clear vision of good teaching permeates all coursework and clinical experiences.
- Curriculum is grounded in knowledge of child and adolescent development, learning, social contexts, and subject matter pedagogy taught in the context of practice.
- Extended clinical experiences are carefully developed to support the ideas and practices presented in simultaneous, closely interwoven coursework.
- Explicit strategies help students to confront their own deep-seated beliefs and assumptions about learning and students and to learn about the experiences of people different from themselves.

In their report, Darling-Hammond and Bransford (2005) present a framework for exploring the kinds of knowledge, skills, and commitment that enable teachers to be effective. Specifically, Darling-Hammond and Bransford identified three general areas of knowledge that teachers must acquire:

- Knowledge of learners and how they learn and develop within social context
- Conceptions of curriculum and social purposes of education
- Understanding of teaching

This framework may be used to support teacher development to improve their teaching practice. Ultimately, this type of reflective practice may serve in creating highly qualified teachers.

In our review of the most recent research on the preparation of teachers serving Hispanics—many of which are learning English in their classrooms, we find much in common with the factors represented in high-quality teacher preparation as noted by Darling-Hammond (2006) and Darling-Hammond and Bransford (2005). We acknowledge the commonalities between the knowledge related to learners, curriculum, and understanding teaching as they are applied to developing knowledge for culturally responsive teachers. The literature on preparing cultur-ally responsive teachers and knowledge related to Hispanics focuses on contextualizing knowledge of students within their communities, un-derstanding the nexus between identity and language, and the sociocul-tural impact of communities on students and classrooms. We recognize that teachers develop this knowledge through the context of their students' communities, and we call for teacher preparation to promote understanding of Hispanics through field experiences grounded in their communities.

RESPONSIVE TEACHER PREPARATION

We frame this discussion in a broad educationally relevant theoretical continuum. At one end of this continuum, it is argued that addressing linguistically and culturally diverse populations calls for a deeper understanding of the interaction of a student's language and culture and the prevailing school language and culture (García, 2001b). This cultural significance position is supported by a rich contribution of research, which suggests that the educational failure of "diverse" student populations is related to this culture clash between home and school. In essence, these researchers have suggested that without attending to the distinctiveness of the contribution of culture, educational endeavors for these culturally distinct students are likely to fail.

Pre-service and practicing teachers must be given opportunities to thoroughly explore and comprehend their own cultural and personal values, their identities, and their social beliefs. It has been well documented in the literature that teachers' attitudes and beliefs serve as filters for what they learn, what they teach, and how they manage their classrooms (Pajares, 1992; Richardson, 1996). In addition, research suggests the influence of teachers' attitudes and beliefs on their expectations of ELLs, interactions, and instructional practices (García-Nevarez, Stafford, & Arias, 2005; Reeves, 2004; Youngs & Youngs, 2001). In their study on mainstream teachers' attitudes toward ESL students, Youngs and Youngs (2001) found that teachers that had taken foreign language classes were significantly more positive toward teaching Hispanics then those teachers that had not taken a course. Based on the results of their investigation, they suggest that both in-service and pre-service teachers would benefit from more opportunities with diverse learners and diverse experiences.

García (2005) refers to "pedagogy of empowerment" as a responsive pedagogy that expands students' knowledge beyond their own immediate experiences while using those experiences as a sound foundation for appropriating new knowledge. He characterizes the school-wide and teacher practices, which reflect this pedagogy. Included in the school-wide practices are a school vision, which values diversity, professional collaboration, and teacher practices, which focus on language development through meaningful interactions and communications and awareness of the role of language and language policy in schools.

Culturally Responsive Pedagogy

The work on culturally responsive pedagogy can be divided into two broad themes: beliefs and values of teachers and characteristics of culturally responsive teaching practices. Four predominant experts in the field who address beliefs and values of teachers include Ladson-Billings, Villegas, Lucas, and Gay. Based on her work with African American students, Ladson-Billings (1995) states that teachers must "develop a broader sociopolitical consciousness that allows them to critique the cultural norms, values, mores, and institutions that produce and maintain social inequities" (p. 162). Through their review of the research and work with teachers in culturally and linguistically diverse classrooms, Villegas and Lucas (2002) propose that, in order to become culturally responsive teachers, teachers must develop a "sociocultural consciousness," recognizing that each individual's "perspective reflects his or her location in the social order" (p. 42). Villegas and Lucas state that the task of teacher educators is to help prospective teachers move toward a greater consciousness that includes understanding themselves as individuals (race, class, ethnicity, gender) and developing an understanding of the distribution of power in society that causes inequities and oppression.

In her review of the research and her work with national projects, Gay (2002) defines culturally responsive teaching as

> using the cultural characteristics, experiences, and perspectives of ethnically diverse students as conduits for teaching them more effectively. It is based on the assumption that when academic knowledge and skills are situated within the lived experiences and frames of reference of students, they are more personally meaningful, have higher interest appeal, and are learned more easily and thoroughly. (p. 106)

Culturally responsive teaching practices must be grounded in an understanding of students' cultural background (Gay, 2000; Ladson-Billings, 1994; Villegas & Lucas, 2002). Villegas and Lucas (2002) report common characteristics of culturally responsive teaching practices that include building on what students already know, understanding how students construct knowledge, demonstrating a sociocultural consciousness, knowing and understanding about the lives of their students, and affirming the views of their students. These practices cannot be conducted in isolation but rather must be supported and situated within specific learning communities. In teacher-preparation programs, this speaks to field placements where prospective teachers may actively participate in the community where they teach and their students live. Research strongly suggests the benefits of experiencing such culturally diverse field placements (Hollins & Guzman, 2005; Zeichner, 1996). These experiences provide opportunities for prospective teachers to change the way they are thinking about their students.

Situated Learning

One route to responsive pedagogy is to propose that teacher preparation include a service-learning component, which situates teaching and learning in the ELL community. Boyle-Baise and McIntyre (2008) reviewed the research on preparing teachers in two contexts for teacher education, one professional development schools and the other community oriented settings. Professional development schools focus on student academic achievement and develop teachers' academic expertise, and "aim to be centers of educational excellence" (p. 313). Based on the community-oriented context, the authors state that service learning "eases a community orientation into teacher education," "allows pre-service teachers to work with and learn from local youth and adults while doing something worthwhile," and "fosters greater comfort with people unlike oneself" (p. 309).

Service learning experiences provide opportunities for prospective teachers to engage in the school's community. For example, in the American Indian Reservation Project, Stachowski and Frey (2005) reviewed the service learning activities performed by student teachers placed in the Navajo Nation. Student teachers were immersed in the lives and cultures of the people with whom they lived and worked. Through this community involvement, student teachers gained cultural insights, developed a deeper appreciation for "other peoples' lives," experienced the multiple realities of the classroom and community setting, and in turn, promoted an acceptance by community members. Whereas Cooper (2007) described ways pre-service teachers responded to cultural immersion community-based activities located in the home communities of their learners that challenged their previous beliefs and stereotypes about the students they teach. Results from her study suggest these types of community experiences incorporated into teacher-preparation programs may facilitate new discoveries about the students and their families and the community's strength. In addition, Seidl (2007) explained how a group of prospective teachers participating in an African American community began to develop culturally relevant pedagogies. Voluntary internships were arranged at an African American Baptist church where pre-service teachers worked with adults from the church in projects for children such as tutoring and other community-sponsored events. Students also completed coursework and readings on African American history, racism, culture, and privilege.

Through these guided experiences, pre-service teachers were engaged in the community, and began to implement culturally responsive approaches to their teaching. Similar to what Ladson-Billings writes about preparing culturally responsive teachers, these particular pre-service teachers were immersed in the cultural experiences of the community with situated educational opportunities and, as a result, learned to personalize cultural and political knowledge.

Imbedded in this is the understanding that language, culture, and their accompanying values are acquired in the home and community environment. Children come to school with some knowledge about what language is, how it works, and what it is used for that children learn higher-level cognitive and communicative skills as they engage in socially meaningful activities; and that children's development and learning is best understood as the interaction of linguistic, sociocultural, and cognitive knowledge and experiences. A more appropriate perspective of learning, then, is one that recognizes that learning is enhanced when it occurs in contexts that are both socioculturally and linguistically meaningful for the learner. García (2005) further emphasized that students learn best and teachers feel most satisfied when both become allies in the learning process and are encouraged to actively cooperate and share. Therefore, a more appropriate perspective of teacher development, then, is one that recognizes that development and learning is enhanced when it occurs in contexts that are socioculturally, linguistically, and cognitively meaningful for the learner.

Such meaningful contexts have been notoriously inaccessible to linguistically and culturally diverse children. On the contrary, schooling practices and teachers who are the architects and engineers of instruction, often contribute to educational vulnerability. The monolithic culture transmitted by the U.S. schools in the form of pedagogy, curricula, instruction, classroom configuration, and language dramatizes the lack of fit between the culturally diverse student and the school experience. The culture of the U.S. schools is reflected in such practices as

- The systematic exclusion of the histories, languages, experiences, and values of these students from classroom curricula and activities.
- "Tracking," which limits access to academic courses and which justifies learning environments that do not foster academic development and socialization or perception of self as a competent learner and language user.
- A lack of opportunities to engage in developmentally and culturally appropriate learning in ways other than by teacher-led instruction.

Practices such as these perpetuate inequitable schooling and hinder student progress and achievement (Nieto, 2004).

CONSTRUCTING RESPONSIVE PEDAGOGY AND LEARNING COMMUNITIES

The implication of this re-thinking has profound effects for the teaching-learning enterprise related to culturally diverse students (García, 2005). This new pedagogy is one that redefines the classroom as a community of learners in which speakers, readers, and writers come together to define and redefine the meaning of the academic experience. It might be described by some as pedagogy of empowerment, by others as cultural learning, and others as a cultural view of providing instructional assistance/guidance. In any case, it promotes teachers who respect and integrate students' values, beliefs, and histories; patterns of thoughts and behaviors; and experiences. In addition, it recognizes the active role that students must play in the learning process. Teachers must also recognize that the cultural characteristics that each student brings to the classroom are continually influenced by family norms and the larger society (Cloud, 2002). Their instruction should take into account what students know and can do. Therefore, a *responsive pedagogy* is one that encompasses practical, contextual, and empirical knowledge and a "world view" of education that evolves through meaningful interactions among teachers, students, and other school community members. This responsive set of strategies expands students' knowledge beyond their own immediate experiences, while using those experiences as a sound foundation for appropriating new knowledge.

Of course, a teaching and learning community that is responsive to the dynamics of social, cultural, and linguistic diversity within the broader concerns for high academic achievement both requires and emerges from a particular schooling environment. While considerable work has been devoted to restructuring schools and changing the fundamental relationships among school personnel, students, families, and community members, seldom have these efforts included attention to the unique influences of the linguistic and sociocultural dimensions of these same relationships and structures. The environments that potentially support and nurture the development of responsive learning communities are not unlike those promoted by leading school reform and restructuring advocates. However, we further suggest that the incorporation of social, cultural, and linguistic diversity concerns creates a set of educational principles and dimensions that are more likely to address the challenges faced by schools that must attend to the needs of growing populations of diverse students.

Responsive Learning Communities

The learning environments that we consider essential to the development of a responsive pedagogy are referred to as Effective Schooling (García, 1999, 2001, & 2005). The focus on the social, cultural, and linguistic diversity represented by students in today's public schools further challenges us to consider the theoretical and practical concerns relative to ensuring educational success for diverse students. That is, responsive learning communities must necessarily address issues of diversity in order to maximize their potential and to sustain educational improvement over time.

Examples of responsive learning communities are found in the work of Michelle Fine and her colleagues (2007), who illustrated successful public school models for working with Hispanics in New York City. These schools work against the negative effects of high-stakes education policy, and produce strong academic and civic outcomes. Their school-wide practices were grounded in understanding the student population, and their commitment to maximizing students potential. At these schools, teachers and staff focus on supporting students in the use of their individual experiences to benefit themselves and their classmates.

University-school partnerships are an example of collaboration that supports teacher preparation in communities. One example of such a partnership effort is provided by the Arizona State University Office of the Vice President for Educational Partnerships in eight urban districts in 2004. This long-term community collaboration involved various opportunities to support the development and enhancement of early childhood programs, supporting teachers by providing endorsements for Sheltered English Immersion (SEI) and ESL to prepare them for working with Hispanics, providing scholarship opportunities for student teachers to teach in partnership schools, supporting educational leaders by providing leadership institutes and leader certification, and providing support to students, schools, and families. The goal of the partnership is for all students attending these schools to attain educational success through their access to effective teachers.

RESPONSIVE TEACHING PRACTICES

Although there are many effective teacher characteristics in the literature, we have taken the prerogative to compile a table that includes our characterization of effective teaching practices that serve young Hispanic children. As a quick overview, Table 6.1 provides a quick summary of the skills that are essential for an effective teacher of young Hispanics. We have tried to

Table 6.1. Characteristics of Effective Teachers for Hispanics

An effective teacher *cares* by	An effective teacher *organizes* by	An effective teacher *implements instruction* by	An effective teacher *monitors* by
creating a supportive classroom climate that demonstrates interest and concern about students' lives outside of home • Family journals	establishing routines for all day tasks and orchestrating them efficiently and consistently thru smooth transitions • Daily schedule	employing various instructional strategies while attending to the lesson pace and student engagement • Plans informal assessments	relating homework to the content being taught and grading and discussing homework when appropriate • Logo homework
showing respect to all students by creating situations where students are treated equally and encouraged to succeed • Cooperative structures	using classroom space efficiently, so students are able to identify where materials and learning contexts are located • Labeled areas but flexible when needs are identified	giving clear examples and offering guided practice while expecting improvement and growth for each student • Lesson template	targeting questions and accountability to lesson objectives • Lesson template
interacting with students, maintaining a professional role, and always valuing what students say • Conversational Table	implementing rules of behavior fairly and consistently while using proactive discipline • Students and teacher identify rules and consequences	asking students to demonstrate understanding of meaning rather than memorizing • Holds literacy as a priority in all content areas	giving clear, specific, and timely feedback to avoid misconceptions that may occur • Makes notes that document specific student or area

An effective teacher *cares* by	An effective teacher *organizes* by	An effective teacher *implements instruction* by	An effective teacher *monitors* by
demonstrating a dedication to teaching and accepting responsibility for student outcomes • Implementing new instructional strategies	clearly articulating high expectation for student responsibility and accountability • Total Response techniques	identifying questions in advance that reflect the type of content that is being taught • Wait time is planned and differentiated	using a variety of grouping strategies that meet student needs • Lesson template
reflecting on how to improve teaching/learning while setting high expectation for self and students • Professional portfolios • Student collections	planning and developing objectives, questions, and activities that reflect higher and lower cognitive skills • Content and language objectives	attending to the clarity of information and explanation while being aware of lesson pacing • Student-engagement checklist	monitoring student progress with a clear knowledge of students as individuals in terms of ability, needs, and achievement • Data collection with reflections and dialogue

identify a teacher strategy or classroom context that was discussed previously in this volume by placing them in capitals.

We have actually seen teachers with these characteristics at work and often studied their outcomes (García & García, 2009). We realize it is often difficult to determine effectiveness, but any observer entering a classroom with a teacher at work with these characteristics would be impressed. And more than likely the academic outcomes produced by that teacher would be very well received.

For these teachers, the school day is planned and orchestrated to meet student needs as well as reflect the theory of learning that they bring to a classroom. Teachers need to believe and understand that students are learning content through the language that is being used by the teacher and students. That in fact, English language development happens through the content that is being taught and that content learning happens through the language that is being used. How do we teach if not through oral and written language and more importantly, how do students share what they are learning if not orally or in written text? It is clear that students can share their knowledge through filling in bubbles, but the bubbles do not inform teachers of the level they have understood and learned. Their use of language, written or oral, creates a more detailed account of their thinking and learning.

We will begin to address specific issues that relate to the daily organization as well as the physical organization of the classroom. Teachers who are effective with Hispanic students attend carefully to these forms of organization. What follows is particular attention to a recommended daily schedule and classroom map.

Daily Schedule

Having a daily schedule that is predictable for students helps them to anticipate as well as focus on what is being communicated each and every day. Teachers who believe in these ways create optimal learning that ensures that each student will listen, will read, will write, and will talk in different groups throughout the day. In these classrooms they ask questions and belong to groups in which they are busy hearing the language and practicing the new words in order to solve problems or creating new ideas. Working in pairs and small groups allows children the redundancy of answers and exposure to different ways words are used by different peers. It allows them to "give it a go," listening to their peers to reframe their words when they are not using them quite correctly.

The day begins with a sign-in sheet where each child answers a question that will be used later during Math Time (see Chapter 3 for specifics).

Students come to their table of four and then participate in putting their homework away using a cooperative structure called Numbered Heads. Their desks are placed together to form a small table with each desk labeled with a number from 1 to 4. The student at desk #1 asks the group to take homework out, student #2 reminds the group to write their names on the homework, student #3 collects homework and places it in a specific basket, and student #4 collects work and returns them to a different basket. Then all four students put their hands up to show they have completed their tasks. This type of interaction helps students become responsible for their work as well as to each other. It is not unreasonable that some students will share with the teacher that so and so has not done their work and ask the teacher to intervene. Some students might ask if they can help their peer sometime during the day to finish his/her homework. And the day begins with individual students concerned and supporting each other. Figure 6.1 is a daily schedule that has been followed by many effective teachers.

It is important to note that the schedule includes all of the content areas as well as language development contexts that require cooperative work by each student. The schedule reflects how the four domains of language, reading, writing, speaking, and listening will be used throughout the day.

Figure 6.1. Daily Classroom Schedule

AM	
8:00	Sign-in and Homework Bags
8:15	Community Circle/Calendar
	Mystery Morning Message
8:45	Read Aloud/Dialogic Reading
9:15	Word Work/Vocabulary
9:40	Teacher Led Groups/Centers
10:45	Writing Mini Lesson
11:00	Writers Workshop
11:30	Lunch/Recess
PM	
12:15	Reading on Their Own
12:40	Math and Centers
1:45	Theme/Science/Social Studies
2:30	Sharing: "What We Learned"

Classroom Organization

The effective organization of a classroom reflects set times, routines, and centers. This classroom arrangement supports the daily schedule and is an example of a responsive classroom, shown in Figure 6.2.

The physical classroom is planned around what students will be doing during the day, specifically where language, literacy, and learning will be shared by all members of the learning community. Four desks are placed together with students in chairs looking at each other. This demonstrates to students that they will be speaking and listening to each other as they cooperate in many of the activities they engage in. (It is important that teachers select which students sit at which tables to optimize the language sharing that will happen throughout the day.) There are center areas that include a listening table with recorded books, a computer area with two students at each computer, a writing table with different types of paper and writing implements, a math area with books and manipulatives, an art table filled with materials, and a discovery table where students can touch and discuss what is there. This table has word cards, maps, and graphic organizers that support their learning as they discover.

There are two large areas that are used during all times of the day. The book area contains many types of books in baskets, and usually has a rug area where students can comfortably read their self-selected choice of books. Students are here early in the morning when they arrive in the classroom, during centers, during the read-to-self time, when they finish an activity their teacher has assigned, and often at the end of the day while waiting for parents or siblings. The other large area is the whole group rug area. This is where the day begins and where it usually ends. This is where whole group instruction occurs, where the vocabulary list for the week is written on the chart, and specifically where the content and language objectives for each lesson are written. This is the area where most structured language learning occurs. Language is often exchanged between pairs using a cooperative structure like "Think, Pair, and Share." (Other cooperative structures are described in Chapter 5.)

In this responsive classroom organization students can participate in large group work in the rug area, in small group learning with the teacher at the discovery table, with a partner as they work together in a center, and as an individual sitting in his or her own desk. The classroom is filled with books, charts, and manipulatives always made available by where they are placed. The literacy and language learning opportunities happen in instructional contexts that have been created and planned for by the teacher using centers, selective seat assignments, and the large rug area. This type of responsive organization has paid attention to who is in the learning community as well as to how students learn content and develop language.

Figure 6.2. A Responsive Classroom Map

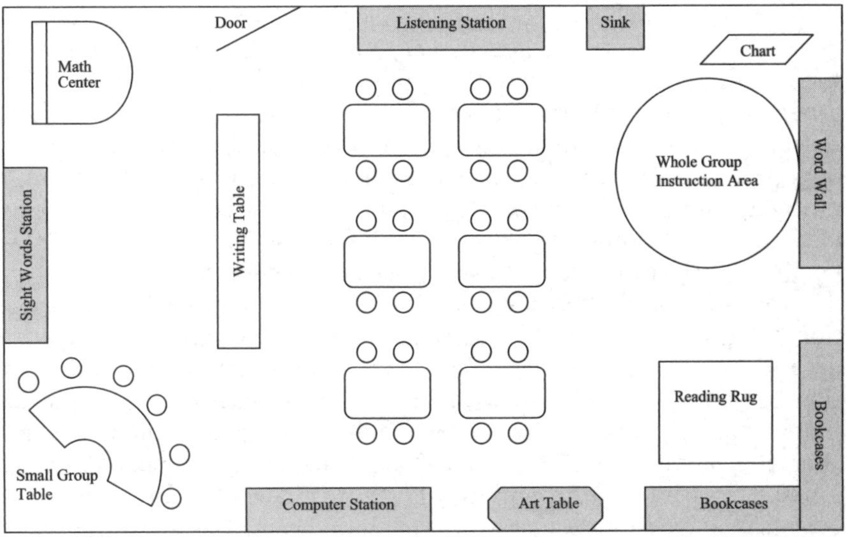

We will use an example of a 5-day vocabulary routine to highlight how the classroom organization supports content and language achievement. In classrooms where students are being academically challenged as well as performing academically, two types of vocabulary learning occurs. Students gain new words from center and small group work into their oral and written communications. The second type of learning occurs daily at the same time and over a 5-day structured routine (see Table 3.1). The vocabulary words may come from any of the content areas, selected by the teacher. The work is incorporated into 5-by-8 inch blank page booklets compiled by the teacher. (The 5-day routine follows their area of the classroom noted at the end of each day.) This type of classroom organization supports instruction. During the structured routine, students are able to work in whole groups, in pairs, at centers, and by themselves. This type of classroom is respectful and friendly, with an organization that encourages students to ask questions and practice academic vocabulary that have been explicitly targeted.

Focusing on Academic Language

For Hispanics in particular, effective teachers are cognizant of the requirement that our classrooms must continually consider the academic language in every instructional opportunity. Learning academic language allows children to understand and use that language to communicate effectively within the learning venues offered in the schooling process. Therefore, we must always remind teachers that English is, not only the acquisition of vocabulary, but also developing control of the use of language conventions and nuances that are part of all classroom learning—we have referred to this in previous chapters as academic discourse. In order for Hispanic students to be successful using academic language, teachers must examine the type of language used within their constructed learning opportunities. They must explicitly teach academic English, develop opportunities where it can be practiced, and continually monitor and assess student progress toward this goal. What follows is an example of how academic language can be taught using a specific model.

The recent work by Seidlitz and Castillo (2010) is the basis for instruction being used in effective classrooms that have taken the responsive organization of the daily schedule and classroom map into their instruction. Seidlitz and Castillo (2010) identify seven language and literacy steps that align nicely with empirical research findings related to more general characterizations of effective teachers and teaching for Hispanics (García, 2001). However, Seidlitz, and Castillo (2010) have also created a set of professional development activities that have been attended by hundreds of teachers. After attending the professional activities, teachers who use the seven steps are assisted through a coaching model to implement the steps in their own classrooms. According to data provided by these authors, this emphasis on the seven steps, coupled with professional development and coaching, produces very positive outcomes for teachers and their students. Teachers report having a much better understanding of the teaching/learning process, for which augmented coaching provides a significant support structure, and that students have become more actively engaged in acquiring academic English and related content time, higher levels of language proficiency indicators, and participation in cooperative structures (Seidlitz & Castillo, 2010).

We have seen this process ourselves, and offer an example of the type of professional development and related coaching support teachers need to consider for their students and for Hispanic students in particular. The first step addressed asks teachers to consider ways to *teach students what to say when they do not know what to say.* It is important that students learn to monitor whether they understand what is being communicated. Teachers understand that this monitoring strategy is to help students evaluate whether they understand or are still not sure of what is being said or taught. In these classrooms, we see teachers asking students to respond with one of four statements provided on a chart if they are not sure of their answer. Two of these are, "May I ask a friend?" and "May I have some time to think?" These options are particularly responsive and respectful to all students and specifically to those whose academic language is developing. It could be the case that learners need more time to understand the academic language of the question and/or generate an academically featured response. It is also appropriate to include sentence frames that can be used by students, particularly those who have the content knowledge and their academic language is still developing: "I need to know _____"; "I am not sure about _____."

As we have discussed earlier, effective teachers realize that students must go beyond vocabulary words and learn the form and structure of the academic language that they will be sharing. In step two, teachers are asked to model these language structures *using complete sentences.* From the first 5 minutes that students enter classrooms, teachers must speak, question, and respond in complete sentences. Teachers must also require and support our students to do the same. Having students share and respond to the teacher and other students by using complete sentences will support their development as an academic language speaker. This second step sounds so simple, but many teachers struggle to personally address this spontaneously and, therefore, they need to plan the language frames they will be using to support the development of academic language before they teach a lesson.

Step three focuses on student engagement. When teachers *randomize and rotate* they are systematically determining who will respond to their questions, ensuring that all students become participants. Many teachers use the "popsicle stick" method for randomizing and ensuring that each student has had an opportunity to speak. After presenting material, teachers will pull a stick with a student's name and ask a question. Sometimes students are not able to answer or they may ask for more information, so the teacher would pull another stick and ask another student. This popsicle stick ensures more random participation and allows the teacher to stay cognizant of who has or still needs to participate. There are other methods to ensure participation by all students. The critical issue is planning for and implementing these types of engagement processes.

Step three asks teachers to carefully plan questions related to the lesson, ask them, and then be patient in getting student answers: prepare, ask, and wait. This provides students with more time to think, process the answer, and generate their response. As teachers randomize and rotate who will answer their questions they are demonstrating student efficacy. When teachers follow step three they ask thoughtful and purposeful questions that then fosters reflective answers leading to higher levels of learning.

Understanding how important it is for Hispanic students to participate in classroom instruction is the basis for step four. The *use of total response signals* ensures that they can participate without always having to be dependent on language. The teacher is asked to afford the opportunity to respond to lesson related queries: Through the use of pre-made signal cards, physical thumbs, or pens up/down (agree/disagree), rank with your fingers, green card–red card (stop/proceed with lesson), and number wheels (paper made wheels with numbers related to options of answers to a teacher question). We have seen teachers use these effectively to mitigate that absence of verbal responding by students while keeping all students engaged. Total response signals also facilitate the assessment of students' receptive academic and language skill development.

Developing content and language objectives is step five, and its focus is on what standards students should know and be able to do. Teachers use their local- or state-content standards to inform students what content concepts they will be teaching and in which language domain(s) students will share what they have learned. When content objectives are implemented teachers are able to connect lessons with the standards. Language objectives determine the language skills and structures that will be developed during the lesson. Unfortunately, in our own experience, we often visit classrooms in which there are no content and language objectives communicated to students. Often content and language objectives are not developed or documented in lesson plans. This step represents an understood principle of teaching and learning—that when students know what and why they are learning a specific skill or content they learn it sooner and with more breadth.

The remaining two steps are step six, *have students participate in structured conversations,* and step seven, *have students participate in structured reading and writing,* focus on what needs to be taught: speaking, listening, reading, and writing skills. Teachers who structure explicit instruction in these areas also plan many opportunities for practice. These two steps should begin with the background knowledge that students bring to the content area, so as to build on this information in lessons. Teachers should always plan how conversations will be structured so students can share what they are learning. This can be done with a writing prompt or a sentence frame using a cooperative structure that will ensure that all students are participating in the conversations.

The use of the seven steps and this type of professional knowledge helps teachers reflect on what learning is happening in their classroom. Teachers should always reflect on which of these seven steps they already have in place and which step they might want to begin to work on.

This model by Seidlitz and Castillo has provided teachers with steps that will support the academic achievement that all students are successfully attaining on a daily basis. We refer you to the publication by Seildlitz and Castillo (2010) for more details.

Of course this example of teachers operating on academic learning with Hispanics is not the only method available. Another example is Sheltered Instruction Observational Protocol (SIOP), which is a method we have seen for ourselves that has had very positive results. However, like any other method of organizing instruction to ensure rich language environments (see Chapter 5), these methods generate classroom environments organized by teachers to engage all students in the intersecting development of language and content.

CONCLUSION

In summary, we suggest that developing responsive and effective teachers for young Hispanics requires a setting for developing teacher knowledge that has its roots in processes both in the school and community. This focus on developing responsive teachers encourages professional efforts that support prospective and already engaged teachers to construct and reconstruct meaning and to seek reinterpretations and augmentations to past knowledge within compatible and nurturing schooling contexts. This mission requires an understanding of how individuals with diverse sets of experiences, packaged individually into cultures, "make meaning," communicate that meaning, and extend that meaning, particularly in the social contexts we call schools. Such a mission requires in-depth treatment of the processes associated with producing diversity and issues of socialization in and out of schools, coupled with a clear examination of how such understanding is actually transformed into pedagogy and curriculum that results in high academic performance for all students—acquiring the content and the language forms and nuances of the academic setting.

CHAPTER 7

The Significance of Family Engagement

New teachers express the clear need for insight and practical strategies to successfully address the diverse learning needs of their students. Not surprisingly, they also want more information about how to best communicate with the parents of their students. Parents often come from cultures that differ from that of the teacher, and teachers often need to interact with parents who speak languages other than English. (Brophy & Good, 2008, p. 43)

Parents and families of Hispanic students can play a critical role in supporting children's growth and development. Specifically, family engagement in the early years is essential for laying the foundation that promotes a child's learning and later school success (Rodriguez-Brown, 2010). Yet, many families may not know how to help their children at home or in school—or may not perceive this role as "appropriate"—and best reserved for the "professional teacher." Often Hispanic parents do not speak English and may feel disconnected from the school environment (García, Schribner, & Cuellar, 2009). Furthermore, the ways parents from diverse Hispanic immigrant families do get involved may not coincide with the system's expectations of involvement. Teachers, administrators, and staff often do not engage in efforts to understand the culture of families in the school context and build rapport through ongoing communication.

FAMILY CHARACTERISTICS

Even though variability within the Hispanic groups exists (García, 2001c), these populations share certain demographic and sociocultural traits, mainly in family characteristics, parenting and home language, learning experiences, and childcare and early education.

Within the wider Hispanic population, families share similar characteristic factors, such as large family households, low parental education achievement, low-wage jobs, and high rates of poverty (García, Jensen, &

Cuellar, 2006). Even though socio-economic factors may have a negative bearing on the infant's development, other family characteristics may exert a protective influence on their development. For example, Hispanics households, with a higher rate of grandparents and relatives, may be conducive to communal caregiving and participation in infants' early learning experiences (Golan & Petersen, 2007). This may be particularly valuable for families with low income.

Compared to other ethnic groups, regarding household income, the percentage of two-parent households, percentage of married parents and maternal depression, Hispanic families generally out-perform African American and American Indian families, but do not fare as well as European American and Asian American families. In relation to maternal education attainment and employment, Hispanic mothers' educational backgrounds lag behind mothers in other ethnic groups, and they are less likely to be part of the workforce than mothers in other groups (Lopez, Barrueco, & Miles, 2006).

However, when looking at families in the poverty sample of the Early Childhood Longitudinal Study—Birth Cohort (ECLS-B) data set, Hispanic families seem to fare generally better than most of the other groups. For example, in terms of maternal depression, European American mothers show higher depression rates than Hispanic mothers.

Parenting and Parent-Child Interaction

There is an exhaustive body of research documenting the sociocultural patterns of Hispanic parents and the ways in which they influence child development. (National Task Force on Early Childhood Education for Hispanics, 2007). This research has found that there are a number of salient factors within the Hispanic family, including respect, famialism, and a sociocentric view on children's enculturation. Furthermore, these studies have shown Hispanic parents' belief systems, practices, and expectations to be significantly influenced by socio-economic factors, maternal educational background, and level of socialization.

In their analysis of the differences between Hispanic infants and those from other ethnic groups, using ECLS-B data, Lopez, Barrueco, and Miles (2006) found that there seem to be no significant race/ethnicity differences between infant developmental outcomes in Hispanic families and those from other ethnic groups. They say that rather than education, socio-economic resources, or ethnicity, child development depends on parents' emotional well-being, behavior, and parenting skills. However, they go on to say that while family resources, such as income and maternal education, did not directly associate with child development, they do have a bearing on parenting behaviors. For example, the socio-economic and educational backgrounds led to differences in mothers' observed teaching and responsive behavior, as well as frequency of reading, song singing, and story-telling. In relation to reading, several studies have found that Hispanic parents admit having few books and literacy materials in their homes and reading less often to their children. These factors, research shows, contribute to lower performance on cognitive, language, and literacy activities (National Task Force on Early Childhood Education for Hispanics, 2007). In fact, when asked to define parental involvement, Hispanic parents reported participating more in the children's lives more often than in their academic involvement (García, 2001b).

Hispanic Family Composition

Although, Hispanic children often start school under disadvantaged academic characteristics and circumstances (Galindo & Reardon, 2006), the literature has shown that Hispanic families possess positive attributes that are likely to work as a safeguard against these risk factors. For example a foundational attribute in Hispanic families is familism. Familism expresses important values such as family identification, obligation, and support (Vélez-Ibáñez & Greenberg, 1992). Furthermore, familism has been found to positively affect Hispanic students' academics (Valenzuela & Dornbusch, 1994). In this study Valenzuela and Dornbusch (1994) used survey data from 3,158 (2,666 Anglo and 492 Mexican origin) high school students to investigate the impact of familism on students' academics. Behavioral, attitudinal, and structural dimensions of familism were related to students' self-reported grades. What the authors found was that for both the White and Mexican American groups, familism was important, but the Mexican group was able to achieve academic gains because of it. It is crucial to explain that this was the case for the students of Mexican descent, whose parents had at least 12 years of education. For instance, for the Mexican descent group, neither familism nor parental education related to higher educational outcomes on their own. However, it was the interaction of the two variables that accounted for the gains.

Another important attribute is the high percentage of intact families within the Hispanic community. Specifically, Mexican immigrant families have the highest percentage of intact families when compared to all immigrant families and all U.S. native families (Hernandez, 2006). Research shows that children who grow up in stable, two-parent households achieve higher levels of education, earn higher incomes, enjoy higher occupational status, and report less symptoms of depression when compared to children who lack these attributes, even after controlling for parental income and education (Amato, 2005). Specifically, for Mexican families, it has been suggested that the high rate of intact marriages helps contribute to Mexican American children's high levels of psychological well-being (Crosnoe, 2006).

How researchers and practitioners think about the socialization of Mexican American children continues to be shaped by notions of *cultural models,* or core norms, advanced by parents within the Hispanic community (e.g., García, 2001a; García & Gonzalez, 2006). While illuminating the strengths and coherent scripts found within many families, these models fail to explain variation in children's socialization found among diverse Hispanic families, often corresponding to generation, acculturation, and class position.

The life-history of the individual is first and foremost an accommodation to the patterns and standards traditionally handed down in his or her community. From the moment of birth, the customs shape experience and behavior. It is important to emphasize that these "customs" involve everyday activities, from sleeping conventions with young children to how dinners are socially organized. Such activities host "cultural messages" that signal what is normatively expected to be a proper member of the family or group (García, 2001b). Conceptually, this understanding allows us to focus on how social environments shape individual social as well as cognitive processes.

The accumulation of studies across varying groups has yielded evidence on how parents' economic activities and material contexts may condition socialization practices. Youngsters raised in agricultural communities, for example, were often socialized to be obedient and place paramount importance on the family's well-being (Barry, Child, & Bacon, 1959). This led to particular comparative generalizations of how children are raised, for instance, into the dichotomous characterization of individualistic versus collective forms (e.g., Greenfield, Keller, Fuligni, & Maynard, 2003). Others have contrasted the parental beliefs of different ethnic or linguistic groups regarding the underlying nature of young children. One example is Whiting and Edwards' (1988) distinction between the belief that a child's destiny is predetermined, versus the notion in the middle-class American community they studied that the "infant was a bundle of potentialities" to be advanced through home practices.

To the extent that group membership is delineated and members share particular cultural or taken-for-granted socialization practices, everyday activities reflect normative expectations regarding how young children are to behave, as well as which adults retain authority to enforce the rules for becoming a member of the group. This line of work continues to emphasize central tendencies, not variability among group members; it establishes how a "typical" member of group A behaves or believes vis-à-vis a typical member of group B.

More complex portrayals of child socialization appeared in the 1980s, as research approaches with Mexican American and other Hispanic families developed. An elaborated social architecture was revealed that stressed particular values or cultural models—from the heritage culture—which seemed to *distinguish* these families, still moving from a comparative, between-ethnic group perspective. A growing number of social scientists have noted that the differences between the socialization goals of ethnic minority parents and those of the majority White parents are rooted in their distinct cultural norms (García, 2001a) Cauce and Domenech-Rodriguez (2002) wrote, "Values that have been considered distinctly Hispanic include *familismo, personalismo, marianismo,* and *machismo.*" Other anthropologists, cultural psychologists, and sociologists illuminated related themes underlying how children are raised in Hispanic families, including the importance of *bien educado* (Reese, Balzano, Gallimore, & Goldenberg, 1995), *respeto* (Halgunseth, Ispa, & Duane, 2006; for review, García Coll, Meyer, & Brillon, 1995) and *confianza* (Rodriguez-Brown, 2009).

Beyond delineating these themes, some students of Hispanic socialization have focused on behavioral scripts, identifying chains of parental beliefs or practices that are enacted inside the home and hold implications both for mother-child interactions and decision-making about childcare. Reese and Gallimore (2001), for instance, showed how immigrant Hispanics in Los Angeles understood the emergence of literacy skills in their children and how their model of social action was situated in the school and emphasized training by teachers, not skill-building inside the home. In contrast, López (2003) detailed variation among Hispanic mothers: Some have acquired the "family as educator model" from middle-class parents or the media, or through exposure to preschools and local institutions (Harwood, Leyendecker, Carlson, Ascenio, & Miller, 2002). Drawing on Quinn and Holland's (1987) work related to tacitly followed cultural scripts, Holloway and Fuller (1997) showed how the emphasis placed on family or kin networks by employed Hispanic mothers and mediated by familiarity and trust, often led them to select home-based childcare.

Mireles, Bridges, Fuller, Livas, and Mangual (2007) highlight the utility of mapping the daily routines and activities in which young Hispanic children are engaged. Working from detailed notes on each activity and the people involved yielded valid data that could be reliably coded and analyzed with multiple methods. The incidence of activities recorded in these chronological field notes was closely associated with a second method, recording spot observations. At one level, the profiles they report are rather unremarkable: Mothers and their young children spend major portions of time playing, preparing meals, and eating. Mothers urge their children to help pick up and treat visitors politely.

Yet the norms and thematic emphases of socialization goals and practices—so salient in the earlier research on scripts or models specific to Hispanic groups—came to light in many activities. Household responsibilities and routines made up just 8% of all activities but revealed socialization practices stemming from the heritage culture held by these Mexican Americans mothers. Children were often reminded to always greet adults and visitors with appropriate offers and gestures of respect. These instances represent elements of learning how to become *bien educado*, to demonstrate the proper, respectful way of being with guests. Several children were required to clear their dishes following a meal, or fetch various utensils and objects when their mother directed them to do so. But such activities appear to reflect a commitment to *familismo* and respect for the household's interests, as enforced by the mother.

One stark finding of this study was the amount of time that participating 4-year-olds spent watching television, playing video games, or using a personal computer. Almost one-quarter of all activities observed involved television (17%) or another electronic medium (6%). In only 6% of all activities could we infer that children were actively involved in the activity, excluding electronic games, such as reading with an adult, playing cards, doing a puzzle, and working with materials of some kind. If we combine TV, video games, and eating, this represents 47% of all activities observed. We observed from early afternoon to early evening, so the activity profile may have been different if early mornings were included. But exposure to text materials and interactive language with an adult, not appearing on a television screen, was comparatively rare (García, Scribner, & Cuellar, 2009).

Although these patterns should be interpreted cautiously, these investigators reported that young children watched less television if they attended preschool and if their parents were better off economically. Children with better-educated mothers tended to watch less television, although the mean difference in the proportional incidence did not reach statistical significance. In addition, children who watched more television tended to play with materials less (again, as a proportion of all activities). Mothers not employed outside the home demanded more of their 4-year-olds in terms of household responsibilities and routines, compared with children with employed mothers.

These specific findings, related to the growing population of Hispanic, Mexican American children suggest revisiting the importance of early learning opportunities and issues related to parental and family engagement in those opportunities. We turn now specifically to overviews of programs that provides a promising opportunity with regard to this issue.

FAMILY INVOLVEMENT IN EDUCATION

Parent involvement in children's education has been documented as important in the academic well-being of children by the academic literature (Barrera & Warner, 2006; Lee & Bowman, 2006; Raikes et al., 2006) as well as the federal government. For example, the federal government's goals 2000: Educate America Act poses that "every school will promote partnerships that will increase parent involvement and participation in promoting the social, emotional, and academic growth of children" (Goals 2000: Educate America Act).

Qiuyun (2003) explored the relationship between parent involvement and academic gains. The dependent variables were reading, math, and general knowledge achievement at the end of the Kindergarten year. Parent involvement was considered with the following three dimensions; (1) involvement at home, including home literacy environment and home cognitive stimulation; (2) involvement at school; and (3) involvement outside of the home, including extracurricular activities and use of community resources. In Qiuyun's study, the relationship between the parent involvement practices of 16,083 first-time Kindergartners and early literacy students, while controlling for background variables such as child gender, family SES, and family type was examined. The findings suggest that among the parent involvement types studied, school involvement was significantly associated with reading, math, and general knowledge for almost all children, except for Asian children's reading achievement. Importantly, for the Hispanic community that has a large proportion of children in poverty (Hernandez, 2006), among all the parent involvement practices, the percentage of variance explained by parent involvement was greater for minority children than for European American children and for poor children than for the non-poor children.

In a different study, Qiuyun (2006) studied the effects of parent involvement of language minority parents in their children's academic outcomes (reading, math, and science) and social emotional outcomes in the years of Kindergarten through the 3rd grade, in a 4-year longitudinal study. The independent variables were home/center involvement (ethnic/ racial heritage is discussed, family religion is discussed, participates in cultural events and degree expectations for their children) and facilitators of involvement. Facilitators involved included whether the schools made information available to parents regarding how to better know and teach their children at home, information about community services, and whether volunteering opportunities were made available to parents. The findings suggested that ELL children experienced less parent involvement through the years, and that they lagged behind their non-ELL peers at the beginning of Kindergarten and continued to lag behind by the end of the 3rd grade. Although no relationship was found among the social emotional outcomes, facilitators of involvement had a high relationship with ELL academic well-being.

Family Engagement Programs in Early Education

Of all the definitions of family engagement programs, the one provided by the Harvard Family Research Project and, in particular, by Heather Weiss and M. Elena Lopez seems most appropriate and comprehensive. They found that, first, family engagement is a shared responsibility in which schools and other community agencies and organizations are committed to reaching out to engage the families in meaningful ways and in which families are committed to actively supporting their children's learning and development. Second, family engagement is continuous across a child's life and entails enduring commitment but changing parent roles as children mature into young adulthood. Third, family engagement cuts across and reinforces learning in the multiple settings where children learn—at home, in pre-Kindergarten programs, in schools, in faith-based institutions, and in the community (Weisner, 2002).

The federal government has supported the critical role of families in children's learning through a number of policies and programs. However, they lack a common definition and have created a field that is dominated by "random acts of family engagement rather than a coherent strategy" (Weisner, 2002). Research in parental engagement in their children's education indicates that it produces positive results within the educational community and the children's learning (Fuligni & Pedersen, 2002; Rodriguez-Brown, 2009; Lopez, 2003). In addition, the large increase of immigrant children in the United States places significant demands on schools (García & Miller, 2008).

Benefits of parent engagement with schools come in a variety of areas:

Student—improvement of grades, attendance, attitude and behavior, homework completion, ability to self-regulate, social skills, and state test results

Family—self-efficacy and empowerment
School—communication, collaboration, ability to solve problems, and
     staff morale

However there are several barriers that make this engagement problematic and have to be overcome in a respectful, participatory manner that allows families to have input into what is done at school (Furger, 2006). First is family's cultural understanding of U.S. education and expectations, language, and culture of families; family work schedules; family education level; understanding of English; and negative attitudes toward and understanding of the parent's culture by school personnel.

Leaders in the field such as Joyce Epstein, Anne Henderson, and Karen Mapp have reported that parental involvement is more important to school success than a parent's education or income level, and that students whose parents are involved in their education tend to do better in school, stay in school longer, and have fewer disciplinary problems (Greaves, 2009). Throughout the United States, schools are faced with a large number of immigrant families, of which the majority is Hispanic, mainly Mexican (García, Scribner, & Cuellar, 2009). At times these families are treated as lower-class citizens, directly by specific anti-immigration policies and, more often indirectly, by the disadvantageous anti-immigrant climate that may reside inside and outside educational venues (Freeman, 2009).

The following programs have been found to have a positive effect specifically for Hispanic immigrant parents and family engagement, and this participation in these programs has been found to positively affect their children's education: AVANCE, Abriendo Puertas, Project FLAME, PIQE, and HIPPY. They are reviewed her in an effort to inform both policymakers and practitioners of the enormous positive possibilities of family engagement for our immigrant populations.

AVANCE. AVANCE, a non-profit organization established in 1973 with the mission of "Unlocking America's potential by strengthening families within at-risk communities through effective parent education and support programs" (p. 1), is a parent-child education program that focuses on parent education, early childhood development, brain development, literacy, and school readiness. The program largely supports Hispanic immigrant families under conditions of economic stress in underserved communities and aims to prepare parents to be supporters and role models for their children to succeed in school.

The AVANCE program (AVANCE, 2007), with chapters throughout Texas and in Los Angeles, California, is a 9-month course built on the assumption that parents can improve their parenting skills, that they are the most influential teachers and role models for their children, and that the years between childbirth and three are critical to influencing a child's educational success.

The program serves parents with children from 0 to 3 years of age and operates in housing projects, schools, and community centers. AVANCE instructors make parents aware of the learning and development their children undergo, including the emotional, physical, social, and cognitive processes. This awareness-raising practice is based on the discussion of topics that range from the importance of effective discipline and nutrition to reading and math. Parents are also encouraged to attend classes in literacy, learning English, and preparing for the GED.

Abriendo Puertas. Abriendo Puertas is an evidence-based parenting, leadership, and advocacy training program for low-income, primarily Spanish-speaking parents of children from birth to 5 years of age.

The program developed by and for Hispanic parents aims to improve the outcomes of the nation's Hispanic children by building the capacity and confidence of parents to be strong and powerful advocates in the lives of their children.

Curriculum is a ten-session leadership and advocacy training program centered on the cultural values, strengths, and experiences of Hispanic families and uses popular education and folk wisdom (Bridges & Gutierrez, 2011). This approach engages parents at a very personal level and results in transformative learning. The executive summary on the evaluation of Abriendo Puertas key findings noted that participants reported significant increases in areas of parenting, health services, social support, and community involvement (Bridges & Gutierrez, 2011). The program is based on the premise that enhancing parenting skills early in a child's life leads to economic and social benefits.

The primary objective of Abriendo Puertas is to increase the number of Hispanic children in the United States who enter school ready to learn and able to succeed in life. The objective is reached by increasing parent's confidence in their parenting skills, knowledge, available health services, social support and social connections in the community, desire for community involvement, and empowerment to get involved in the community and their child's education.

FLAME. The FLAME (Family Literacy: Aprendiendo, Mejorando, Educando) program was established with the purpose to improve the parent involvement and academic achievement of children of limited English proficient parents (Rodriguez-Brown & Shanahan, 1989). FLAME is housed at the University of Illinois-Chicago and is carried out in public schools. Presently, the program model has been nationally circulated to over five sites to train family literacy professionals. FLAME offers wide-ranging services to Hispanic families with children between the ages of 3 and 9 with the purpose of increasing parents' abilities to provide literacy opportunities for their children, increasing parents' ability to act as positive literacy models for their children, improving parents' literacy skills so that they may efficiently initiate, encourage, support, and extend their children's learning; and improving the relationship between parents and school officials. An important aspect of Project FLAME is the emphasis on using the language in which the parents feel the most comfortable. Understanding and valuing individual cultural beliefs of educational preparation can determine how they can further educate and involve parents in home literacy prior to going to school.

PIQE. Parent Involvement for Quality Education (PIQE) is a program whose underlying assumption is that the most promising way to enhance their children's education is by transforming the working partnership between parents, school, and community. It aims to teach parents how to become important supporters of their children's educational performance and development (Vidano & Sahafi, 2004).

The fundamental premise of PIQE is that low-income, recently immigrated parents to the United States need information about the dynamics of the U.S. educational system, about how to collaborate with the school and teachers, and about how to assist their children at home. PIQE offers this information through a program that consists of eight 90-minute sessions in which a range of topics is discussed, including home–school collaboration, the home, motivation, self-esteem, communication and discipline, academic standards, how the school functions, and the road to university (Chrispeels & Rivero, 2001; Chrispeels, González, & Arellano, 2004; Golan & Peterson, 2002).

Each PIQE session emphasizes the centrality of parents to their children's future and encourages parents to interact with each other and with the instructor to talk about the topic at hand. Instructors are selected because they share the student's parents' similar life experiences. Multiple classes are scheduled to accommodate the family's needs (e.g., morning or evening classes). The classes are conducted by instructors from the same culture as the participants who speak the language fluently.

PIQE centers on inner-city minority children of immigrant Hispanic parents due to this population's unique needs and difficulties that restrict parent involvement. PIQE's mission is built upon four principles: All parents love their children and want a better future for them; every child can learn and deserves the opportunity to attend and complete college education; parents and teachers need to work together to ensure the educational success of every child; learning, for children, is a natural process that parents and teachers facilitate (Vidano & Sahafi, 2004).

Since its inception, PIQE has graduated over 154,000 parents from schools all over California, and has begun its expansion outside of California, opening new offices in Dallas and Phoenix. Moreover, PIQE programs have been implemented in parent courses at two other National Council of La Raza (NCLR) affiliates in Kansas.

Research on and evaluations of PIQE have suggested that as a result of parents' participation in its program, they have become more engaged with their children, the school, and especially the teacher. Parents have also developed new relationships with their children, spouse, and their children's teachers; have become more aware of the importance of setting goals for their children; and have established more explicit goals for their childrens' future (Chrispeels & Rivero, 2001; Chrispeels, González, & Arellano, 2004). Likewise, data from a performance evaluation that focuses on the children of parents that graduated from the PIQE program in San Diego suggest that the PIQE has had a bearing on school persistence, reduced the dropout rate, and increased college enrollment (Chrispeels & González, 2004; Chrispeels, González, & Arellano, 2004; Vidano & Sahafi, 2004). PIQE instructors have played a key role in achieving these goals by utilizing specific collaborative and supportive practices that effectively retain parents and remove barriers to their participation, as well as using parent- and community-centered activities that encourage parents to conclude the 8-week sessions of the program.

HIPPY. The Home Instruction for Parents of Preschool Youngsters (HIPPY) program is a free, 2-year, home-based early intervention program for 4- and 5-year-old children. The HIPPY program is an internationally acclaimed early childhood education program presently used in 157 sites, 26 states, and 7 countries. In the United States, it is intended to provide educational enrichment to at-risk children from poor and immigrant families, increase school readiness, and foster parent involvement in their children's education (HIPPY USA, 2007). The main purpose of the program is to increase school readiness and to foster parent involvement in their children's education and in community life. The 30-week HIPPY curriculum is an explicit, direct instructional program. The lessons are designed to develop a child's skills in three major areas: language development, problem solving, and sensory and perceptual discrimination (HIPPY USA, 2007).

A study conducted by García (2006) investigated the academic effects of HIPPY on Hispanic English language learners (ELL) in Texas.

Specifically, using standardized measures in reading, mathematics, and language arts, the author compared Hispanic youngsters who attended HIPPY starting at age 4 (HIPPY 4–Preschool) and age 5 (HIPPY 5–Kindergarten) to Hispanic students who attended an early childhood school as 4-year-olds and did not participate in HIPPY. The curriculum used was in Spanish. The treatment group statistically outperformed the control group in the reading, language, and mathematics long after they experienced the intervention. These statistically significant results were still found at the end of 3rd grade.

The majority of the teachers who work with Hispanic students are not participating in programs like the ones that have been described. With a clear understanding of why they must establish home–school connections, teachers create homework that requires families to participate in their child's homework. These often include acknowledging that they have checked math problems, listened to their child read a list of words, observed and timed how much their child read that night, and so forth. They are then required to provide a signature showing that their child completed the assigned homework. Parents often share that they are willing to go beyond a signature and perhaps share some of their own educational resources. Luis Moll's work at the University of Arizona expands on the importance of home–school connections. His conceptualization of the "funds of knowledge" requires that teachers become familiar and utilize home-based resources for instructional resources (Moll, 2009).

LEARNING FROM OUR COMMUNITIES

We have emphasized that learning environments must be constructed responsively and congruently with the child's home environment. Parent/family journals are another way a teacher and family can maximize the individual and collective understandings of the home and school environment. Keeping parent/family journals establishes a weekly sharing between those caring for the child at home and the teacher. The writing that is shared often includes the skills their child might need as well as the skills the child is bringing to the classroom. It also informs teachers with the "thinking" that parents have about what is happening in schools, their own understanding of specific content as well as their students' academic achievement.

Interactive Family Journals

Interactive parent/family and teacher journals are notebooks that are filled with entries that are responded to on a weekly basis by each participant, the teacher and a family member. The choice of language, topic, and amount of response are negotiated by the "need" of the responder. "Parent journals have become interactive informers of my families' lives, experiences, and expectations of the schooling process. They have informed what I teach and why" (García, 1999, p. 8). The entries become informational histories that support teachers in their instructional decisions. It is understood by educators that our students' homes and communities hold knowledge that provide us with strategic resources. These resources should inform our classroom practices and promote student learning. It is our responsibility to find ways to create opportunities where our students' families are able to share their lives, their experiences, and their expectations for the academic learning of their children. This type of interaction will enhance each student's schooling experience.

A critical piece of information that is shared within these journals is the literacy levels of the family member or members who are responding to the entries that are being shared weekly. These journals are a systematic and consistent effort to expand the communication between the teacher and the family.

Interactive family journals help to:

1. Establish a direct way for families to become active informants of their child's schooling process.
2. Create "authentic" and purposeful communication between families and teachers on a weekly basis.
3. Allow for greater insights into the social and cultural context of their students' families and specifically their child and the teacher's student.
4. Promote open-ended dialogue leading to unexpected insights into the cultural and linguistic resource each student brings to the classroom.
5. Become a year-long documentation of the what topics and concerns were shared by the family member and teacher.

It is the teacher's responsibility to acknowledge parents whose oral language has become the resource to their child's literacy learning. When it became evident that a parent of one of Erminda's students did not have writing skills, she would call the home and take notes that allowed her to continue gaining information about the family and the child. She also had siblings who often became the reader and writer of the entry for their parents. This type of engagement required the family to understand that their responses as well as topics they initiated were supporting their child's learning.

As this communication enhancement is being implemented, several questions should be asked about how journals help to clarify implementation and purpose.

How should I begin? Begin with a short note formatted like a letter that "talks" to parents about who you are, what you enjoy doing, and so forth. The letter sets the tone for sharing about who students are and states that the written conversation may not always be about "school" but about their student and his/her family.

What topics should I cover or not cover? The journal allows you to initiate topics that focus around learning and teaching, about their home lives and experiences, what they see in the future for their child, and so forth. Since you also must respond to the topics they initiate you might need to establish that you would rather not respond to specific topics.

When a family who was going through a divorce began to discuss personal information, Erminda responded that she was uncomfortable with the topic and that they needed to refocus on what their child was doing in the classroom. Both parents then responded with "thanks for thinking about our child, we have not been thinking about his needs for a while."

With which parents/family should I use a journal? Send journals home with at least five students; two whose parents you need to inform *more* about their *needs*; one whose parents have found it difficult to come into the classroom or attend meetings; and two whose parents have been supporting your efforts with positive comments. Your goal is to write journals with all your students. How you structure the response time will also help you. You may want to send out journals to half of your class the first part of the year and the second half during the second semester.

How long should my response be or should parents' responses be? The length is not important. What you need to remember is that you are establishing an avenue that offers you information you need to use when considering vocabulary words for that student, about interests that informs what books you bring into the classroom and make available for the student, or perhaps personal connections you make when responding to his or her journal. It is also important that this information be used during your appointment at the conversation table (see Chapter 4).

What if I do not speak or write some of the languages that my students speak? Establish which languages the parents of their students are literate in. Also, ask if there are other siblings in the school who are literate in English and establish that having their sibling read and translate the teacher's journal entries to the family will be an important activity. The sibling will also translate into English the family's response and new questions that they might have for the teacher.

What if one of my families does not read or write? There might be families in your classroom in which neither parent can read or write in English or in their own native language. There might be families in which the student in your classroom is the first child to go to school. These families are encouraged to plan for a day and time when a phone call from the teacher is established and the journal dialogue is done orally. The teacher should date and document what is being discussed, then send it home when the other children take their journals home.

A few years ago, Erminda selected a family in her 1st grade to participate in parent/family journals and sent it home on a Thursday expecting a written response the following Thursday. She did not receive a response and reintroduced the idea of the journals and a bit more about herself. After the third attempt and 6 weeks had gone by she called home. The parent shared that they did not read or write in any language. Erminda was surprised because the initial homework "Who is the family?" was completed and returned, as all the daily homework had been. She let me know that they had listed Spanish as their home language, implying they could read Spanish because a neighbor in the next apartment had agreed to read and support the child with all of her homework. She also felt she could not ask the neighbor to help with one more thing. Erminda agreed with her, and they established a specific day and time when she would call the family. A few months later, the student asked if Erminda would be writing in the family journal that week. Erminda was surprised by the questions, took a peek, and realized that her student had written an entry with a question for her to answer. Yes the journal had become a *family* journal, and by the end of the year Erminda no longer called but wrote entries that the student could ask her family. She then would respond, using her best effort to write what her parents would share with her.

Like the other family engagement programs, parent/family journals provide an interaction with Hispanic families that focuses on maximizing communication, understanding, and, mutual respect among key individuals who are shaping a child's development and learning opportunities. We have found them, once instituted, to be well embraced by family members and teachers, and to provide useful foundations for further conversations that invoke practices at both home and school that benefit students.

A Vocabulary Lesson That Involves Parents

It is important that homework help inform instruction as often as possible. It should honor families and values that they share and demonstrate to students that what was shared at home during their homework time is important enough to be used in a lesson. Not only do children bring content from their families, they also engage in a purposeful literacy event. The level of language literacy being used at home is also reflected in the homework.

In order to invite parents to join our new learning, we send the ABC Word Chart (Figure 7.1) home at the beginning of any new theme or literacy unit, or at the introduction of a new concept in any content area. The ABC Word Chart has already been established by different strategies that students experience since the first week of school. We earlier introduced the phonological sound word wall that moves into a phonics ABC Word Wall and is used throughout the school year. Send home the ABC Word Chart with a short note that asks parents to discuss the theme (for example, plants, insects, weather, etc.). Then they identify a set of words focused on the theme, write and possibly draw the word in the appropriate letter square. We recommend that the parents/family find a word related to the topic using at least ten letters. When students return their homework, they bring their charts to the large group area. Each child uses their charts to "read" the words that their family has written. On the large (24" x 36") chart with ABC squares, the words are written and shared.

This type of vocabulary work continues to demonstrate how much information families can share. The words may be written in Spanish and the teacher must decide how to honor this knowledge (two charts—one in Spanish and one in English) or to rename them in English and let the children know how all the words are being used. This all serves as a base for learning. You may have children draw pictures of the words (nouns) or find pictures on the Internet. These charts will be used for many learning opportunities. Students will use them to create their own ABC word charts that can be used during journal writing, a new book they will begin, or a learning poster they will create and later share orally with their classmates.

We are always surprised by the amount of interest that this type of family homework generates. Not only do families comment on how "easy" it is, but wonder if other families fill in the same words. We recall one particular chart for which a students and her family generated five different words for the small rolly poly "bug" that most of us thought only had one name. More importantly, in this exercise, connections are made between students, families, and teachers while engaging in an important learning opportunity.

CONCLUSION

Now that there is a recognized set of conduits for collaboration with parents and families, schools must begin to reduce the affective filters that parents/families and schools often co-construct. The recommendation

Figure 7.1. ABC Word Chart

(Child's name) family,

We will begin a new unit on (ex., insects) this Friday. We need your help. Please take time to talk with your child about insects that you know or remember from when you were a 1st-grader. Help your child write the insect's name and draw a picture. Try to fill in at least ten ABC squares. Please return this homework tomorrow. Thank you once again for sharing information with your child and participating in the homework.

A	B	C	D	E	F
G	H	I	J	K	L
M	N	O	P,Q	R	S
T	U	V	W	X,Y,Z	Topic

of research and practice reviewed in this chapter indicates that parents/ families will need to become involved more comprehensively with the education of their children, and educators will need to provide multiple venues for engagement (Henderson, 2007). Support for what families can do at home in support of student academic learning includes the use of the families' home language and recognizing that the home language literacy also contributes to development of English literacy providing access to appropriate literature resources. The objective of the engagement is a collaborating partnership with families and educational colleagues at every level.

Recommendations for enhancing family engagement:

- Expand the meaning of parent involvement to include all family members.

- Capitalize on resources of family members by sharing their native language(s) culture(s).
- Empower parents and families by providing resources and programs tailored to their needs more comprehensively.
- Provide a variety of opportunities that welcome families at the school site.
- Provide a parent "facilitator" or coordinator to establish procedures for ongoing communication between and among parents and professionals.
- Provide informal and formal avenues for teacher-family and family-family communication.
- Include written materials and information regarding community and school resources, translated into the appropriate native language.
- Ensure the professional development of staff members toward becoming culturally and linguistically sensitive to the individual needs of parents and families.
- Devise ways to interact positively with the entire family in family-originated venues.

Successful parent participation in the child's learning process depends upon recognizing individual strengths, establishing positive parent-professional relationships, and providing support and resources for parents/families. With educative experiences and support, parents are more apt to become advocates and partners in their child's education. Creating connections for parents between their natural interactions with their children (e.g., book reading, cooking activities) and what is happening in the classroom is a way to bridge the home-school connection. Increased linguistic and cultural sensitivity will also help to include all family members in the educational process. Because immigrant families rely on extended families for care-giving roles, supporting familial relationships will indirectly foster the child's development.

CHAPTER 8

Policy and Young Hispanics

The under-education of racial and ethnic minorities in the United States is certainly not a new phenomenon, nor a novel concern to policymakers. Research literature is ripe with decades of data documenting the low academic performance and educational attainment (i.e., school completion rates) of children of African American, Native American, and Hispanic origins (Paik & Walberg, 2007). So what is it we can say that has not already been said? What new contributions can we offer policymakers concerned with the under-education of children from racial and ethnic minority groups in this country?

The value of this discussion is found in its focus on a specific ethnic group during a specific age range: those of Hispanic origins ages 3 to 8 years. We argue that this group deserves special attention from policymakers for several reasons. In the first section of this chapter, we identify and explain these reasons. Then we propose what policymakers can do to improve the early educational opportunities for young Hispanic (or Latino, in some federal, state, or local policy discussions of Hispanics) children. We share empirical evidence on the benefits of early programs and practices for these children and discuss additional research and development needs to see that such programs are expanded, implemented well, and improved, and that new and innovative strategies are pursued. While a consensus has emerged concerning the economic returns (Heckman & Masterov, 2004) and cognitive benefits (Ramey & Ramey, 1998; Shonkoff & Phillips, 2000) of schooling interventions for children ages 3 to 8 years, in general, much is still unknown concerning the efficacy of instructional and curricular strategies across socio-economic segments. But why should we differentiate Hispanic children from those of other racial/ethnic groups? What makes them different? Are their needs different? Below we offer answers to these questions.

EARLY INTERVENTION

Empirical evidence suggests that certain interventions during the early years are a wise investment to improving learning opportunities and outcomes for Hispanic children. A substantial body of reliable knowledge shows that instructional programs, teaching strategies, and educational policies can improve literacy and academic development for young Hispanic children. Because a majority of young Hispanic children come from homes in which Spanish is used—and there are important associations between language development in Spanish and English and the development of certain cognitive features (especially those needed to do well in school)—early educational programs for Hispanic children ought to be explicit and strategic concerning the integration of language and culture. This means instruction, curricular content, and schooling practices are developed and evaluated to account for their linguistic and sociocultural circumstances so as to leverage home resources and parental support and to optimize student learning (Genesee, Geva, Dressler, & Kamil, 2006; Goldenberg, Gallimore, Reese, & Garnier, 2001; Goldenberg, Rueda, & August, 2006; Reese, Garnier, Gallimore, & Goldenberg, 2000; Scheffner Hammer & Miccio, 2004; Shannon, 1995; National Task Force on Early Childhood Education for Hispanics, 2007).

Recent research—including syntheses, meta-analyses, and other reviews—offers clearer conclusions (August, Calderón, Carlo, & Nuttall, 2006). In a meta-analysis of 11 studies—which included standardized test scores of 2,719 elementary school students, 1,562 of whom were enrolled in bilingual programs, in 13 states—Greene (1998) found that bilingual programs overall produced 0.21 of a standard deviation improvement on reading tests and 0.12 of a standard deviation improvement on math tests measured in English. Moreover, the overall gain on Spanish test scores was 0.74 of a standard deviation. The author noted that while these data showed the general academic benefits of bilingual programs, a few critical programmatic concerns were left unclear. Namely, this study did not ascertain the ideal length of time students should be in bilingual programs, the ideal amount of native language used for instruction, and the age groups in which these techniques are most appropriate.

Recent research, therefore, suggests academic benefits of bilingual over English-only programs—on average, an increase of 0.2 to 0.3 standard deviations in test performance. This is enough to close one-fifth to one-third of the overall Hispanic-White achievement gap in reading in the early years of schooling.

One of the problems with broad comparisons of program types is that there is not one "bilingual" program or approach (García, 2005; García, Jensen, Miller, & Huerta, 2005) but several. As mentioned above, programs differ in terms of required teacher qualifications, curriculum, the student population they are designed to serve, instructional approaches, variations of Spanish/English use, among other aspects.

Relatively new in the United States, dual language (DL) programs—also known as two-way immersion (TWI)—offer a unique approach to bilingual education. Designed to teach English to ELL students and Spanish to native English speakers through dual-language content and instruction in a shared classroom (i.e., English-plus-Spanish [EPS] approaches), available research suggests positive effects for young Hispanics as well as for language majority populations (García & Jensen, 2006). It is important to note that the implementation of these programs varies in terms of the amount of time they devote to each language (e.g., 50-50 versus 90-10 models), the grade levels they intend to serve, language and curriculum division, and the populations they intend to serve (Center for Applied Linguistics [CAL], 2005). On the other hand, DL programs are unified by common notions of learning (based heavily on Vygotsky [or sociocultural] notions of social interaction and naturalistic learning), second language acquisition, the importance of teaching language through content, and the goal of producing bilingual students (Genesee, 1999).

Extant research shows that DL programs are able to promote bilingual oral and academic skills for young ELL Hispanics as well as for their language majority counterparts (Barnett, Yarosz, Thomas, & Blanco, 2006; Cazabon, Lambert, & Hall, 1999; Christian, 1994, 1997; Christian, Genesee, Lindholm-Leary, & Howard, 2004; Cobb, Vega, & Kronauge, 2005; Figueroa, 2005; García & Jensen, 2006; Howard, Sugarman, & Christian, 2003; Lindholm, 1999; Sugarman & Howard, 2001). While the methodological rigor between studies varies from randomized trials controlling for student background, school environment quality, and the integrity of program implementation to measuring the academic progress of a small group of DL participants over time (Howard, Sugarman, & Christian, 2003), conclusions converge on comparisons between DL and other programs and comparisons between Hispanic ELLs and native English speakers.

Comparisons between programs for Hispanic ELLs and native English speakers show that DL participants score as well or better on standardized achievement tests in English and Spanish than same-age peers educated in other programs (Howard, Sugarman, & Christian, 2003). Indeed, studies document native Spanish speakers participating in DL programs to outperform other Spanish speakers enrolled in other programs in English reading and mathematics as well as Spanish pre-reading, reading, writing, and mathematics (Barnett, Yarosz, Thomas, & Blanco, 2006; Christian, 1994; Cobb, Vega, & Kronauge, 2005). Other studies have found no significant differences in outcomes for Hispanic ELL students (Cazabon, Lambert, & Hall, 1999; Howard, Sugarman, & Christian, 2003).

A final topic regarding the schooling of young Hispanics concerns pre-Kindergarten programs. In recent years access to state-funded pre-Kindergarten programs has expanded in several states where Head Start and other initiatives have come up short (García & Jensen, 2007). The motivation in most cases to get children in school at age 4 (and often age 3) concerns the economic (Heckman & Masterov, 2004) and cognitive (Ramey & Ramey, 1998; Shonkoff & Phillips, 2000) benefits of early education. Moreover, recent research shows that young Hispanics are particularly positioned to benefit from pre-Kindergarten involvement (García & González, 2006; Gormley, Gayer, Phillips, & Dawson, 2005), even though, overall, they are less likely to be enrolled than their White, Asian, and African American peers (García & Jensen, 2007).

The general academic benefits of participation in pre-Kindergarten programs have been documented repeatedly, yet the sizes of the effects vary across programs and between racial/ethnic groups. Indeed, an evaluation of the public pre-Kindergarten program in Tulsa, Oklahoma, found that while benefits for all racial/ethnic and SES groups were found, gains for Hispanic students in letter-word identification, spelling, and applied problem solving were each greater than for African American, Native American, and White children (Gormley, Gayer, Phillips, & Dawson, 2005). Yet no discussion was rendered concerning the curricular or instructional strategies that generated these results or their impact over time.

Head Start

On December 12, 2007, President Bush signed into law the Improving Head Start for School Readiness Act of 2007 (P.L. 110–134). This was the first reauthorization of Head Start in nearly 10 years. Given the growing diversity and rapidly changing demographics across the country, Latino children and families had a lot at stake in the reauthorization process of the nation's premiere early childhood education program. It is a well-known fact that access to high-quality early childhood education programs has the potential to close the academic achievement gap and that Latino children enter school less prepared to learn than their White peers. As such, the reauthorization of Head Start plays an important role in a broader effort to enhance Latino educational attainment. Various provisions were included in the new law that will help to ensure that Latino and limited English proficient (LEP) children—the vast majority of whom are Latino—fully benefit from Head Start's services.

Historically, Latinos have been underrepresented in Head Start; however, their participation rates are steadily increasing and Latino children are reaching rates of parity in the program. From 1992 to 2006, Latino enrollment in Head Start increased more than 10%. The percent of Latino children in Head Start has grown steadily since 1992, when only about

19% of Latino children were served in the program. By the 2007 school year, this increased to more than 32% (National Task Force on the Early Childhood Education for Hispanics, 2007). Notwithstanding this steady progress, participation in Head Start remains a challenge for some Latino children, particularly those who reside in states where Latinos have not traditionally lived. In addition, a lack of resources to expand the Migrant and Seasonal Head Start (MSHS) and Early Head Start (EHS) programs thwarts the participation of hundreds of thousands of Latino children eligible for these programs. The following section discusses these challenges in greater detail and describes the new opportunities for expansion through the reauthorization. One of the most challenging obstacles preventing large numbers of children of farmworkers from accessing MSHS services is limited funding for program expansion. According to the *Descriptive Study of Seasonal Farmworker Families*—a 2001 congressionally mandated study—MSHS programs serve a mere 19% of eligible children on average. According to the same study, only 10% (4,987 of 46,972) of eligible children in California—the largest agricultural state in the United States—have access to MSHS services (National Task Force on the Early Childhood Education for Hispanics, 2007).

Children of migrant and seasonal farmworkers have limited access to MSHS programs in part due to under identification and unreliable data that show where these children and families live and describe their demographic characteristics. The transitory nature of farmworkers makes gathering accurate and consistent information difficult. As a result, many estimates run the risk of under-counting and misrepresenting this vulnerable population. Head Start legislation has not mandated an MSHS study since 1998, out of which came the 2001 study noted above. Since that time, there have been no other studies conducted to provide a more accurate portrait of need and demand for MSHS services.

The Improving Head Start for School Readiness Act of 2007 provides a framework for expanding MSHS in two important ways. First, it creates a mechanism for accurately determining the percentage of eligible children compared to the number children served on a consistent basis. Second, the legislation requires that the HHS secretary ensures a plan be developed to identify and alleviate enrollment barriers to MSHS programs. The reauthorization also improves the funding structure for MSHS programs over the next 5 years. The new funding formula is structured so that when overall Head Start funding is sufficient to cover the cost-of-living adjustments (COLA), MSHS programs have the potential to receive as much as $10 million annually for expansion, with a $50 million maximum over a 5-year period. In the case that Head Start is not funded enough to cover the full COLA, a graduated plan will fund partial cost-of-living expenses and expansion funding. In the event that Head Start funding is not sufficient to fund 50% of the cost-of-living expenses, MSHS programs will not benefit from expansion dollars. This new funding structure shifts the discretion of funding from the HHS secretary and creates a more equitable funding formula for MSHS.

Access to Early Head Start. Latino children face enormous barriers in the earliest years of life that impact their preparedness for the first day of school. More than a quarter of Latino children live in linguistically isolated households, and more than 50% of Latino infants and toddlers live in homes with incomes below 150% of the federal poverty level. In addition, Latino children are less likely to have access to reading activities and resources. Early Head Start (EHS), which provides high-quality child development and family support, serves children from birth to three years old and pregnant mothers and can play a significant role in improving the school readiness and healthy development of young Latino children. In 2002, a Congressionally mandated evaluation of EHS found that Latino children receiving EHS services improved in cognitive and language development and that Latino parents were more likely to read to their children daily than parents who did not receive EHS services. This study is the most rigorous study to date examining the effects of high-quality early learning programs for Latino children under the age of three.

Unfortunately, EHS is not available to the vast majority of eligible families. Much like MSHS, insufficient funding limits the reach of EHS programs. Although EHS has been praised for being a successful program, Congress and the Administration have not made the resources available to expand it. For example, EHS has not had a significant increase since its inception in 1995. In fiscal year 1997, Early Head Start funds were 4% of the total Head Start appropriation, or $159.2 million, and served just more than 5,000 children. By 2006, almost 10 years later, EHS was funded at $679 million and served only 62,000 children. These figures indicate that EHS has only been expanded by approximately 6,000 children per year between 1997 and 2006. Current estimates suggest that EHS is serving only 3% of all eligible infants and toddlers in the country, making the need for increased funding all the more critical.

The new reauthorization bill signals the intention to expand the EHS program in two key ways. According to the new Head Start funding formula, EHS is eligible to receive half of all new funding made available for program expansion. In addition, under the new law, Head Start centers have the option and flexibility to convert spaces dedicated to serving preschool-age children to EHS programs serving infants and toddlers. To convert preschool slots to EHS slots, programs must document that the preschool-age children already had adequate access to Head Start services and that there is a need to serve younger children with EHS.

Access in Emerging Communities. While national participation rates show that Latinos enjoy greater access to Head Start services, their enrollment remains a concern in communities that have experienced a recent and rapid Latino population growth. During the last 15 years, states in the Midwest and Southeast have experienced the fastest growth among Latino children. For example, North Carolina and Arkansas have experienced rapid increases in the Latino child population under age 3. Data collected from the Census Bureau (Garcia & Frede, 2010) reveal that between 1990 and 2000, North Carolina and Arkansas experienced a 546% and 504% growth of Latino children ages 0 to 2, respectively. Other southeastern states, including Tennessee, Georgia, and Alabama, have also experienced up to 462% growth rate and make up the top states with the fastest growing Latino child population under 3 years old. Anecdotal evidence suggests that Head Start programs in these communities may have a difficult time enrolling Hispanic and LEP children. While the reasons for this are complex, the lack of staff that speak multiple languages in these programs and a lack of culturally and linguistically appropriate outreach to new populations are among some of the challenges.

It is critical that Latino and LEP children benefit from Head Start services in new growth communities. Foremost, the high-quality early education experience that Head Start provides will help to prepare these children for the first day of school. Moreover, the comprehensive nature of Head Start services can help integrate diverse families into the school system and community by building parents' understanding of the school system and helping families navigate social services systems. The Head Start reauthorization legislation strives to ensure that Head Start programs serve all children on a level playing field. The bill improves the monitoring of community needs assessments that Head Start grantees prepare on a triannual basis. This is important because these needs assessments include demographic characteristics regarding Head Start–eligible children in a grantee's target area. Although Head Start agencies have been required to conduct a needs assessment in the past, the federal review and monitoring of progress did not hold programs accountable for addressing the enrollment shortages found in the community needs assessment. It is also important to note that the new legislation requires Head Start agencies to provide culturally and linguistically appropriate outreach approaches to underserved populations.

Child Development and Educational Performance Standards. Head Start is highly regarded for having comprehensive child outcomes and high standards for children's progress and accomplishments. Notwithstanding this, performance standards and guidance for LEP instruction have been rather limited and narrow. For example, the Outcomes Framework, which is used to guide Head Start program's assessment of student progress, explicitly mentions English language acquisition, but does not include guidance to help LEP students make meaningful progress in all content areas through a culturally and linguistically appropriate approach. This is of particular concern given the growing amounts of research supporting the use of home language instruction for developing a second language.

While the acquisition of the English language is an important outcome for LEP children, research tells us that the development of a child's proficiency in the native language is important for the development of a second language. In addition, there is evidence that bilingual exposure has a positive impact on the linguistic, cognitive, and reading development of young children. Given these findings, providing instruction for children in a culturally and linguistically appropriate manner ensures the success of acquiring English and further supports the broader goals outlined in the Head Start Outcomes Framework. Under the new law, LEP students are required to make progress, not only in English language acquisition, but in each of the domains, including literacy, mathematics knowledge, and science knowledge, through the use of culturally and linguistically appropriate instruction. This new provision has the potential to positively shape the development of new outcomes and benchmarks for children in each domain, including measuring progress in the native language.

Teacher Quality. A mounting body of research has linked a well-trained, highly-skilled workforce with a quality learning environment and academic gains. Given this mounting evidence, Head Start has moved toward increasing teacher requirements. In 1998, the revised Head Start Act set a nationwide goal of having 50% of Head Start teachers obtain an Associate of Arts degree (AA). The new reauthorization bill requires that 50% of teachers in Head Start classrooms have at least a Bachelor of Arts degree (BA) in early childhood education or a related field by 2013. EHS has moved in a similar direction; teachers are required to have at least an AA while half of EHS teachers are required to have a BA by 2012. Clearly, increasing training requirements is an important step for improving the quality of services to all children; however, this policy can have an unintended effect of altering the diversity of the teacher workforce, which can undermine the services and instruction of Head Start children. Currently, the Head Start workforce is fairly reflective of the child population; however, anecdotal evidence suggests that many Hispanic teachers had difficulty meeting the 1998 AA requirement for Head Start lead teachers and remained in the classroom as assistant teachers. Facing the challenge of low wages, time constraints, and language barriers, many Hispanic teachers were unable to meet the requirements.

Maintaining diversity in the workforce is all the more critical given the growing diversity and growing presence of LEP children in Head Start classrooms across the country. Thus, building a diverse workforce will require that teachers, particularly those who encounter significant barriers to accessing higher education, have support to help them obtain higher levels of training. In addition, training must go beyond simply having a BA but must ensure that higher education programs prepare teachers to work with a diverse group of children. Recent research has documented significant gaps in the training of the early childhood teachers in regards to working with diverse children, revealing that among higher education programs dedicated to teacher preparation in early childhood, very few requirements are related to understanding the needs of children from diverse communities and children with special needs.

Under the re-authorization, programs will be required to collect and report data about classroom instructors' early childhood education credentials and will be desegregated by race and ethnicity. Documenting the progress of teachers' attainment of higher credentials over time by race and ethnicity will shed light on how teachers are obtaining higher levels of training and whether there are any differences based on race and ethnicity. The implications of this data are far-reaching, given that we have very little information related to the early childhood education workforce and its progress toward meeting the 1998 requirements. Further, the collection of this data will greatly inform strategies for developing effective career ladder programs and professional development. The law codifies existing relationships with Hispanic-serving institutions and higher education institutions. In 1999, the Head Start Bureau began the Head Start Higher Education Hispanic/Latino Service Partnerships program that supported the development of education and training models between institutions of higher education and Head Start agencies. The reauthorization bill gives the secretary the authority to award demonstration grants to Hispanic-serving institutions to create career ladders by providing coursework to allow Head Start staff to meet the teacher qualification standards and offering professional development. These grants codify relationships established in the 1999 program.

WHAT SHOULD POLICYMAKERS DO?

The recommendations below are offered to improve educational opportunities for young Hispanics in the United States. In general terms, they highlight the need for federal and state education policies in early education (i.e., pre-Kindergarten through grade 3) to directly address language development issues, and for curricular and instructional approaches to embrace principles of appropriateness and relevance in early education programs. While available evidence on schooling, language development, and related policy remain limited—particularly in the development and testing of classroom strategies for diverse segments of the Hispanic child population—current evidence suggests rich language environments, dual-language programs, universal pre-Kindergarten programs, and high-quality teachers can improve learning opportunities and outcomes for these children (National Task Force on Early Childhood Education for Hispanics, 2007). Below we touch on each of these areas, offering specific recommendations to the federal, state, and local governments.

We conclude with some thoughts regarding future collaborations between researchers and policymakers to continue to explore and implement effective practices in early education programs. Because the design, testing, and evaluation of programs and strategies can take 10 to 15 years, we present these recommendations using a long-term (5–20 years) time frame. Ongoing research will entail impact evaluations, implementation evaluations, longitudinal considerations, and analyses of Hispanic subgroups (by parent education, national origin, immigrant generation status, primary language spoken in the home, and other related social factors). Moreover, the extent to which our recommendations are considered and successfully implemented will depend on the collaborative efforts between those who produce knowledge (i.e., researchers) and those who enact legislation (i.e., policymakers) (Reimers & McGinn, 1997), as well as innovations in approaching research/policy collaborations.

The Federal Government

There are specific activities through which the federal government can improve classroom environments of young Hispanic children. These are concerned with implementing evidence-based practices at scale, as well as directed efforts to expand the available knowledge base of best practices. Here we offer four related recommendations.

First, we recommend that the federal government underwrite tests of programs designed to produce large increases in the number of culturally knowledgeable preschool and early elementary teachers proficient in English and Spanish. The most fundamental element in the provision of rich language environments and high-quality, dual-language programs across the pre-K–3 spectrum is high-quality teachers. This means teachers are bilingual, proficient in both English and Spanish, and knowledgeable regarding the cultural and linguistic circumstances of Hispanic families, particularly the educational strengths and needs of their children. Indeed, research shows that the transfer of academic skills between languages is heightened, and early achievement outcomes increased for young bilingual and emergent bilingual students, when teachers use Spanish in the classroom. The most successful teachers are fluent in both languages, understand learning patterns associated with second language acquisition, have a mastery of appropriate instructional strategies (i.e., cooperative learning, sheltered instruction, differentiated instruction, and strategic teaching), and have strong organizational and communication skills.

Second, we recommend that the federal government fund and experiment with teacher-preparation programs to recruit more Spanish-speaking undergraduates and teachers who are trained in second language acquisition to work as language specialists. The responsibility of "language specialists" is to help classroom teachers in schools and preschools with substantial numbers of ELL students to be responsive to their linguistic and academic needs. Language specialists serve as consultants to teachers and aides in the classroom to help ELL students learn and achieve, recognizing and leveraging existent strengths. Having a language specialist in the classroom can also help monolingual teachers make essential links with Spanish-speaking parents. Ongoing relationships with parents are an invaluable resource to connect educational practices between the home and school and thereby increase student engagement and learning (García, Schribner, & Cuellar, 2009).

Third, we recommend that the federal government (through Head Start, Early Head Start, and other grant programs) continue to explore and expand dual-language (DL) programs. Young Hispanic children should have access to high-quality DL programs (i.e., two-way immersion), which teach English and Spanish language skills through content. Integrating native English speakers and native Spanish speakers in the same classroom, thereby fostering linguistic and ethnic equity among students, DL programs have been shown to support literacy development in English for Hispanic students without compromising Spanish skills. Moreover, research shows that academic achievement levels of young Spanish-speaking Hispanics as well as their native English-speaking peers enrolled in DL programs are equivalent or, in many cases, superior to outcomes of students in mainstream, monolingual classrooms.

The Center for Applied Linguistics (CAL, 2005) offers a set of recommendations to help school personnel establish and maintain high-quality DL programs:

1. create and maintain an infrastructure that supports an accountability process;
2. use curriculum which promotes and maintains the development of bilingual, biliterate, and multicultural competencies for all students;
3. use student-centered instructional strategies derived from research-based principles of dual-language education;
4. recruit and retain high quality dual-language staff;
5. have knowledgeable leadership who promote equity among groups and support the goals of additive bilingualism, biliteracy, and cross-cultural competence;
6. have a responsive infrastructure for positive, ongoing relations with students' families and the community; and
7. be adequately funded and supported by school staff, families, and the community.

Finally, we recommend that the federal government expand the scope of the national and international databases developed to assess student performance. We recommend expanding national, longitudinal studies (e.g., ECLS-B, ECLS-K) to allow for more extensive analysis of Hispanics and other subgroups by national origin, SES (e.g., parent education), nativity, immigrant generation status, and primary language spoken in the home. Additionally, we recommend that U.S. participation in international assessments of student performance be expanded to allow for more detail in monitoring how segments of the Hispanic population compare to students in other nations, particularly Latin American countries of origin. In many cases this means sampling at the state level and oversampling for Hispanics.

State Governments

Our recommendations to state governments are also concerned primarily with improving the delivery of early education practices, yet improved data collection efforts are also needed to evaluate the successful implementation of early education programs and practices. In most cases the sort of work needed from state governments necessitates meaningful collaborations with school districts and other community-based organizations.

First, we recommend that state governments collaborate with local communities to offer high-quality educational experiences with a variety of schedule options. Young Hispanic children ages 3 and 4 years should be given access to free, state-funded preschool in which enrollment is on a volunteer basis. Evidence suggests that high-quality pre-Kindergarten programs improve school readiness for young Hispanic children and decrease achievement differences between racial/ethnic groups at Kindergarten entry. As mentioned, these programs should have bilingual and culturally competent staff to effectively engage students and to develop sustainable relationships with family members. As Hispanic enrollment in preschool programs remains low compared to other racial/ethnic groups, state governments would be particularly wise to work alongside Hispanic organizations and other local institutions to provide information to parents on these programs and encourage meaningful collaborations between the home and school.

In states where access to state-funded pre-Kindergarten is not yet universal—that is, available to all children—policymakers and program administrators should expand definitions of eligibility to include children with LEP. This should be an intermediate step, intended to increase Hispanic enrollments and serve more at-risk children until the larger goal of universal access is attained. Where possible, summer programs should be developed and instituted.

Second, we recommend that state governments provide pay and benefits to qualified preschool teachers that are equal to those of public school teachers. This would provide the economic incentive to recruit and maintain a well-educated, reasonably stable group of preschool professionals. Again, high-quality teachers to young Hispanic children are fluent in both languages, understand learning patterns associated with second language acquisition, have a mastery of appropriate instructional strategies, and have strong organizational and communication skills. With these skills, teachers are able to interact with Hispanic parents appropriately and encourage them to engage in literacy-related activities with their children in the home. Moreover, bilingual teachers are better able to find out details concerning students' language and educational backgrounds and, therefore, to develop creative and accurate assessments of Hispanic children's linguistic ability and progress.

Third, along with the federal government, we recommend that state governments continue to fund and experiment with teacher-preparation programs to recruit more Spanish-speaking undergraduates and teachers who are trained in second language acquisition to work as language specialists. As mentioned previously, the responsibility of language specialists is to help classroom teachers in schools and preschools with substantial numbers of ELL students to be responsive to their linguistic and academic needs.

Fourth, we recommend that state governments establish information systems to be used by school districts and state education departments to disaggregate their students into subpopulations. These subpopulations are defined simultaneously in terms of race/ethnicity, parent education level, family income, immigrant generation status, national origin, and primary language spoken in the home. With this information states could monitor the academic progress of student subpopulations more effectively. Moreover, longitudinal data can assist evaluation efforts of program (and policy) effectiveness over time and determine important differences across mentioned student background variables.

Local Governments

As Hispanic enrollment in preschool programs remains low compared to other racial/ethnic groups, and there is a substantial gap between what we currently know to be best educational practices for young Hispanics and what is actually implemented in schools throughout the country, local governments (including school districts and other community organizations) should serve as liaisons between families and state governments. To this end, we offer two recommendations.

First, we recommend that local governments collaborate with state governments and the federal government to provide information to parents on pre-K, Head Start, and Early Head Start programs in order to increase Hispanic enrollments. Continuing to increase preschool enrollment remains important considering available demonstrating linking preschool attendance with improvements in school readiness for young Hispanic children, and decreases in achievement differences between racial/ethnic groups at Kindergarten entry.

Second, local government should propose plans to governments on particular strategies to develop the workforce needs. Suggestions from the community to improve teacher recruitment, for example, could serve as a means to engage the families and local institutions on ways state governments might increase the number of highly qualified teachers and language specialists. The mere engagement between families, schools, and local and state governments is meaningful.

CONCLUSION

We hope that the data shared, interpretations rendered, and the stated recommendations provide sufficient impetus for the federal, state, and local governments to give serious consideration to the educational well-being of young Hispanic children in this country. With our best efforts, improvements occur incrementally. The design, testing, and evaluation of programs and strategies require calculated investment and time. Moreover, successful implementation of programs and practices are facilitated as research and policy initiatives are pursued jointly. We remain optimistic that innovative collaborations can expedite improved academic performance among young Hispanic children and, therefore, the "intergenerational mobility" of the largest racial/ethnic minority group in the country. We conclude by offering some recommendations for innovative research, including activities in which non-governmental actors (i.e., private foundations, Hispanic organizations, and education researchers) might involve themselves.

In addition to the recommended research agenda for the federal government and state governments, we recommend that private foundations fund long-term efforts to design, test, and evaluate language and academic development strategies for Hispanic children in preschool through 3rd grade from all SES groups (particularly across levels of parent education and immigrant status). These include systematic, value-added studies to explore, develop, and determine the efficacy and scalability of instructional and curricular approaches. In order to maximize the chances of determining if the strategies are able to contribute to improvements in school readiness at scale, formal grant programs should be designed to provide 10 or more years of support for promising approaches. In addition, private foundations should seriously consider creating two or three new foundations specialized in funding these areas, thereby ensuring that sustained investments in strategy development are made in the long term. These new foundations would be chartered to support strategy development for other groups that continue to lag academically in addition to Hispanic children.

Hispanic organizations (and other community-based organizations) should assist all levels of government and private foundations to carry out the stated objectives. A major contribution of these organizations will be to continue to function as a liaison between families and institutions, including research bodies, government departments, and schools. They should shine as leaders in providing literacy development information, materials, and other support to parents and families of all SES segments. Moreover, assuming their near connection with the concerns and needs of families, they should be intimately involved in the process of program design, testing, and evaluation. Contributions from Hispanic organizations could be especially beneficial in exploring proposals to increase the number of highly qualified teachers to serve Hispanic children.

As indicated in Chapter 1, children of Mexican origin represent the largest group of Hispanic children nationwide. An approach of growing interest to develop improved educational practices and student-learning opportunities during the early years of schooling (and across the pre-K–12 spectrum) is through binational collaborations between researchers, practitioners, and policymakers in the United States and Mexico (Jensen, 2008b). To date, the Foreign Affairs Office of the Mexican government has launched a number of programs (including teacher exchange, online courses, community plazas, the "transfer document," among others) to enhance educational opportunities for Mexicans living in the United States (Gándara, 2008). A preliminary study of these programs found they have a great deal of potential to serve Mexican American children and families (not to mention the expansion of binational cooperation in education), but are constrained by low visibility, inadequate funding, poor integration with U.S. institutions (particularly the schools), and limited research and evaluation (Gándara, 2008). Ongoing study of programs like these, in addition to other binational initiatives, provide opportunities to explore, develop, and determine effective and scalable strategies to increase school engagement and learning for Mexican American children, and is an example of the sort of innovation needed to enhance early educational opportunities for at-risk subgroups of Hispanic children in this country.

CHAPTER 9

Conclusion

In the Introduction we gave our deepest appreciation to the National Task Force on Early Childhood Education for Hispanics (2007) for its important comprehensive analysis of early learning and young Hispanics. That report noted that, from an educational standpoint, Hispanics are in a complex situation. They have made substantial educational progress over the past several decades. Yet, as a group, they are far from converging on the educational attainment and academic achievement patterns of Whites and Asian Americans in the United States, or on the attainment and achievement norms of most industrialized nations.

As this volume has emphasized, the most formidable challenge in these circumstances is to build a much stronger early childhood education system for the children of the very large number of adult Hispanic immigrants with little formal education and limited knowledge of the academic dimensions of the English language. Available evidence suggests that far too many of their children are struggling academically in the early years of school, not only in English literacy, but in other key subjects including mathematics.

Moreover, as the under-representation of low-SES Hispanics in preschool programs attests, many of these children are not even gaining access to that key part of the early childhood education system. Beyond basic access to pre-Kindergarten is the need for a much more time-extensive system at the pre-K and K–3 levels for many of these youngsters. In addition, it would be extremely essential if that system's capacity to work with these youngsters in both English and Spanish was much more robust. That is the case because, as noted previously, many of these children are educationally at-risk when viewed from either language—they lack through no fault of their own rich language environments.

Fortunately, there is a growing body of evidence that high-quality pre-Kindergarten programs and K–3 education produce meaningfully higher levels of school readiness and academic achievement for Hispanic children from low-SES and middle class circumstances. Growing understanding of literacy development also provides a great deal of guidance regarding how early childhood programs might be strengthened from a school readiness and academic achievement standpoint.

RECOMMENDATIONS FROM RESEARCH, BEST PRACTICES, AND EXPERIENCE

In an effort to more formally summarize, we leave you with what we conclude are foundations from our research, review of best practices, and our own teaching experience.

1. Foster English acquisition and the development of mature literacy. Development and learning venues used native language abilities to develop literacy that promoted English literacy development. Programs in these locales were more interested in this mature development than transitioning students quickly into English language instruction. This approach paid off in English language development at levels that allowed students to be successful in English instruction.

2. Deliver grade-level content. Challenging work in the academic disciplines was perceived and acted on simultaneously with the goals of English language learning. Teachers organized lessons to deliver grade-level instruction through a variety of native language, sheltered English, and ESL activities. Organize instruction in innovative ways. Examples of innovations included (1) "schools-within-schools" to more responsively deal with diverse language needs of the students; (2) "families" of students who stayed together for major parts of the school day; (3) "continuum classes" in which teachers remained with their students for 2 to 3 years, helping teachers become more familiar with and respond to student diversity; and (4) grouping of students more flexibly on a continuous basis so as to respond to the developmental differences between their native and second language.

3. Protect and extend instructional time. Schools used after-school programs, supportive computer-based instruction, and voluntary Saturday schools and summer academies. These school activities multiplied the opportunities for students to engage in academic learning. Regular teachers or trained tutors were used to extend this learning time. Not surprisingly, a majority of students took advantage of these voluntary extensions. Care was taken not to erode the daily instructional time that was available—erosion often related to auxiliary responsibilities placed on teachers that take valuable time away from instruction.

4. Expand the roles and responsibilities of teachers. Teachers were given much greater roles in curricular and instructional decision-making. This decision-making was much more collective in nature to ensure cross-grade articulation and coordination. Teachers in these schools became full co-partners. They devised more "authentic" assessments that could inform instruction and developed assessment tools and scoring rubrics in reading and mathematics.

5. Address students' social and emotional needs. Many venues we worked in are located in low-income neighborhoods serving poor families. Therefore, a proactive stance with regard to issues in these communities was adopted. An after-school activity that was aimed at families, particularly dealing with issues of alcohol and drug abuse, family violence, health care, and related social service needs, brought the school staff together with social service agencies at one school site. Similar examples of actual family counseling and direct medical care were arranged at other sites.

6. Involve families in their children's education. Some of the schools were magnet schools. Parents had chosen to send their children to these schools. Family engagement was part of the magnet school contract in these schools. Other areas of family engagement included participation in school committees, school festivals and celebrations, student field trips, and other activities. In non-magnet schools, parent outreach services were an integral part of the school operation. In all cases, communication was accomplished on a regular basis in various home languages. Parent participation in governance of the school was a common attribute, although levels of parent participation were highly variable.

A PERSONAL SET OF RECOMMENDATIONS: THE FOUR "R"S—*LOS CUATRO* "R"S—AND A "T"

These summonses to change educational practices in the face of continued Hispanic student underachievement are not to be ignored. And our own personas have not been silent regarding these calls (García, 2001a; García, 2005; García and García, 2009). We have often been called upon to translate such calls in ways that might be helpful to educators and the general public. In doing so, we often draw from a set of recommendations that use a particular mnemonic, "remember the four *R*'s and the *T*." Educational programs, initiatives, strategies, and policies that assist Hispanic students are: *Respectful, Responsive, Responsibility, Resourcefulness,* and *Theoretically* viable. We admit that we particularly like this focus on the "r" because in Spanish the pronunciation takes the form of a trilled "r," phonetically it is like placing multiple "r"s together as in the roar of a motor "bah-r-r-room"—the term *"Respeto"* is pronounced "r-r-speto." So much for Geno's and Erminda's love of the Spanish "r" and its significance as a mnemonic. In short, attending to these four "R"s *and* the "T" should serve as a shorthand guide for those concerned with practical translation of today's theory and research and their implication for the education of Hispanic children and their families.

1. Respect. Everyone wants respect. Parents want to be respected and want their children respected. Over and over again, it is common to hear from Hispanic parents and their children that in schools they do not receive that respect. They are too often seen as the foreigner, the immigrant, the non-English speaker, the disadvantaged, someone who does not belong, is "less than," and the schools mission is to change them so they can belong. The most detrimental lack of respect for Hispanics might be identified as *el pobrecito* or *el benditio* syndrome—"Oh, you poor thing—unwashed, of and in poverty, immigrant, non-English speaking; we sympathize with your circumstances and lower our expectations for what you might be able to learn." Sympathy is not what Hispanic students need. This is when an educator or an educational system actually begins the slippery slope of lowering expectations and academic standards, begins to devise selection devices that separate the deserving from the non-deserving, the smart from the dumb, those with and those without a future. Hispanic students find themselves at the bottom end of this continuum through no fault of their own. Educational programs, teachers, and administrators that serve Hispanics will respect the students for what they bring—their language, culture, world view—and do not see disadvantages that place students only "at-risk" but as we see in these students' resources that can be marshaled to meet learning goals, particularly high learning goals. There is an acceptance and a respect that is to be honored and displayed for all students and the families and the communities from which they come. *Pobrecitos* they are not.

It was at a middle school in California that we first encountered this *pobrecito* phenomenon. The school was primarily serving Mexican American students, many children of first-generation immigrant parents. Some teachers actually felt that these students should not be in the country and by that logic in this school. Since they did not speak English, were poor, were members of gangs, and came from farmworker families, the majority of educators at the school felt the most they could do for these students was provide them a basic, no-frills education. Provide enough of an education to take them out of the fields. After we performed an analysis of the math and literacy curriculum for 7th graders, we found that teachers, over an extended period of time, had arrived at teaching 5th-grade skills to these 7th graders. This was not an instructional staff that purposely set out to downgrade instruction. They were not sinister in their goals or in their instructional behavior. When asked why they were teaching at these lower levels, the response came back, "We sympathize with their disadvantages and don't want them to fail." In other words, they were *pobrecitos*. That same staff, realizing and acting upon the need to begin respecting the language and culture of the students, and raising standards and academic expectations, developed and implemented organizational and instructional changes that resulted in significant gains in academic achievement in literacy, mathematics, and science (García, 2001b). For Hispanic students in particular too much sympathy for their circumstances can be highly detrimental; too much respect is never handicapping.

In San Antonio, Texas, we encountered the program AVANCE. Here was a program that served young Hispanic mothers and their children from before the time of birth until the beginning of Kindergarten. It delivered family support services and did so within culturally and linguistically respectful parameters, helping families adjust to immigrant circumstances through bilingual staff and programming. It began with the basic premise that these families needed to be respected for all the assets they brought to the developmental processes, and those cultural, social, linguistic, and cognitive assets were to be used to advance their own abilities to support and assist their children and families. And it worked, producing positive adult, child, and family outcomes. AVANCE is now a model for other immigrant family intervention programs, garnered national prizes and expanded to the national arena. (See Chapter 6 for details of this and other family engagement programs that serve Hispanics well.) AVANCE began and still begins with *Respeto*.

2. Responsive. It is not enough just to have respect. Educational programs and those individuals who serve in them must be directly responsive to the students and families that they serve. This requires an active assessment of the learning tools that the student brings to the schooling process coupled with the utilization of those tools that optimize student learning. It means shifting the emphasis from "needs assessments" to "asset inventories." However, it is not enough just to know your students well, teachers must take that knowledge and make it come alive in organizing and implementing teaching and learning environments for those students. Borrowing from an educational colleague: "The general can only be understood in its specifics." That is, we can come to know our Hispanic students in various intellectual ways, but until we can translate that knowledge into the very specific ways in which we teach them, maximum benefits of the intellectual knowledge will go unrealized.

We are now encountering in states where we have worked, specifically California and Arizona, a policy response to their predominantly Hispanic, Spanish-speaking children that bans the use of their primary language during instruction. These policies are premised on the notion that since English is the official language of the United States, these children's primary responsibility should be to learn English and to do so by immersing them in English-only instructional environments. These policies are responsive to the will of the people of these states, since they were passed by a majority of voters in state level referendums. But, they are clearly not responsive to the theoretical and empirical underpinnings of what we know works for these students. These restrictive language policies have been shown empirically to be highly detrimental to the students in these states (Gandara & Orfield, 2010). Ignoring what we know conceptually and empirically works because public officials are garnering electoral advantages at the educational costs of Hispanic children is unacceptable.

Quite the opposite, our first encounter with dual language (DL) programs in the San Francisco School District exemplifies a truly responsive instruction option for these same students (see Chapter 3). While the vast majority of the district programs offer instruction in Spanish and English, there are also DL programs that target Korean, Chinese, and Tagalog. These efforts have three responsive goals: to help children to learn English and find success in U.S. schools; to help these children become competent in their own language without sacrificing their own success in school; and to promote linguistic and ethnic equity among the children, encouraging children to bridge the gaps between cultures and languages. Evidence in various district sites has emerged indicating that DL programs can be an excellent model for academic achievement for both Hispanic and non-Hispanic bilingual and monolingual children (García, 2005). Studies have shown DL programs to promote English language learning as well or better than other special programs designed for bilingual children with positive and no negative effects on monolingual children participating in these programs.

This phenomenon continues today with programs expanded in the district and extended to middle school and high school. It is a real and productive example of educational *responsiveness* to Hispanic students. It took those ingredients that make up this student and adapted the curriculum and instruction to maximize learning (our grandson, Joaquin, is a student in one of the district DL schools and truly bilingual).

3. Responsibility. In considering federal legislation related to the reauthorization of the Elementary and Secondary Education Act (ESEA) we were continually confronted with the unequal achievement outcomes for selected students in U.S. schools (see Chapter 1 for details of these academic achievement incongruences for Hispanics.) It becomes evident that nationally we did not have policy mechanisms in place for holding educational institutions accountable for these disparate educational results. Moreover, general aggregation of achievement data did not reveal how sub-groups of students were actually doing. For this reason, the ESEA, known more commonly as No Child Left Behind, now requires states, school districts, and schools receiving federal Title I funds to report student achievement by race, ethnicity, gender, and socioeconomic status.

Unfortunately, local schools and states do not always adopt disaggregation practices for achievement data on the bases of historically and new relevant demographic categories. For Hispanics, failures to make distinctions in this data for immigrants versus non-immigrants, Spanish-speakers versus English-speakers, and previous educational background make interpreting these data confusing and unproductive. Most significantly, Hispanic limited English-speaking students are often out of the bounds of accountability simply because they were not assessed at all. In this case, educational entities have no knowledge regarding the academic effects of schooling for this population. Absence of such achievement data has often been defended on the basis that it is best not to take such measures rather than do so with inappropriate (unreliable and invalid) assessments. Confused at this policy level is the failure to develop appropriate assessments as opposed to use inappropriate ones. These are clearly two different issues, each placing Hispanic students outside any system of accountability.

The state of Texas has taken an important lead in resolving this set of issues. A statewide accountability system administers achievement tests to each student in its schools on a yearly basis, publishes the results of those tests by school, and provides school-based rewards in the form of new resources to those schools that make substantial progress. In addition, Hispanic students who are limited English proficient and have been receiving instruction in Spanish are administered academic achievement assessments in Spanish. Some have observed that the tests may still not meet high standards of content and may even be suspect due to their questionable reliability and validity. Yet, we now have in one state a system that attempts to seriously address the issues of educational accountability for Hispanic students. This type of *responsibility* is still the exception not the rule. It must become commonplace, as Hispanic students grow in number throughout the United States, in order to inform practices that can hold education agencies accountable for the educational progress of these and all students.

4. Resourcefulness. We often are encouraged, particularly in education, that less is more and that throwing money at a problem is not the solution. Jaime Escalante, as portrayed in the popular movie, *Stand and*

Deliver, takes low-achieving Hispanic students and with little more than engendering *ganas* in these students, produces a cadre of mathematics success stories. For many Hispanics, these adages sound hollow in the face of the challenges that they confront in everyday educational settings. *Ganas* is good, but a systematic effort to improve education on a variety of fronts is not enough.

We learned in our own work that the key resources for Hispanic children are the presence of high-quality staff and teachers that serve these children and their families. These resources are sometimes hard to find, yet are the most critical ingredient related to academic success for these children. We have also learned that taking good care of these teachers and staff members through ongoing professional development and in classroom coaching can be a substantive investment in positive outcomes for children. Teachers, staff members, and institutional leaders that understand the cultural and linguistic assets these children, families, and communities bring to the teaching-learning enterprise are critical. The types of curriculum and assessment and the expertise of these providers are critical resources in need of attention if Hispanic students are to do well. Teachers with bilingual and English development instructional skills and reduction of class size and resources (time and money) for professional development can enhance the educational *responsiveness* in preschools and during the early grades.

After-school programs, specifically targeted in-school reading programs and community-based support programs are not free. They require public and private resourcefulness that are usually non-existent. And, it doesn't always take a lot of resources. We are struck by the development and implementation of a K–3 program in Albuquerque, New Mexico, that addressed very directly this issue of *resourcefulness* in response to a low achievement of Hispanic students. Simply, the schools redeployed a cadre of its teachers to prepare its lowest achieving students in after-school programs 2 days a week. These teachers worked for an hour after school on Mondays and Wednesdays to prepare a half dozen students for the lessons all their classmates would engage in the next school day. The pre-preparation ensured that these students would engage in that lesson and may even take on a leadership role with their classmates in an academic context. Academic achievement of these low-achieving Hispanic students tripled within one year. Its added costs were estimated at approximately $220/year, but its benefits, as articulated by parents, students, teachers, and administrations, undeniably justified this added expenditure. We pay for what we receive—Hispanics and the general society will need to find the resources.

5. Theory. We all have theories. They guide our everyday activity and often we do not realize how powerful they are. In our families, our mother's had a common and important theory: When in need, pray to *la Virgen de Guadalupe*. If that does not resolve the problem, pray the rosary, and do not hesitate to light a candle at the local church. Our fathers had yet another common theory: Work hard. If that does not resolve the problem, work harder, and even harder. We realize that Hispanics have a high sense of spirituality and inclination to work hard—and we wonder where that comes from.

We, and you as educators, have theories as well and they guide our every action as we develop and implement practices that we trust will assist children develop and learn. For many educators, children who come to them are to be served by meeting a set of agreed upon expectations, standards. We may not always agree with those standards, or we might modify some, yet how we get those children to those standards is up to us. We have to often realize that far too many individuals who serve Hispanic children are operating on a set of assumptions or theories that are too generic and do not take into consideration the complexities of this population—the language, cultural, and development diversity that they bring.

We find in the work of our Arizona colleague Luis Moll and his theory of "Funds of Knowledge" (Moll, 2009), that we all need to understand the cultural, social, linguistic, and academic "funds" that these students bring to the schooling enterprise. That capital going unrecognized leads only to the faulty construction of developmental and early learning environments that are unresponsive and potentially deleterious to those whom they were specifically designed to assist. Following from this, we suggest adopting a conceptual framework, a new *theory*, with regard to Hispanics: Their *reices* are a resource not a problem.

PREPARING YOUNG HISPANICS AND THE UNITED STATES FOR THE FUTURE

As the United States advances its educational pursuits, it is even more important to understand the seismic changes in technology, globalization, and democratization that are reflected in similar seismic changes in demography. Unfortunately, the general U.S. population is far more attuned to and comfortable with engaging in aspects of the technological, globalization, and political challenges, rather than those challenges confronting us by our demographic changes. They are almost characterized as having a blind spot when it comes to the new demographic reality; they are "demographically challenged."

To educate our underachieving but growing Hispanic students is a no-brainer. Hispanic youth will serve as our foundation for national preeminence in the fields of high technology in a global workplace that promotes democratic principles and practices. These circumstances pose a particular challenge to educators and those among us who look to educational agencies for help in realizing the moral imperatives of equity and social justice. These agencies are being called on to develop and implement models of culturally competent practices in treating and delivering services to growing numbers of Hispanic students and families. This volume, with its emphasis on the early education of Hispanics in the United States, has attempted to further contextualize our understanding of the education in this country through the discussion of culture. If class and race count, so does culture.

We want to end on an optimistic note for Hispanic students and American society in general. If these findings are valid, then one could predict that, as more Hispanic children enter the "right" kind of early learning venues, barriers to their academic, social, and economic success and mobility will fall. As ethnic majorities become more attuned to the cultural diversity around them, and the resources adopted in that diversity, we can look forward to a blending of cultural distinctions with other features of our society and the formation of a more egalitarian and multicultural society.

Recommended Books as Windows and Mirrors

All teachers have a set of favorite books that they read to students every year. These lists need to include books that become windows and mirrors for students. Windows are books that help students see and hear the words that describe places, activities, languages, and perhaps characters that are different from themselves. Mirrors are books that are filled with pages that have pictures and words that look like them, sound like them, live in houses that look like theirs, and perhaps participate in experiences that they do. We would like to share our list of favorite books that are read during read aloud. Many of these books serve as windows and mirrors for our students.

Argueta, Jorge. (2005). *Mooney Luna*. San Francisco: Children's Book Press.

Auch, Mary Jane, and Herm Auch. (2003). *Superchicken*. New York: Holiday House.

Beaumont, Karwn. (2005). *I Ain't Gona Paint No More!* New York: Harcourt, Inc.

Brown, Margaret Wise. (1949). *The Important Book*. New York: HarperCollins.

Charlip, Remy, and Lilian Moore. (1975). *Hooray For Me!* New York: Four Wind Press.

Choi, Yangsook. (2001). *The Name Jar*. New York: Alfred A. Knopf.

Clement, Debbie. (1997). *You're Wonderful*. Columbus, OH: Rainbows Within Reach.

Falwell, Cathryn. (2001). *David's Drawing*. New York: Lee & Low, Inc.

Fosberry, Jennifer. (2008). *My Name is Not Isabella*. Hong Kong: Sourcebooks, Inc.

Gottlieb, Dale. (1991). *My Stories by Hildy Calpurnia Rose*. New York: Alfred A Knopf.

Henkes, Kevin. (1991). *Chrysanthemum*. New York: Greenwillow Books.

Hopkins, Lee Bennett. (2003). *Alphathoughts: Alphabet Poems*. Honesdale, PA: Boyds Mills Press Inc.

Morris, Ann. (2000). *Families*. Monterey, CA: Hampton Brown-National Geographic.

Neubecker, Robert. (2007). *Wow! School!* New York: Hyperion Books for Children.

Rappaport, Doreen. (2001). *Martin's Big Words.* New York: Hyperion Books for Children.

Walsh, Melanie. (2002). *My Nose, Your Nose.* Boston: Houghton Mifflin.

Wong, Janet S. (2004). *Apple Pie 4th of July.* New York: Harcourt, Inc.

Velthuijs, Mas. (1989). *Frog in Love.* New York: A Sunburst Book/Farrar, Straus and Giroux.

Recommended Wordless Books

A teaching strategy that helps students use their language to create text involves the use of wordless books. This strategy invites students to create their own meaning for each of the pages that are being shared by the teacher. Often this becomes the bridge from talk to reading and then to writing books. We understand that reading is learned in schools and is generally acquired through explicit teaching. Understanding the "why" related to explicit teaching leads teachers to plan what they will explicitly teach: the "when" and the "how." To be successful in learning this complex process, students must know and understand alphabet skills—knowing the names, shapes, and sounds of the letters. Teaching alphabet-related skills needs to be part of the instruction that is purposefully planned and taught by teachers during whole group, small group, and individual instructional time as well as in centers.

We have had the opportunity to use highly engaging wordless books with our young Hispanic students, finding them to be engaging and supportive. Here is a list of our favorites:

Alborough, Jez. (2009). *Hug.* Somerville, MA: Candlewick..

Baker, Jeannie. (2004). *Home.* New York: Greenwillow Books.

Briggs, Raymond. (1978). *The Snowman.* New York: Random House.

Carle, Eric. (1992). *Do You Want to Be My Friend?* New York: Trumpet Club.

Day, Alexandra. (1985). *Good Dog, Carl.* La Jolla, CA.: Green Tiger.

DePaola, Tomie. (1991). *Pancakes for Breakfast.* New York: Scholastic.

Fleischman, Paul, and Kevin Hawkes. (2004). *Sidewalk Circus.* Somerville: Candlewick Press.

Jay, Alison. (2008). *Welcome to the Zoo.* New York: Dial for Young Readers.

Lee, Suzy. (2008). *Wave.* San Francisco, CA: Chronicle.

Lehman, Barbara. (2004). *The Red Book.* Boston: Houghton Mifflin.

Liu, Jae Soo, and Dong Il Sheen. (2002). *Yellow Umbrella.* La Jolla, CA: Kane/ Miller Book.

Mayer, Mercer. (2003). *A Boy, a Dog, and a Frog.* New York: Dial for Young Readers.

Pinkney, Jerry. (2009). *The Lion & the Mouse*. New York: Little, Brown for Young Readers.

Raschka, Christopher. (1998). *Yo! Yes?* New York: Orchard.

Rathmann, Peggy. (1993). *Goodnight, Gorilla*. New York: Putnam.

Rockhill, Dennis. (2004). *Polar Slumber*. Green Bay, WI: Raven Tree Press.

Wiesner, David. (1991). *Tuesday*. New York: Clarion.

Wilson, April. (1998). *April Wilson's Magpie Magic: A Tale of Colorful Mischief*. New York: Dial for Young Readers.

References

Amato, P. (2005). The impact of family formation change on the cognitive, social and emotional well-being of the next generation. *The Future of Children, 15,* 76–96.

Arzubiaga, A., Rueda, R., & Monzó, L. (2002). Reading engagement of Latino children. *Journal of Latinos and Education, 1*(4), 134–243.

Au, K. H., & Mason, J. M. (1981). Social organizational factors in learning to read: The balance of rights hypothesis. *Reading Research Quarterly, 17*(1), 115–152.

August, D., Calderón, M., & Carlo, M. (2002). *Transfer of skills from Spanish to English: A study of young learners.* Washington, DC: Center for Applied Linguistics.

August, D., Calderón, M., Carlo, M., & Nuttall, M. (2006). Developing literacy in English-language learners: An examination of the impact of English-only versus bilingual instruction. In P. D. Mccardle and E. Hoff (Eds.), *Childhood Bilingualism: Research on Infancy Through School Age.* Bristol, UK: Multilingual Matters, pp. 111–131.

AVANCE (2007). About AVANCE. Retrieved from http://www.avance.org

Baker, C. (2000). *The care and education of young bilinguals: An introduction for professionals.* Clevedon, UK: Multilingual Matters.

Banks, J., Banks, S., & Loren, J. (2007). *Learning in and out of school in diverse environments: Life-long, life-wide, life-deep.* Seattle, WA: The LIFE Center.

Barnett, W.S. (2006). Research on the Benefits of Preschool Education: Securing High Returns from Preschool for All Children. Presentation at the Second Annual Conference on Building the Economic Case for Preschool. New York, NY, January 10.

Barnett, W. S., Yarosz, D. J., Thomas, J., & Blanco, D. (2006). *Two-way and monolingual English immersion in preschool education: An experimental comparison.* New Brunswick, NJ: National Institute for Early Education Research.

Barrera, J. M., & Warner, L. (2006). Involving families in school events. *Kappa Delta Pi Records, 42*(2), 72–75.

Barry, H., Child, I., & Bacon, M. (1959). Relations of child training to subsistence economy. *American Anthropologist, 61,* 51–63.

Bean, F., & Tienda, M. (1987). *The Hispanic population of the United States*. New York, NY: Russell Sage Foundation.

Bialystok, E. (2001). Metalinguistic aspects of bilingual processing. *Annual Review of Applied Linguistics, 21*, 169–181.

Borman, G., Hewes, G. M., Overman, L., & Brown, S. (2003). Comprehensive school reform and student achievement: A meta-analysis. *Review of Educational Research, 73*(2), 125–230.

Borman, G. D., Hewes, G. M., Reilly, M., & Alvarado, S. (2006). *Comprehensive school reform for Latino elementary-school students*. Report to the National Task Force on Early Childhood Education for Hispanics. Tempe, AZ: Arizona State University.

Boulton, M. J. (1995). Patterns of bully/victim problems in mixed race groups of children. *Social Development, 3*, 277–293.

Boyle-Baise, M., & McIntyre, D. J. (2008). What kind of experience? Preparing teachers in PDS or community settings. In M. Cochran-Smith, S. Feiman-Nemser, & D. J. McIntyre (Eds.), *Handbook of research on teacher education: Enduring questions in changing contexts* (3rd ed.) (pp. 307–330). New York, NY: Routledge.

Bransford, J. D., Brown, A. L., & Cocking, R. R. (2000). *How people learn: Brain, mind, experience, and school*. Washington, DC: National Academies Press.

Bransford, J., Derry, S., Berliner, D., Hammerness, K., & Beckett, K. L. (2005). Theories of learning and their roles in teaching. In L. Darling-Hammond & J. Bransford (Eds.), *Preparing teachers for a changing world: What teachers should learn and be able to do*. San Francisco, CA: Jossey-Bass.

Bridges, M., & Gutierrez, S. (2011). *Beyond a haircut, lunch pail, and new shoes: Opening doors to school readiness for Latino children and their parents*. Berkeley, CA: Zero to Three.

Brooker, L. (2002). "Five on the first of December!" What can we learn from case studies of early childhood literacy? *Journal of Early Childhood Literacy, 2*(3), 292–313.

Brophy, J., & Good, T. (2008). Teacher behavior and students achievement. In M. C. Wittrock (Ed.), *Handbook of research on teaching* (3rd ed.). New York, NY: Macmillan, p. 43.

Brown, A. L., & Campione, J. C. (1994). Guided discovery in a community of learners. In K. McGilly (Ed.), *Classroom lessons: Integrating cognitive theory and classroom practice*. Cambridge, MA: MIT Press.

Brown, J. S., Collins, A., & Duguid, P. (1989). Situated cognition and the culture of learning. *Educational Researcher, 18*(1), 32–42.

Buriel, R., & Cardoza, D. (1988). Sociocultural correlates of achievement among three generations of Mexican American high school seniors. *American Educational Research Journal, 25*(2), 177–192.

Capps, R., Fix, M., Murray, J., Ost, J., Passel, J., & Herwantoro-Hernandez, S. (2005). *The new demography of America's schools: Immigration and the No*

Child Left Behind Act. Washington, DC: Urban Institute.

Carter, T. P. (1968). The negative self-concept of Mexican American students. *School and Society, 96,* 271–219.

Cauce, A., & Domenech-Rodriguez, M. (2002). In J. Contreras, K. Kerns, & A. Neal Barnett (Eds.), *Latino children and families in the United States* (pp. 3–25). Westport, CT: Praeger.

Cazabon, M., Lambert, W., & Hall, G. (1999). *Two-way bilingual education: A report on the Amigos Program.* Washington, DC: Center for Applied Linguistics.

Center for Applied Linguistics (CAL). (2005, March). *Guiding principles for dual language education.* Washington, DC: Author.

Chavez, L. (1991). *Out of the barrio: Toward a new politics of Hispanic assimilation.* New York, NY: Basic Books.

Chavez, L. (1995, February). Bilingual education and its problems. *Readers Digest,* 81–96.

Chrispeels, J., & González, M. (2004). *Do educational programs increase parents' practices at home? Factors influencing Latino parent involvement.* Cambridge, MA: Harvard Family Research Project.

Chrispeels, J., González, M., & Arellano, B. (2004). *Evaluation of the effectiveness of the Parent Institute for Quality Education in Los Angeles Unified School District September 2003 to May 2004.* Santa Barbara: University of California.

Chrispeels, J. H., & Rivero, E. (2001). Engaging Latino families for student success: How parent education can reshape parents' sense of place in the education of their children. *Peabody Journal of Education, 76*(2), 119–169.

Christian, D. (1994). *Two-way bilingual education: Students learning through two languages.* Washington, DC: Center for Applied Linguistics.

Christian, D. (1997). *Directory of two-way bilingual programs.* Washington, DC: Center for Applied Linguistics.

Christian, D., Genesee, F., Lindholm-Leary, K., & Howard, L. (2004). *Project 1.2 two-way immersion: Final progress report.* Center for Research on Education, Diversity & Excellence. Berkeley: University of California

Cobb, B., Vega, D., & Kronauge, C. (2005, April). *Effects of an elementary dual language immersion school program on junior high school achievement of native Spanish speaking and native English speaking students.* Paper presented at the American Education Research Association annual conference in Montreal, Canada.

Cole, M. (1996). *Cultural psychology: A once and future discipline.* Cambridge, MA: Harvard University Press.

Cole, M., & Cole, S. R. (2001). *The development of children.* New York, NY: Worth.

Cole, M., & Engeström, Y. (1993). A cultural-historical approach to distributed cognition. In G. Salomon (Ed.), *Distributed cognitions: Psychological and educational considerations.* New York, NY: Cambridge University Press.

Cooper, J. E. (2007). Strengthening the case for community-based learning in teacher education. *Journal of Teacher Education, 58*(3), 245–255.

Crosnoe, R. (2006). *Mexican roots, American schools: Helping Mexican immigrant children succeed.* Palo Alto, CA: Stanford University Press.

Darling-Hammond, L. (2006). *Powerful teacher education: Lessons from exemplary programs.* San Francisco, CA: Jossey-Bass.

Darling-Hammond, L., & Bransford, J. (Eds.). (2005). *Preparing teachers for a changing world: What teachers should learn and be able to do.* San Francisco, CA: Jossey-Bass.

Dolson, D. P. (1984). *The influence of various home bilingual environments on the academic achievement, language development, and psychological adjustment of fifth and sixth grade Hispanic students.* (Unpublished doctoral dissertation). University of San Francisco.

Dolson, D. P. (1985). The effects of Spanish home language use on the scholastic performance of Hispanic pupils. *Journal of Multilingual and Multicultural Development, 6*(2), 135–155.

Driscoll, M. P. (2000). *Psychology of learning and instruction* (2nd ed.). Needham Heights, MA: Allyn & Bacon.

Duquette, G. (1991). Cultural processing and minority language children with needs and special needs. In G. Duquette & L. Malve (Eds.), *Language, Culture, and Cognition* (pp. 54–66). Philadelphia, PA: Multilingual Matters.

Durán, B. J., & Weffer, R. E. (1992). Immigrants' aspirations, high school process, and academic outcomes. *American Educational Research Journal, 29*(1), 163–181.

Ellis, S. (1997). Strategy choice in sociocultural context. *Developmental Review, 17,* 490–524.

Ercikan, K., & Roth, W. M. (2006). What good is polarizing research into qualitative and quantitative? *Educational Researcher, 35*(5), 14–23.

Espinosa, L. M. (2010). Classroom teaching and instruction "best practices for young English language learners." In E. E. García & E. C. Frede (Eds.), *Young English language learners: Current research and emerging directions for practice and policy* (pp 143–164). New York, NY: Teachers College Press.

Faltis, C., & Coulter, C. (2007). *Teaching English learners and immigrant students in secondary schools.* Upper Saddle River, NJ: Merrrill/Pearson.

Fantini, A. E. (1985). *Language acquisition of a bilingual child.* Clevedon, Avon, UK: Multilingual Matters.

Figueroa, L. (2005, April). *The development of pre-reading knowledge in English and Spanish: Latino English language learners in a dual-language education context.* Paper presented at the American Education Research Association annual conference in Montreal, Canada.

Fine, M., Jaffe-Walter, R., Pedraza, P., Futch, V., & Stoudt, B. (2007). Swimming: On oxygen, resistance, and possibility for immigrant youth under siege. *Anthropology & Education Quarterly, 38,* 76–96.

Freeman, M. (2009). Knowledge is acting: Working-class parents intentional acts of positioning within discursive practice of involvement. *International Journal of Qualitative Studies in Education, 76* (3), 181–198.

Freire, P. (1970). *Pedagogy of the oppressed.* New York, NY: Herder & Herder.

Furger, R. (2006, March). Parents are a secret weapon just waiting to be discovered. *Edutopia,* 46–49.

Fuligni, A., & Pedersen, S. (2002). Family obligations and the transition to young adulthood. *Developmental Psychology, 38,* 856–868.

Fuller, B. (2007). *Standardized childhood: The political and cultural struggle over early education.* Stanford, CA: Stanford University Press.

Fuller, B., & Clark, P. (1994). Raising school effects while ignoring culture? Local conditions and the influence of classroom tools, rules, and pedagogy. *Review of Educational Research, 64*(1), 119–157.

Galindo, C., & Reardon, S. F. (2006). *Hispanic students' educational experiences and opportunities during kindergarten.* Tempe, AZ: National Task Force on Early Childhood Education for Hispanics.

Gándara, P. (2008). A preliminary evaluation of Mexican-sponsored educational programs in the United States: Strengths, weaknesses, and potential. In E. Szecsy (Ed.), *Resource book, Second Binational Symposium.* Tempe, AZ: Arizona State University. Retrieved from http://simposio.asu.edu/docs/2007/cdrom/book/gandara_PDF.pdf

Gándara, P., & Orfield, G. (2010). Moving from failure to a new vision of language policy. In P. Gandara & M. Hopkins (Eds.), *Forbidden languages: English learners and restrictive language policies.* New York, NY: Teachers College Press.

Gándara, P., Rumberger, R., Maxwell-Jolly, J., & Callahan, R. (2003). English learners in California schools: Unequal resources, unequal out-comes. *Education Policy Analysis Archives, 11*(36). Retrieved from http://epaa.asu.edu/epaa/ v11n36

García, E. E. (1983). *Bilingualism in early childhood.* Albuquerque, NM: University of New Mexico Press.

García, E. E., (1991). Factors influencing the English reading test performance of Spanish-speaking Hispanic children. *Reading Research Quarterly, 26*(4), 371–392.

García, E. E. (1994). *Understanding and meeting the challenge of student cultural diversity.* Boston, MA: Houghton Mifflin.

García, E. (1999). *Student cultural diversity: Understanding and meeting the challenge* (2nd ed.). Boston, MA: Houghton Mifflin.

García, E. E. (2001a). *Hispanic education in the United States: Raíces y alas.* Lanham, MD: Rowman & Littlefield.

García, E. E. (2001b). *Rethinking school reform in the context of cultural and linguistic diversity: Creating a responsive learning community.* Berkeley, CA: University of California.

García, E. E. (2001c). *Understanding and meeting the challenge of student diversity* (3rd ed.). Boston, MA: Houghton Mifflin.

García, E. E. (2002). Bilingualism in schooling in the United States. *International Journal of the Sociology of Language, 155*(156), 1–92.

García, E. E. (2005). *Teaching and learning in two languages: Bilingualism and schooling in the United States.* New York, NY: Teachers College Press.

García E. E., & Barry. C. (1990). Interactive journals and teacher interactions. *Discourse Processes, 12* (3), 89–97.

García, E. E., & Carrasco, R. (1981). An analysis of bilingual mother-child discourse. In R. Duran (Ed.), *Latino Discourse* (pp. 46–61). Norwood, NJ: Ablex.

García, E. E., & Cuellar, D. (2006). Who are these linguistically and culturally diverse students? *Teachers College Record, 108*(11), 2220–2246.

García, E. E., & Frede, E. C. (2010). *Young English language learners.* New York, NY: Teachers College Press.

García, E. E., & García, E. H. (2009). Language development and the education of dual-language-learning children in the United States. In Guofang Li & Patricia A. Edwards (Eds.), *Best practices in ELL instruction* (pp. 44–58). New York, NY: Guilford Press.

García, E. E., & Gonzales, D. M. (2006). *Pre-K and Latinos: The foundation for America's future.* Washington, DC: Pre-K Now.

García, E. E., & Jensen, B. T. (2006). Dual-language programs in the U.S.: An alternative to monocultural, monolingual education. *Language Magazine, 5*(6), 30–37.

García, E. E., & Jensen, B. T. (2007). Advancing school readiness for young Hispanic children through universal prekindergarten. *Harvard Journal of Hispanic Policy, 19*, 25–37.

García, E. E., & Jensen, B. (2009). Early educational opportunities for children of Hispanic origins. *Social Policy Report, 23*(2), 1–20. The Society for Research in Child Development.

García, E., Jensen, B., & Cuellar, D. (2006). Early academic achievement of Hispanics in the United States: Implications for teacher preparation. *The New Educator, 2*, 123–147.

García, E. E., Jensen, B. T., Miller, L. S., & Huerta, T. (2005). *Early childhood education of Hispanics in the United States.* Tempe, AZ: National Task Force on Early Childhood Education for Hispanics. Retrieved from http://www.ecehispanic.org/work/white_paper_Oct2005.pdf

García, E. E., & Miller, L. S. (2008). Findings and recommendations of the National Task Force on Early Childhood Education for Hispanics. *Child Development Perspectives, 2*(2), 53–58.

García, E., Scribner, K., & Cuellar, D. (2009). Latinos and early education: Immigrant generational differences and family involvement. In E. L. Grigorenko &

R. Takanishi (Eds.), *Immigration and diversity* (pp. 95–111). New York, NY: Routledge.

García, G. E. (1991). Factors influencing the English reading test performance of Spanish speaking Hispanic children. *Reading Research Quarterly, 26*(4), 371–392.

Garcia, M. (2006). *The impact of the home instruction for parents of preschool youngsters on reading, mathematics and language achievement of Hispanic English language learners.* (Unpublished doctoral dissertation). University of North Texas.

Garcia Coll, C., Meyer, E. C., & Brillon, L. (1995). Ethnic and minority parenting, In M.H. Bornstein (Ed.) *Handbook of parenting* (Vol. I) (pp.189–209). Mahwah, NJ: Lawrence Erlbaum Associates.

Garcia-Nevarez, A. G., Stafford, M. E., & Arias, B. (2005). Arizona elementary teachers' attitudes toward English language learners' and the use of Spanish in classroom instruction. *Bilingual Research Journal, 29*(2), 295–318.

Gardner, H. (2006). *The development of education of the mind.* New York, NY: Routledge.

Gay, G. (2000). *Culturally responsive teaching: Theory, research and practice.* New York, NY: Teachers College Press.

Gay, G. (2002). Preparing for culturally and responsive teaching. *Journal of Teacher Education, 53*(2), 106–116.

Genesee, F. (Ed.). (1999). *Program alternatives for linguistically diverse students.* Center for Research on Education, Diversity & Excellence (CREDE). Berkeley, CA: University of California, Berkeley.

Genesee, F. (2003, April). *The capacity of language faculty: Contributions from studies of simultaneous bilingual acquisition.* Paper presented at the 4th International Symposium on Bilingualism, Tempe, AZ.

Genesee, F., Geva, E., Dressler, C., & Kamil, M. (2006). Synthesis: Cross-linguistic relationships. In D. August & T. Shanahan (Eds.), *Report of the national literacy panel on language minority youth and children.* Mahwah, NJ: Lawrence Erlbaum Associates.

Genesee, F., Lindholm-Leary, K., Saunders, W., & Christian, D. (2005). English language learners in U.S. schools: An overview of research findings. *Journal of Education for Students Placed at Risk, 10*(4), 363–386.

Genesee, F., Lindholm-Leary, K., Sanders, B., & Christian, D. (2006*). Educating English language learners: A synthesis of research evidence.* New York, NY: Cambridge University Press.

Genishi, C. (1981). Code switching in Chicano six-year olds. In R. Duran (Ed.), *Latino language and communicative behavior.* Norwood, NJ: Ablex.

Golan, S., & Petersen, D. (2007). *Promoting involvement of recent immigrant families in their children's education.* Palo Alto, CA: SRI International.

Goldenberg, C. (1987). Low income Hispanic parents' contributions to their first-grade children's word recognition skills. *Anthropology and Education Quarterly, 18*(3), 149–179.

Goldenberg, C. N., & Gallimore, R. (1991). Local knowledge, research knowledge, and educational change: A case study of early Spanish reading improvement. *Educational Researcher, 20*(8), 2–14.

Goldenberg, C. N., Gallimore, R., Reese, L., & Garnier, H. (2001). Cause or effect? A longitudinal study of immigrant Latino parents' aspirations and expectations and their children's' school performance. *American Educational Research Journal, 38*, 547–582.

Goldenberg, C. N., Reese, L., & Gallimore, R. (1992). Effects of literacy materials from school on Latino children's home experiences and early reading achievement. *American Journal of Education, 100*(4), 497–536.

Goldenberg, C., Rezaei, A., & Fletcher, J. (2005, April). *Home use of English and Spanish and Spanish-speaking children's oral language and literacy achievement.* Paper presented at the annual meeting of the American Educational Research Association, Montreal, Canada.

Goldenberg, C., Rueda, R., & August, D. (2006). Synthesis: Sociocultural contexts and literacy development. In D. August & T. Shanahan (Eds.), *Report of the national literacy panel on language minority youth and children.* Mahwah, NJ: Lawrence Erlbaum Associates.

Gonzalez, G. (1990). *Chicano education in the segregation era: 1915–1945.* Philadelphia, PA: The Balch Institute.

González, J. (2005, March). *Speculations on the future of the Spanish language in the United States of America.* Paper presented at the 5th International Symposium on Bilingualism, Barcelona, Spain.

Gonzalez, N., Moll, L., & Amanti, C. (2005). *Funds of knowledge: Theorizing practices, households, communities, and classrooms.* Mahwah, NJ: Lawrence Erlbaum Associates.

Gormley, W. T., Gayer, T., Phillips, D., & Dawson, B. (2005). The effects of Universal pre-K on cognitive development. *Developmental Psychology, 41*(6), 872–884.

Grantmakers for Education. (2010). *Investing in our next generation: A funder's guide to addressing the educational opportunities and challenges facing English language learners.* Portland, OR: Author.

Greaves, M. C. (2009). Why parent involvement? A perspective of the Cranston Family Center. *NCEA, 39*, 45.

Greene, J. P. (1998). *A meta-analysis of the effectiveness of bilingual education.* Claremont, CA: Thomas Rivera Policy Institute.

Greenfield, P., Keller, H., Fuligni, A., & Maynard, A. (2003). Cultural pathways through universal development. *Annual Review of Psychology, 54*, 461–490.

Greenwood, C. R., Horton, B. T., & Utley, C. A. (2002). Academic engagement: Current perspectives on research and practice. *School Psychology Review, 31*(3), 328–349.

Grosjean, F. (1982). *Life with two languages.* New York, NY: Cambridge University Press.

Guthrie, J. T., Rueda, R., Gambrell, L., & Morrison, D. (2008). Roles of engagement, valuing, and identification in reading development of students from diverse backgrounds. In L. Morrow, R. Rueda, & D. Lapp (Eds.), *Handbook of Research on Literacy Instruction: Issues of diversity, policy, and equity.* New York, NY: Guilford.

Gutierrez, K., & Rogoff, B. (2003). Cultural ways of learning: Individual traits and repertoires of practice. *Educational Researcher, 32*(5), 19–25.

Hakuta, K., Ferdman, B. M., & Diaz, R. M. (1987). Bilingualism and cognitive development: Three perspectives. In S. Rosenberg (Ed.), *Advances in applied psycholinguistics, volume II: Reading, writing and language learning.* (pp. 284–319). Cambridge, UK: Cambridge University Press.

Halgunseth, L. C., Ispa, J. M., & Duane, R. (2006). Parental control in Latino families: An integrated review of the literature. *Child Development, 77*(5), 1282–1287

Hammer, C. S., Miccio, A. W., & Wagstaff, D. A. (2003). Home literacy experiences and their relationship to bilingual preschoolers' developing English literacy abilities: An initial investigation. *Language, Speech, and Hearing Services in Schools, 34,* 20–30

Hancock, D. R. (2002). The effects of native language books on the pre-literacy skill development of language minority kindergartners. *Journal of Research in Childhood Education, 17*(1), 62–68.

Hansen, D. A. (1989). Locating learning: Second language gains and language use in family, peer, and classroom contexts. *NABE: The Journal of the National Association for Bilingual Education, 13*(2), 161–180.

Harry, B., & Klingner, J. (2006). *Why are so many minority students in special education? Understanding race & disability in schools.* New York, NY: Teachers College Press.

Hart, B., & Risley, T. (1995). *Meaningful differences in the everyday experience of young American children.* Baltimore, MD: Paul H. Brookes Publishing Co.

Hart, B., & Risley, T. R. (1999). *Learning to talk: The social world of children.* Baltimore, MD: Paul H. Brookes Publishing Co.

Harwood, R., Leyendecker, B., Carlson, V., Ascenio, M., & Miller, A. (2002). Parenting among Latino families in the United States. In M. Bornstein (Ed.), *Handbook of parenting* (2nd ed.) (pp. 21–46). Mahwah, NJ: Lawrence Erlbaum Associates.

Hasson, D. (2004, April). *Perceived language abilities in bilingual Hispanic university students: Did bilingual education help*? Paper presented at the American Educational Research Association annual conference, April 13, 2004, San Diego, CA. Heath, S. B. (1983). *Ways with words: Language, life and work in community and classrooms.* Cambridge, UK: Cambridge University Press.

Heath, S. B. (1986). Sociocultural contexts of language development. In California State Department of Education (Ed.), *Beyond language: Social and cultural factors in schooling language minority students* (pp. 143–186). Los Angeles: Evaluation, Dissemination, and Assessment Center, California State University.

Heckman, J., & Masterov, D. (2004). *The productivity argument for investing in young children.* Chicago, IL: Committee for Economic Development.

Henderson, A. (2007). *Beyond the bake sale: The essential guide to family-school partnership.* New York, NY: The New Press.

Hernandez, D. (2007). *Young Hispanic children in the U.S.: A demographic portrait based on Census 2000.* A report to the National Task Force on Early Childhood Education for Hispanics. Tempe, AZ: Arizona State University.

Hernandez, D., Denton, S., & Macartney, N. A. (2007). HIPPY USA. (2007). About HIPPY. Retrieved from http://www.hippyusa.org/About_HIPPY/about_HIPPY.html

HIPPY USA. (2007). About HIPPY. Retrieved from http://www.hippyusa.org/About_HIPPY/about_HIPPY.html

Hollins, E. R., & Guzman, M. T. (2005). Research on preparing teachers for diverse populations. In M. Cochran-Smith & K. M. Zeichner (Eds.), *Studying teacher education: The report of the AERA panel on research and teacher education* (pp. 477–548). Mahwah, NJ: Erlbaum.

Holloway, S., & Fuller, B. (1997). *Through my own eyes: Single mothers and the cultures of poverty.* Cambridge, MA: Harvard University Press.

Howard, E. R., Sugarman, J., & Christian, D. (2003). *Trends in two-way immersion education: A review of the research.* Washington, DC: Center for Applied Linguistics.

Huerta-Macías, A., & Quintero, E. (1992). Code-switching, bilingualism, and biliteracy: A case study. *Bilingual Research Journal, 16*(3–4), 69–90.

Jensen, B. T. (2008a). Immigration and language policy. In J. González (Ed.), *Encyclopedia of Bilingual Education.* Thousand Oaks, CA: Sage.

Jensen, B. (2008b). Raising questions for binational research in education: An exploration of Mexican primary school structure. In E. Szecsy (Ed.), *Resource book, Second Binational Symposium.* Tempe, AZ: Arizona State University. Retrieved from at http://simposio.asu.edu/docs/2007/cdrom/book/jensen_PDF.pdf

Jiménez, R. T. (1997). The strategic reading abilities and potential of five low-literacy Latina/o readers in middle school. *Reading Research Quarterly, 32*(3), 224–243.

Kagan, S. & Kagan, L. (2007). Structures for cooperative learning and active engagement. San Clemente, CA: Kagan.

Kroeber, A. L., & Kluckhohn, D. (1963). *Culture: A critical review of concepts and definitions.* New York, NY: Vintage Books.

Kucer, S. B., & Silva, C. (1999). The English literacy development of bilingual students within a transitional whole language curriculum. *Bilingual Research Journal, 23*(4), 347–371.

Ladson-Billings, G. (1994). *The dreamkeepers: Successful teachers for African-American children.* San Francisco, CA: Jossey-Bass.

Ladson-Billings, G. (1995). But that's just good teaching! The case for culturally relevant pedagogy. *Theory into Practice, 34*(3), 159–165.

Lambert, W. (1974). Culture and language as factors in learning and education. In F. E. Aboud & R. D. Meade (Eds.), *The fifth western symposium on learning.* Bellingham, WA: Western Washington State College.

Lee, J., & Bowman, N. (2006). Parent involvement, cultural capital, and the achievement gap among elementary school children. *American Educational Research Journal, 43*(2), 193–218.

Lesgold, A. (2004). Discussion—Contextual requirements for constructivist learning. *International Journal of Educational Research, 41*, 495–502.

Lieberson, S., Dalto, G., & Johnston, M. (1975). The course of mother tongue diversity in nations. *American Journal of Sociology, 81*(1), 34–61.

Lindholm, K. J. (1999). *Two-way bilingual education: Past and future.* Presentation at the American Education Research Association, Toronto, ON.

Loeb, S., Bridges, M., Bassok, D., Fuller, B., & Rumberger, R. (2005). How much is too much? *The influence of preschool centers on children's social and cognitive development.* (Working Paper 11812). Cambridge, MA: National Bureau of Economic Research.

Lopez. L. (2003). Adapting a family as educator model for young Latino children. Cambridge, MA: Harvard University Department of Human Development (unpublished manuscript).

López, L. (2005, March). *A look into the homes of Spanish-speaking preschool children.* Paper presented at the 5th International Symposium on Bilingualism, Barcelona, Spain.

López, M. L., & Barrueco, S., & Miles, J. (2006). *Latino infants and families: A national perspective of protective and risk factors for development.* A report to the National Task Force on Early Childhood Education for Hispanics. Tempe, AZ: Arizona State University.

Markos, A. (2006). Language development chart for ELL students. Personal Communication.

Márquez-López, T. (2005). California's standards movement: How English learners have been left out of the equation for success. In P. Pedraza & M. Rivera (Eds.), *Latino education: An agenda for community action research* (pp. 205–230). Mahwah, NJ: Lawrence Erlbaum Associates.

Matuti-Bianchi, M. E. (1990). *A report to the Santa Clara County School District: Hispanics in schools*. Santa Clara, CA: Santa Clara School District.

Matuti-Bianchi, M. E., & Ogbu, J. (1988). Understanding sociocultural factors: Knowledge, identity and school adjustment. In California Bilingual Education Office (Eds.), *Beyond language: Social and cultural factors in schooling of language minority students*. Sacramento, CA: California Department of Education.

McClure, E. (1981). Formal and functional aspects of the code-switched discourse of bilingual children. In R. Duran (Ed.), *Latino language and communicative behavior*. Norwood, NJ: Ablex.

McDermott, R., & Varenne, H. (1995). Culture as disability. *Anthropology & Education Quarterly, 26*(3), 324–348.

Menken, K., & Antunez, B. (2001). *An overview of the preparation and certification of teachers working with limited English proficient (LEP) students*. Washington, DC: National Clearinghouse for Bilingual Education.

Mireles, L., Bridges, M., Fuller, B., Livas, A., & Mangual, A. (2007, April). *Mexican mothers' school involvement: Looking at what predictors most identify parent participation*. American Education Research Association Conference, Chicago, IL.

Moll, L. (2009). The civil rights of language minority students and their funds of knowledge. *Educational Researcher, 39*(4), 163–171.

Monzó, L., & Rueda, R. (2001). *Constructing achievement orientations toward literacy: An analysis of sociocultural activity in Latino home and community contexts*. (CIERA Report No. 1-011). Ann Arbor, MI: Center for the Improvement if Early Reading Achievement.

Nasir, N. S., & Hand, V. M. (2006). Exploring sociocultural perspectives on race, culture, and learning. *Review of Educational Research, 76*(4), 449–475.

National Center for Education Statistics. (2007). *The condition of education, 2007*. Washington, DC: Author.

National Institute for Early Childhood Education Research. (2010). *Yearbook of Preschool Circumstances in the United States: 2010*. Rutgers, NJ: National Institute for Early Education Research.

National Task Force on Early Childhood Education for Hispanics. (2007). *Para nuestrosniños: Expanding and improving early childhood education for Hispanics—Main report*. Tempe, AZ. Retrieved from http://www.ecehispanic.org/work/expand_MainReport.pdf

Nieto, S. (2004*). Affirming diversity: The sociopolitical context of multicultural education* (4th ed). New York, NY: Allyn & Bacon.

Nord, C. W., Lennon, J., Liu, B., & Chandler, K. (1999). *Home literacy activities and signs of children's emerging literacy, 1993 and 1999*. (NCES 20000-026). Washington, DC: U.S. Department of Education, National Center for Education Statistics. Retrieved from http://nces.ed.gov/pubs2000/2000026.pdf

Ogbu, J. (1987). *Minority education and caste: The American system in cross-cultural perspective*. San Diego, CA: Academic Press.

Oller, D. K., & Eilers, R. E. (2002). *Language and literacy in bilingual children*. Clevedon, UK: Multilingual Matters.

Padilla, A., & Liebman, E. (1975). Language acquisition in the bilingual child. *Bilingual Review, 2*, 34–55.

Paik, S. J., & Walberg, H. J. (2007). *Narrowing the achievement gap: Strategies for educating Latino, Black and Asian students*. New York, NY: Springer.

Paul, B. (1965). Anthropological perspectives on medicine and public health. In K. Skipper, Jr., R. C. Leonard (Eds.), Social interaction and patient care, (pp. 187–224). Philadelphia, PA: J. B. Lippincott.

Pajares, M. F. (1992). Teachers' beliefs and education research: Cleaning up a messy construct. *Review of Educational Research, 62*, 307–332.

Passel, J. (2003, November). *Hispanic projections: The future and the past*. Presented at the National Research Council Panel on Hispanics in the U.S., Washington, DC.

Pelto, P., & Pelto, G. H. (1975). Intra-cultural variation: Some theoretical issues. *American Ethnologist, 2*(1), 1–45.

Perie, M., Grigg, W., & Donahue, P. (2005). *The nations report card: Reading 2005* (NCES 2006-453). U.S. Department of Education, National Center for Education Statistics. Washington, DC: U.S. Government Printing Office.

Poplack, S. (1981). Sometimes I'll start a sentence in Spanish y termino en español: Toward a typology of code switching. *Linguistics, 18*, 581–618.

Portes, P. (2005). *Dismantling educational inequality: A cultural-historical approach to closing the achievement gap*. New York, NY: Peter Lang.

Portes, P. (2007). *Culture and education in U.S. schools*. New York, NY: Basic Books.

Princiotta, D., & Flanagan, K. (2006). *Findings from the fifth-grade follow-up of the Early Childhood Longitudinal Study, Kindergarten class of 1998–99*. Washington, DC: U.S. Department of Education, National Center for Education Statistics.

Pucci, S. L., & Ulanoff, S. H. (1998). What predicts second language reading success? A study of home and school variables. *International Review of Applied Linguistics, 121-122*, 1–18.

Qiuyun, L. (2003). *Parent involvement and early literacy*. Retrieved from http://www.gse.harvard.edu/hfrp/projects/fine/resources/digest/literacy.html

Qiuyun, L. (2006, April). *Beyond cultural deficit approach: Disentangling language minority parents' involvement in the early grades.* Paper presented at the American Educational Research Association, San Francisco, CA.

Quinn, N., & Holland, D. (1987). Culture and cognition. In D. Holland & N. Quinn (Eds.), *Cultural models in language and thought* (pp. 3–42). Cambridge, UK: Cambridge University Press.

Raikes, H., Pan, B. A., Luze, G., Tamis-LeMonda, S. C., Brooks-Gunn, J., Constantine, J., . . . & Rodriguez, E. T. (2006). Mother-child bookreading in low-income families: Correlates and outcomes during the first three years of life. *Child Development, 77*(4), 924–953.

Ramey, C., & Ramey, S. (1998). Early intervention and early experience, *American Psychologist, 53*(2), 109–120.

Ramirez, A. (1985). *Bilingualism through schooling.* Albany, NY: State University of New York Press.

Reardon, S. F., & Galindo, C. (2006, April). *K–3 academic achievement patterns and trajectories of Hispanics and other racial/ethnic groups.* Paper presented at the Annual AERA Conference, San Francisco, CA.

Reardon, S. F. & Galindo, C. (2006). *Patterns of Hispanic students' math and English literacy test scores.* Report to the National Task Force on Early Childhood Education for Hispanics.

Reese, L., Balzano, S., Gallimore, R., & Goldenberg, C. (1995). The concept of "educación": Latino family values and American schooling. *International Journal of Educational Research, 23*(1), 57–81.

Reese, L., & Gallimore, R. (2001). Immigrant Latinos' cultural models of literacy development: An evolving perspective on home-school discontinuities. *American Journal of Education, 108,* 103–134.

Reese, L., Garnier, H., Gallimore, R., & Goldenberg, C. (2000). Longitudinal analysis of the antecedents of emergent Spanish literacy and middle-school English reading achievement of Spanish-speaking students. *American Educational Research Journal, 37*(3), 633–662.

Reeves, J. (2004). Like everybody else: Equalizing educational opportunity for English language learners. *TESOL Quarterly, 38*(1), 43–66.

Reimers, F., & McGinn, N. (1997). *Informed dialogue: Using research to shape education policy around the world.* Westport, CT: Praeger.

Reyes, R. (1998). *A native perspective on the school reform movement: A hot topic paper.* Portland, OR: Northwest Regional Educational Laboratory, Comprehensive Center, Region X and Washington, DC: U.S. Department of Education, Office of Educational Research and Improvement, Educational Resources Information Center.

Reyes, I. (2001). *The development of grammatical and communicative competence in bilingual Spanish speaking children.* (Unpublished doctoral dissertation). University of California, Berkeley.

Reynolds, A., Temple, J., Robertson, D., & Mann, E. (2001). Long-term effects of an early childhood intervention on educational achievement and juvenile arrest: A fifteen year follow-up of low-income children in public schools. *Journal of the American Medical Association, 285*(18), 144–153.

Richardson, V. (1996). The role of attitudes and beliefs in learning to teach. In J. Sikula (Ed.), *The handbook of research in teacher education* (2nd ed., pp. 102–119). New York, NY: Macmillan.

Risley, T. R., & Hart, B. (2006). Promoting early language development. In N. F. Watt et al. (Eds.), *The crisis in young mental health: Early intervention programs and policies*. Westport, CT: Praeger.

Rodriguez, C. E. (1989). *Puerto Ricans born in the USA*. Winchester, MA: Unwin Hyman.

Rodriguez, R. (1982). *Hunger of memory*. New York, NY: Bantam Books.

Rodriguez-Brown, F. V. (2009). *The home-school connections: Lessons learned in a culturally and linguistically diverse community*. New York, NY: Routledge.

Rodriguez-Brown, F. V. (2010). A research perspective on the involvement of linguistic-minority families on their young children. In E. E. García & E. C. Frede (Eds.), *Young English language learners* (pp. 100–118). New York, NY: Teachers College Press.

Rodriguez-Brown, F. V., & Shanahan, T. (1989). *Literacy for the limited English proficient child: A family approach*. Chicago: University of Illinois.

Rogoff, B. (1990). *Apprenticeship in thinking: Cognitive development in social context*. Oxford, UK: Oxford University Press.

Rogoff, B. (2003). *The cultural nature of human development*. New York, NY: Oxford University Press.

Rogoff, B (2011). *Developing destinies*. New York, NY: Oxford University Press.

Rogoff, B., Mistry, J., Göncü, A., & Mosier, C. (1993). Guided participation in cultural activity by toddlers and caregivers. *Monographs of the Society for Research in Child Development, 58*(8), 1–179.

Rogoff, B., Paradise, R., Mejía Arauz, R., Correa-Chavez, M., & Angelillo, C. (2003). Firsthand learning through intent participation. *Annual Review of Psychology, 54*, 175–203.

Rolstad, K., Mahoney, K., & Glass, G. V. (2005). The big picture: A meta-analysis of program effectiveness research on English language learners. *Educational Policy, 19*(4), 572–594.

Rueda, R., August, D., & Goldenberg, C. (2006). The sociocultural context in which children acquire literacy. In D. August & T. Shanahan (Eds.), *Report of the national literacy panel on language minority youth and children*. Mahwah, NJ: Lawrence Erlbaum Associates.

Rueda, R., MacGillivray, L., Monzó, L., & Arzubiaga, A. (2001). Engaged reading: A multi-level approach to considering sociocultural features with diverse learners. In D. McInerny & S. Van Etten (Eds.), *Research on socio-cultural influences on motivation and learning* (pp. 233-264). Greenwich, CT: Information Age.

Saunders, W. M., & O'Brien, G. (2006). Oral language. In F. Genesee, K. Lind-holm-Leary, W. M. Saunders, & D. Christian (Eds.), *Educating English language learners: A synthesis of research evidence.* New York, NY: Cambridge University Press.

Scheffner Hammer, C., & Miccio, A. (2004). Home literacy experiences of Latino families. In B. H. Wasik (Ed.), *Handbook of family literacy.* Mahwah, NJ: Lawrence Erlbaum Associates.

Scheffner Hammer, C., Miccio, A., & Rodriguez, B. (2004). Bilingual language acquisition and the child socialization process. In B. Goldstein (Ed.), *Bilingual language development and disorders in Spanish-English speakers* (pp. 21–52). Baltimore, MD: Paul H. Brookes Publishing Co.

Scheffner Hammer, C., Miccio, A., & Wagstaff, D. (2003). Home literacy experiences and their relationship to bilingual preschoolers' developing English literacy abilities: An initial investigation. *Language, Speech, and Hearing Services in Schools, 34,* 20–30.

Schwartz, T. (1978). Where is culture? In G. Spindler (Ed.), *The making of psychological anthropology.* Berkeley, CA: University of California Press.

Seidl, B. (2007). Working with communities to explore and personalize culturally relevant pedagogies: "Push, double images, and raced talk." *Journal of Teacher Education, 58,* 168–183.

Seidlitz, J., & Castillo, M. (2010). *Language and Literacy for ELLs.* San Francisco, CA: Seidlitz Education.

Shannon, S. M. (1995). The hegemony of English: A case study of one bilingual classroom as a site of resistance. *Linguistics and Education, 7*(3), 175–200.

Shonkoff, J., & Phillips, D. (2000). *From neurons to neighborhoods: The science of early childhood development.* Washington, DC: National Academy Press.

Skinner, C. H., Pappas, D. N., & Davis, K. A., (2005). Enhancing academic engagement: Providing opportunities for responding and influencing students to choose to respond. *Psychology in the Schools, 42*(4), 389–403.

Smith, M. L. (2006). Multiple methodology in education research. In J. L. Green, G. Camili, & P. B. Elmore (Eds.), *Handbook of complementary methods in education research.* Mahwah, NJ: Lawrence Erlbaum Associates.

Spencer, M. B. (1988). Self-concept development. In D T. Slaughter (Ed.), *Black children and poverty: A developmental perspective* (pp. 103–116). San Francisco, CA: Jossey-Bass.

Spiro, M. E. (1951). Culture and personality: The natural history of a false dichotomy. *Psychiatry, 14*(2), 19–46.

Stachowski, L. L., & Frey, C. J. (2005). Student teachers' reflections on service and learning in Navajo reservation communities: Contextualizing the classroom experience. *The School Community Journal, 12*(3), 101–120.

Steele, C. (1994). Ethnic identity and test performance. *Journal of Social Psychology, 47*(3), 114–128.

Sugarman, J., & Howard, L. (2001). Two-way immersion shows promising results: Findings from a new study. *Language Links*. Washington, D C: Center for Applied Linguistics.

Tabors, P. O. (1997). *One child, two languages: A guide for preschool educators of children learning English as a second language*. Baltimore, MD: Brookes.

Tabors, P. O., & Snow, C. E. (2002). Young bilingual children and early literacy development. In S. B. Neuman & D. K. Dickinson (Eds.), *Handbook of early literacy research*. New York, NY: Guilford Press.

Tharp, R. G., & Gallimore, R. (1989). Rousing schools to life. *American Educator, 13*(2), 20–25, 46–52.

Thomas, S. V., & Park, K. B. (1921). *Culture of immigrants*. Cambridge, MA: Newcome Press.

Tienda, M. (2005). *Hispanics in the United States*. Washington, DC: National Research Council.

U.S. Census Bureau. (2003). *The Hispanic population in the United States: March 2002 detailed tables* (PPL-165). Washington, DC. U.S. Dept. of Commerce, Economics and Statistics Administration, Bureau of the Census.

U.S. Bureau of the Census. (2006). *Statistical abstract of the United States* (126th ed.). Washington, DC: Government Printing Office.

Valdés, G. (1996). *Con respeto: Bridging the distances between culturally diverse families and schools—An ethnographic portrait*. New York, NY: Teachers College Press.

Valenzuela, A. (1999). *Subtractive schooling: U.S.-Mexican youth and the politics of caring*. Albany, NY: State University of New York Press.

Valenzuela, A., & Dornbusch, S. M. (1994). Familism and social capital in the academic achievement of Mexican origin and Anglo adolescents. *Social Science Quarterly, 75*, 18–36.

Vélez-Ibáñez, C. I., & Greenberg, J. B. (1992). Formation and transformation of funds of knowledge among U.S.-Mexican households. *Anthropology and Education Quarterly, 23*, 313–335.

Veltman, C. (1983). *Language shift in the United States*. Amsterdam, Netherlands: Mouton Publishers.

Vidano, G., & Sahafi, M. (2004). *Parent Institute for Quality Education: Organization special report on PIQE's performance evaluation*. San Diego, CA: College of Administration & Marketing Department: San Diego State University.

Villegas, A. M., & Lucas, T. (2002). *Educating culturally responsive teachers: A coherent approach*. Albany, NY: SUNY Press.

Vygotsky, L. S. (1978). *Mind in society: The development of higher order psychological processes.* Cambridge, MA: Harvard University Press.

Wallace, A. F. (1970). *Culture and personality* (2nd ed.). New York, NY: Random House.

Weis, L. (1988). *Class, race and gender in U. S. education.* Albany, NY: State University of New York.

Weisner, T. (2002). Ecocultural understandings of children's developmental pathways. *Human development, 45,* 275–281

Well, G., & Mejía Arauz, R. (2005). Toward dialogue in the classroom: Learning and teaching through inquiry. *Working Papers on Culture, Education and Human Development, 1*(4). Retrieved from http://www.uam.es/otros/ptcedh/2005v1_pdf/v1n4eng.pdf

Whiting, B., & Edwards, C. (1988). *Children of different worlds*: *The formation of social behavior.* Cambridge, MA: Harvard University Press.

Whiting, B., & Edwards, C. (1991). *Children of different worlds: The formation of social behavior.* Cambridge, MA: Harvard University Press.

World-Class Instruction Design and Assessment. (2011). *English language proficiency (ELP) standards.* Retreived from http://www.wida.us/standards/elp.aspx

Wilkinson, L. C., Milosky, L. M., & Genishi, C. (1986). Second language learners' use of requests and responses in elementary classrooms. *Topics in Language Disorders, 6*(2), 57–70.

Wong-Fillmore, L., & Snow, C. (2002). What teachers need to know about language. In C. Adger, C. Snow, & D. Christian (Eds.), *What teachers need to know about language* (pp. 7–53). Alexandria, VA: Center for Applied Linguistics.

Youngs, C., & Youngs, G. (2001). Predictors of mainstream teachers' attitudes toward ESL students. *TESOL Quarterly, 35,* 97–120.

Zeichner, K. (1996). Educating teachers for cultural diversity. In K. Zeichner, S. Melnick, & M. L. Gomez (Eds.), *Currents of reform in pre-service teacher education* (pp. 133–175). New York, NY: Teachers College Press.

Zentella, A. C. (1997). *Growing up bilingual: Puerto Rican children in New York.* Malden, MA: Blackwell.

Zentella, A. C. (Ed.). (2005). *Building on strengths: Language and literacy in Latino families and communities.* New York, NY: Teachers College Press.

Zigler, E., Gilliam, W. S., & Jones, S. M. (2006). *A vision for universal preschool education.* Cambridge, UK: Cambridge University Press.

Zumwalt, K., & Craig, E. (2005). Teachers characteristics: Research on the demographic profile. In. M. Cochran-Smith & K. M. Zeichner (Eds.), *Studying teacher education. The report of the AERA Panel on Research and Teacher Education* (pp. 111–156). Washington, DC: American Educational Research Association.

Index

Please note **f** or **t** following a page number refers to a figure or table, respectively.

About the Authors

Dr. Eugene García is Professor Emeritus at Arizona State University. He served as Vice President for Education Partnerships at ASU from 2006–2011 and as Dean of the Mary Lou Fulton College of Education from 2002–2006. He joined ASU from the University of California, Berkeley, where he was Dean of the Graduate School of Education. He has published extensively in the area of language teaching and bilingual development, authoring and or co-authoring more than 150 articles and book chapters along with 15 books and monographs. He chaired the National Task Force on Early Childhood Education for Hispanics from 2006–2008. His research website is http://ecehispanic.org.

Erminda García is presently a 1st-grade teacher in the Higley Unified School District in Gilbert, Arizona. She has taught pre-K and K through 3rd grade for 27 years in primarily Hispanic serving schools and school districts. She is a contributing author to a curriculum series by Scholastic and National Geographic serving bilingual, Hispanic children. She continues to provide invited professional development nationally on early childhood instructional strategies and has been recognized for her professional contributions at local, state, and national levels.